NEALOGICAL TABLE OF
HE HOUSE OF FARNESE

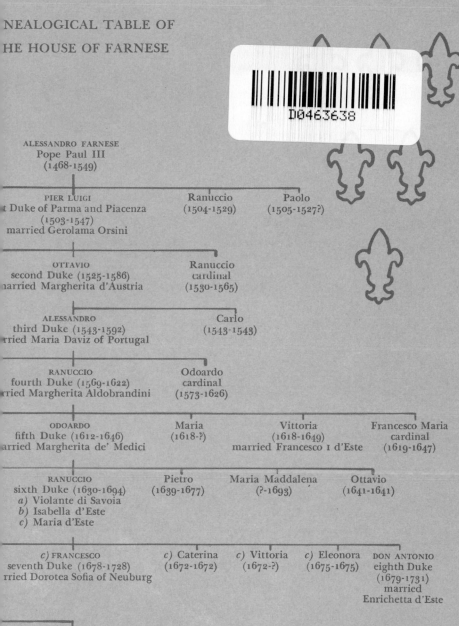

ALESSANDRO FARNESE
Pope Paul III
(1468-1549)

PIER LUIGI
t Duke of Parma and Piacenza
(1503-1547)
married Gerolama Orsini

Ranuccio
(1504-1529)

Paolo
(1505-1527?)

OTTAVIO
second Duke (1525-1586)
narried Margherita d'Austria

Ranuccio
cardinal
(1530-1565)

ALESSANDRO
third Duke (1543-1592)
rried Maria Daviz of Portugal

Carlo
(1543-1543)

RANUCCIO
fourth Duke (1569-1622)
rried Margherita Aldobrandini

Odoardo
cardinal
(1573-1626)

ODOARDO
fifth Duke (1612-1646)
arried Margherita de' Medici

Maria
(1618-?)

Vittoria
(1618-1649)
married Francesco I d'Este

Francesco Maria
cardinal
(1619-1647)

RANUCCIO
sixth Duke (1630-1694)
a) Violante di Savoia
b) Isabella d'Este
c) Maria d'Este

Pietro
(1639-1677)

Maria Maddalena
(?-1693)

Ottavio
(1641-1641)

c) FRANCESCO
seventh Duke (1678-1728)
rried Dorotea Sofia of Neuburg

c) Caterina
(1672-1672)

c) Vittoria
(1672-?)

c) Eleonora
(1675-1675)

DON ANTONIO
eighth Duke
(1679-1731)
married
Enrichetta d'Este

Elisabetta
(1692-1766)
married Philip V of Spain

THE
HOUSE
OF
FARNESE

GIOVANNA R. SOLARI

THE
HOUSE
OF
FARNESE

Translated by Simona Morini and Frederic Tuten

DOUBLEDAY & COMPANY, INC.

GARDEN CITY, NEW YORK

1968

© Arnoldo Mondadori Editore, 1964

In memory of my father

CONTENTS

LIST OF ILLUSTRATIONS

THE
HOUSE
OF
FARNESE

I

Paul III and

"La Fortunazza Paolina"

April 20, 1543 was an important day for the papal court. Titian had at last come to Rome. Princes and kings, doges, men of letters, great ladies and courtesans, all wanted their portraits done by him; and it was an ambition that had become contagious, for even the pope now required the services of the master. But the seventy-year-old painter was so busy and sought-after that the Curia has almost despaired ever of securing, however briefly, his precious brush. At the very moment the Vatican was giving him up, the news arrived that Titian, who had been negotiating with a papal representative, had at last decided to come to Rome. Opening his arms in a gesture of joy, the pope exclaimed, "How lucky we are!"

"Titian," reported the ambassador, "in addition to being talented, seems to be an affable, docile, and well-disposed person, qualities highly valued in so exceptional a man." Indeed, considering that the great artists of the time were all rather whimsical, touchy, hard to please—"Arrogance and painters are born twins," Salvator Rosa wrote later—Titian's exceptionally good character was one more stroke of good luck.

The painter received a hearty reception. The pope gave him hospitality in the Vatican, and the pope's relatives showered him with kindness. Giorgio Vasari escorted him about town. Pietro Bembo, his famous compatriot, welcomed him warmly. Sebastiano del Piombo showed him the newly restored Vatican chambers, St. Peter's (then under construction), the Farnesina, Raphael's ceilings, and the Museum of Antiquities. Titian, who was seeing Rome for the first time, feasted his eyes on its marvels and was frequently heard heaving sighs of admiration. The papal court had persuaded him to leave Venice by pointing out the considerable advantages a sojourn in Rome would bring to his son Pomponio; for Pomponio was entering an ecclesiastical career, and at seventeen already had two rich prebends, one in Milan and the other in Mantua. A third canonry would do no harm, Titian thought, and, with the Abbey of San Pietro in Colle on his mind, he had left for Rome.

The portrait he made of the pope in exchange for this grant is one of his best, and helps us to reconstruct a magnificent story. In it, Pope Paul III is shown as he was: old, fragile, close to death, yet extremely lucid and still ready, as always, to fight his battles as a pontiff and as a man. Struggle and time had furrowed his face with deep wrinkles, yet each wrinkle revealed the energy that had sustained him during the years of his slow but not too difficult ascent to the Vatican.

Paul, or more exactly Alessandro—his name before attaining St. Peter's chair—had been clearly destined for the papal tiara. In fact, never before in papal history had there been so popular an election. Italian, French, English humanists, even German ones tainted with Protestant ideas, sent him congratulations in their beautiful, aulic, solemn Latin. Even Erasmus congratulated him. "Here in Rome we had three consecutive days of feasts and joy, with fireworks and bells and artillery, because His Holiness has suspended all the taxes Pope Sixtus and other popes have long burdened us with." Paul's election satisfied both

Italians and foreigners, and, most of all, Romans who, enthusiastic at the prospect of a Roman pope after exactly one hundred years, had rushed en masse to the conclave hall to touch, brush against, or embrace the newly elected pontiff.

To be exact, Alessandro Farnese was not really a Roman. His family belonged to the minor but venerable country aristocracy of the Latium region, and since the Middle Ages they had owned land and a few castles near Lake Bolsena, where life flowed with rustic, quiet simplicity. For generations, the men in the family had shown an inclination for soldiering, and they distinguished themselves in military ventures on behalf of the various lords involved in the complicated rivalries between Guelphs and Ghibellines. In return for their loyalty, which had not failed even in the tragic days of the Reformation, the popes had rewarded the Farneses with estates and privileges. At the beginning of the fifteenth century, through the marriage of a Farnese heir to a Roman noblewoman, the family rose from the status of provincial nobility to that of urban aristocracy.

The star of Alessandro Farnese, who had entered an ecclesiastical career for social considerations only, began to rise under the auspices of his sister Giulia, who was of such celebrated beauty that in Rome she was known simply as "la bella." The reigning Borgia pope, Alexander VI, then considered "the most sensual man in Rome," had chosen her as his favorite and jealously ensconced her in the Vatican. *Julia sua* [his Julia], wrote the chroniclers of the time, and in that pronoun alone was all the possessiveness and the passion of the aging Borgia pontiff.

As the pope's favorite, it had been easy for Giulia to promote her brother's career. In fact, it was commonly held in Rome that Alessandro owed his scarlet hat entirely to his sister's intrigues, and people commonly referred to him as "the petticoat cardinal." The truth is that Alessandro would probably have succeeded by himself in any case, for the good qualities of the

family had matured and merged in him in such a perfect harmony that, with the slightest amount of good fortune, he would
have secured for the Farneses a place in history.

It is difficult to imagine a more gifted man than Alessandro.
He was healthy, intelligent, shrewd, persevering, amiable, had
patrician manners, and had many other qualities that attracted
everyone's warmest sympathy. In Florence he attended the
Academy of Lorenzo il Magnifico, and in Rome the studio of
Pomponio Leto—the great humanist whose passion for classical
studies had brought him to the threshold of paganism and heresy.
There Alessandro bathed in the humanistic ambience, mastered
the intellectual and spiritual elegance he had set out to acquire,
and won the admiration of his very sophisticated era.

The title of cardinal, given him by Alexander VI as a tribute
to the Farnese family, did not interfere with young Alessandro's
social life. The house of the twenty-five-year-old prince of the
Church was one of the most splendid in Rome. Counting the
grooms, footmen, couriers, and other servants, his staff totaled
360. Very few women's names were linked to his own, although
at the beginning of the fifteenth century he was already the
father of four children, one girl and three boys. But apparently
they all were from the same woman, yet a woman so mysterious
that historians have not been able to establish if her name was
Ruffina, as Rabelais calls her, or Lola, as it appears in a poem
by Tarquinio Molosso. These four children, presented to the
world immediately and without hesitation, legitimized, and later
munificently provided for, demonstrated Alessandro's strong disposition for family life, for at one time he almost renounced his
cardinalatial dignity in order to marry. But luckily, the mentality
of that tolerant age did not prevent him from sharing his
fatherly responsibilities with those of high ecclesiastical office, and
so Alessandro remained a cardinal, and at fifty he took holy
orders and celebrated his first Mass. This marked the beginning
of a transformation which, in a few years, made of this worldly

prelate a man so conscious of his religious duties that he initiated a rigid moral reform, eliminated many ecclesiastical abuses, and founded several new religious orders—a first formal reaction to the threats of schism from that section of Christianity which just then started to question the dogmas of the Church.

Alessandro's new personality coincided with the slow but steady rise of his career and with his increasing political power. He was first made chief treasurer, then cardinal deacon, then Bishop of Corneto and Montefiascone, and then legate to Ancona, and eventually Bishop of Parma, Tuscolo, Ostia, and Benevento. Through a number of other important legations, presidencies, and high offices, Alessandro finally reached a most prominent position, and was counted among the *papabili*—as one of the cardinals likely to be elected pope.

Julius II, the "Iron Pope," and Leo X, the "Pope of the Arts," had both esteemed and loved him, and so did Clement VII, his victorious rival in the 1421 conclave. The Venetian ambassador Marco Foscari wrote: "The pope never consults on affairs of state with any cardinal, except sometimes with the Right Reverend Farnese." "Farnese," wrote another ambassador from Venice, "is foremost among the cardinals. When the pope dies, everyone thinks he will be made pope." And that is exactly what happened after Clement VII's death in 1534. Perhaps it would have happened even earlier, "had not," said Pietro Aretino, "the fraud of simony and of men interfered."

When he donned the papal tiara, Paul III was sixty-seven, an age which justified the general assumption that he would soon have a successor, for he also was "in poor health, worn out, troubled, and feeble." And even in his best moments, when he felt well, he was troubled by bronchitis and frequent colds. But in the end he had a long, powerful old age. A mysterious energy, combined with a careful diet—highly commendable in an age of fantastic gastronomic excesses—contributed to make Alessandro's the longest pontificate of the century.

The old, sick-yet-strong Farnese found himself confronted by a complicated and difficult political situation. In the last thirty years, two major monarchies, France and Spain, had formed and strengthened themselves in Europe. To both, Italy seemed a lucrative political and military prey, and the richer and more civilized it became, the more eagerly was it coveted.

The first to cross the Alps was Charles VIII of France, who for years had yearned to go to Italy "in order to drive out the tyrants and to punish the Church with his sword." Contemporaries said that the only handsome thing about Charles was his large, glittering eyes. And these eyes reflected the wildest dreams of glory, the most quixotic, romantic ambitions imaginable. At Amboise, his favorite castle, he treasured famous and inspiring trophies—the swords of Charlemagne and Saint Louis and the armor of the Maid of Orléans—and he dreamed of enriching his collection with new relics that posterity would associate with his name. Thanks to her last two kings, France then possessed the first national army in history. Charles was longing to test this army in Italy, where he dreamed of carrying on "a splendid war" which, unlike ordinary wars, would win him exotic lands and even extend the boundaries of the faith.

The situation in Italy at the time was very confused. A deceptive, unnatural peace ripened the various antagonisms more each day. The problems were innumerable: the disputes in the turbulent Romagna, the political ambiguity of Venice, the abuses of Ferdinand of Aragon, king of Naples, the dynamic but improvident ambitions of Lodovico il Moro, Duke of Milan. In Florence, Lorenzo de' Medici had just died. Through his patient and subtle diplomacy, while Italy was becoming the stage for a drama of power, ideas, civilization, and religion from which

18

modern history was to draw its essential framework, the Italian princes had been united through a policy of balance of power and federative alliances. When Lorenzo died, Pope Innocent VIII said prophetically: "Peace has ended."

Charles VIII had more than one reason for ending the peace, the most substantial being the ancient claims of his family to the kingdom of Naples, which was then held by Aragon. Instigated by his ambassadors, who sent him word that Naples was as good as his and waited only to be taken, and encouraged by Girolamo Savonarola, who invited him to undertake "the very much needed reformation of the Church," Charles VIII yielded to his dream of glory. He was twenty-two, ill-advised, and had the solemn innocence of the visionary. He never perceived the border line between dream and reality; for him, once a project had been conceived, it was as good as accomplished. In 1494, therefore, his army of 3000 cavalrymen, 5000 Gascon foot soldiers and as many from Switzerland, 4000 Breton archers, 2000 arbalesters, and a long train of artillery hauled by horses instead of oxen—a great novelty in those days—poured down from Mont Cenis. It was an adventure, picturesque, brief, and perfectly useless. Its only result was to unveil to the European nations, and especially to Spain, the beautiful, quarrelsome, defenseless Italian world. For Italy it was the prologue to the great trauma of foreign rule, the beginning of a humiliating, unhappy era. Very few of the Italian states, in the uncertainty of whether Spain or France would prevail, had managed to remain in the good graces of both one and the other. Those who did not were reduced to servile compliance, to begging favors from the two foreign kings around whom Italy's public life by now revolved. "Today we can conclude," wrote Andrea Doria to his friend the Marquis of Mantua, "that the Christian world is divided by two great loves: one for the emperor and the other for the French king; and we are almost obliged to choose between the two." The concept of neutrality had lost its meaning; the wisest statesmen, the most expert politicians—and they were many in those splendid and tragic days—believed that there was no other way but to join one side or the other. Even the sacred college was split in two, and the cardinals, according to political contingencies, influenced the pope in favor of their respective protectors. Generally, however, the Italian princes and cardinals inclined toward Spain. Not that Emperor Charles V was likable. On the contrary, he was a rather unpleasant man, and sad, too, always dressed in black, with a long face, open mouth, and the unmistakable Hapsburg chin. But, as Andrea Doria said, "his projects have strong foundations and are so absolutely certain that we cannot doubt their outcome; while the French are unsure and vague, and their habit is to make stupendous promises which they rarely keep. . . ."

Clement VII, Paul III's predecessor, had been a weak pope, and during his indecisive and passive administration great disasters had occurred: the sack of Rome by the emperor's troops, the increased threat of Spanish supremacy in Italy, the irreparable rift between the Church and Germany, where Luther had already attacked the very structure of the Church by openly advocating rebellion and schism. To make the situation worse, there had been the pope's decision against the divorce of Henry VIII of England, and then the conquest of Tunis by Barbarossa, the dreaded pirate chief. As a consequence of the latter, the coasts of Campania and Latium, and of Rome itself, were now so exposed to Turkish invasion that Clement VII wrote: "Things have gone so far that any day now we shall hear the beat of the enemy's oars." Thus, when the pope died, leaving behind bitter and painful memories, no one seemed better suited to take on this onerous legacy than Cardinal Alessandro Farnese. After the ill-fated alliances of Leo X and Clement VII with France and Spain, Alessandro's past and present policy of independence perfectly suited the most urgent needs of the papacy. "He [Alessandro] behaved in such a way toward the emperor and the king of France, that both Their Majesties had to be content to have him on their side in matters that were reasonable, and have him against them in matters that were not." Which is to say he was on good terms with both. Furthermore Alessandro, anxious to call an ecumenical council to heal somehow the wound inflicted by the Reformation, favored a more liberal attitude toward England. Above all, he was "extremely eager to free Italy from barbarians." A Spanish diplomat thus summarized Alessandro's policy: ". . . to create a lasting peace between the kings of France and Spain so as to resolve definitely the problems of Italy and of Europe, in order to devote himself more effectively to the religious problems in Germany and England; and finally to unite all the powers of Christianity in a great crusade against the Turks." The Turks, meanwhile, in their march west, had attacked Vienna, ejected the Christian Knights from Rhodes, and occupied Egypt and the shores of the western Mediterranean.

The election of Alessandro encouraged the most reasonable hopes. The world liked the way he had of reducing political problems to their essential terms. An ambassador observed that, in Alessandro Farnese, Machiavelli's genial shrewdness had become almost second nature. *"Gentilissimo . . . nobilissimo . . . degnissimo. . . ."* The many sibilants of the Italian superlatives hissed throughout diplomatic reports concerning the pope. A more scholarly pope had never sat on St. Peter's chair; ambassadors never tired of describing to their princes the Farnese pope's unique manner of discussion and negotiation. Not only because of his old age did he speak ceremoniously, precisely, almost syllabizing each word, but also because of his desire "never to utter a word which was not faultless in Italian as well as in Latin and Greek, for he is a master in all three." A generous man, even in discussions, he made it a point to listen to everyone's opinion, though later he might use them with the greatest freedom. He never gave the impression of refusing anything to anyone, but at the same time he managed to leave the diplomats uncertain about the results of their negotiations. The pope's decision would only come later, after long consideration and great *prudentia*—a word which in the fifteenth century had lost its Christian connotation to become exclusively a political term.

In Rome, where he had always been appreciated, Paul III soon became extremely popular. The papal court was then a singular compromise of ecclesiastical pomp and secular style. A man of great taste and pride, Paul lived surrounded by cardinals, prelates, dignitaries, and chamberlains in purple cassocks, and also by a colorful crowd of pages, courtiers, musicians, singers, and court jesters. Fifty footmen followed him everywhere he traveled. A head falconer with a flock of assistants was in charge of organizing the pope's hunts in the environs of Rome, took care of the hawks and the kennels, and imported new breeds of hounds from France. Two cooks prepared food exclusively for the pope who, in deference to custom, ate alone at his own table, but never by himself, for the banquet hall of the Vatican was always open to ambassadors, relatives, and friends. Yet, in the seeming confusion of the Vatican household, the innumerable mace-bearers, squires, halberdiers, attendants, Swiss guards, and secretaries all had precise duties. And so had Luca Gaurico, the most famous astrologer of the time, who regularly consulted the stars on behalf of the pope; and every morning the pope arranged his day according to the reports from the stars.

Of alert and dynamic nature, Paul never stayed in the Vatican for more than a few weeks. He often exchanged the apartments on the second floor of the Belvedere for the chambers of Castel Sant'Angelo. In the spring he moved to Palazzo San Marco—the present Palazzo Venezia—and, as soon as he could, he went to Frascati, to Caprarola, to his villa at Magliana, or to Quirinale where they had started to build a new papal residence. Occasionally he became homesick for his birthplace, and, on a horse decked out with crimson caparison and velvet reins, he visited Valenzano, Gradola, Ronciglione, Capodimonte—the villages of his youth. Meanwhile, in Rome, the Vatican's parasites and sycophants, longing for the prodigal days of Leo X, called Paul a miser. It was a necessary frugality, for only the most accurate bookkeeping and vigilance could have restored the state's finances which had been dangerously depleted by the extravagances of the previous popes.

Strict economy, however, did not prevent Paul from leading a cultivated and aesthetically satisfying life. He had attracted to his court the best among Italian artists and intellectuals: Pietro Bembo, for instance, was his intimate friend (who would have recognized in this portly humanist cardinal the old lover of Lucrezia Borgia?). Among others in the circle were Paolo Giovio, who from his own collection of busts, portraits, and medals was drawing inspiration for the *Biografie;* the devout Sadoleto, and Molza, who was always involved in "love intrigues"; and Giovanni della Casa, the exquisite aesthete who, like Molza, was too dissolute for the high ranks of the Curia. There, too, were Annibal Caro, superb writer, who was to spend almost all his life in the service of the Farneses; Marcantonio Flaminio, then considered the most delicate and successful poet in Rome; and Giorgio Vasari, the painter who wrote in his spare time, not knowing that he would become more famous for his literary hobby than for his canvases.

With Paul III, Rome shed its medieval vestment to assume one worthy of her position as world capital and as the center of Renaissance artistic glory. He ordered the improvement of streets, the creation of new roads, the paving of piazzas; he drained the swamps near St. Peter's, and transformed the Campidoglio. The Vatican was already that unique combination of galleries, halls, corridors, and chapels which is still its chief characteristic, but space was insufficient to maintain the pope's double role of secular and spiritual prince; and so the pope had to expand his stage.

St. Peter's basilica, devastated during the sack of 1527, became an enormous humming workshop under the direction of the architect Antonio di Sangallo, who was always among the workmen, inspecting everything; at times, climbing onto a platform, he commanded like a general. Pope Paul was very fond of him; he was the godfather of Sangallo's children, and in letters Sangallo addressed him as "dear friend." All were sad to see this great architect, who had changed half the face of Rome, die. And it was an inconvenience for the pontiff to have to replace him with Michelangelo, who did not want the job, insisting that he was too old, too tired, and who accepted only when the pope forced him to do so by a formal writ.

Many painters, too, were at home in the Vatican at that time. Daniele da Volterra, who was busy painting his *Deposizione* without thinking that one day he would be called on also to paint drawers on the nudes of the *Last Judgment;* Sebastiano del Piombo, who was in charge of sealing the bulls in the papal chancellery but who, rather than paint and seal, preferred to rest, which he often did, idling away the hours in his beautiful villa outside Porta del Popolo. Goldsmiths, engravers, and jewelers created the most beautiful objects ever seen in Rome. Paul's patronage, however tempered by economy, was always humanistically inclined and surpassed that of his predecessors, adding a precious dimension to the good qualities of a man whom everyone admired and trusted.

❋

"He will be a good pope," had said ambassadors and cardinals the day of Paul's election. And so he was. Especially in politics, Paul kept his promises. In the fifteen years of his rule, crucial years in Italy's and Europe's history, he managed, in the face of his adversaries, to maintain his autonomy. Independence meant to him a return to the old Italian ideal of political wisdom and the only guarantee of peace in a torn and impoverished Italy. In order to avoid an invasion—inevitable, should the Church become associated with either of the Catholic kings—for fifteen years he resisted the flattery, the threats, and even the blackmail through which the two rivals attempted to use him and to bring him to their side. Confronted for fifteen years by people courting, enticing, pressing, frightening him, he discovered how more difficult it is, in turbulent times, to remain neutral rather than to be partisan. To the last, he pursued the fifteenth-century dream of an independent Italy; and when he was asked his opinion about the rivalry between Charles V and Francis I, he answered with a firm and almost heroic smile that he would never change, he would never through his own doing allow war to be brought to Italy. Regularly disappointed, both Spanish and French ambassadors returned home to their rulers with messages, already anticipated, that "there was nothing to be done with the pope," and that Rome ate "bread and neutrality."

Even more than Francis I, Charles V was outraged by the pope's obstinacy—the only resistance, incidentally, besides that of Venice, in a country already at his feet. Naples, Milan, Sicily, Sardinia belonged to him. The most prominent Italians, the Dorias, the Colonnas, a duke of Savoy, were in his pay. In Mantua, even the stones in the street exuded the presence of the emperor. Cosimo de' Medici, along with the Gonzagas, was one of his most faithful followers, and even the Duke of Este was favorably disposed to him, although his own wife was a Huguenot princess. Only the old pope remained carefully impartial, while never ceasing to preach peace. In the very years when the Hapsburgs were consolidating their power, Charles V found an implacable obstacle in the old Farnese. And even when the emperor tried to play on the pope's weakness—his fondness for his family—he came to realize that he was dealing with a man who knew how to turn his weakness into advantage. "The emperor," people said, "comes to Italy and dominates everyone, but he will never dominate Pope Paul, whose soul in invincible."

Capable of pressing the *raison d'état* to the utmost, always ready to make subtle and clever compromises, quick to seize the right moment to extricate himself from dangerous intrigues, the pope could also be extremely vigorous in his approach to internal ecclesiastical politics and was not much different in this respect from other European autocrats. In 1540, for instance, Perugia revolted against the Vatican, ostensibly because of an increase in the salt tax—one of the basic revenue taxes of the time—but actually because of the town's passionate municipal spirit. Pope Paul's repression was ruthless and, as symbolized by the construction of the Rocca Paolina, marked the end of Perugia's autonomy.

Ascanio Colonna was another victim of the pope's severity. Ascanio was one of those cruel and exquisite, civilized yet savage men who were typical of the late Renaissance. The pope crushed his immense feudal power, dismantled the twenty castles Ascanio owned in Latium, annexed his estates, and finally sent him and his followers into exile. That Ascanio was the emperor's friend was of little protection to him.

The pope's attitude toward the "Turkish affair" was equally firm. In 1536, Charles V's expedition drove the pirates out of Tunis, and for a while everyone hoped to see Turkey turn to "the true Christian faith, with God's help." The papal troops, which had participated in the expedition with six galleys and a great deal of good will, brought home the bolt and lock of the gate of Tunis to be kept in St. Peter's, where they still remain. But in only a few months the danger of an impending Turkish invasion was renewed, and the general fear made everything worse. The nightmare of Barbarossa's pirates always on the verge of setting ashore to kill, rape, plunder was shattering the Mediterranean world. Expecting death to come from the sea, the villages and towns in Calabria, Latium, Sicily, and Sardinia could no longer sleep at night. The serious defeat the Turks suffered in Persia reassured the people for a while but did not deceive the pope; it seemed just the other day when the troops of Suleiman, though defeated and worn, had found the strength to conquer Cairo and the Mamelukes. The situation was further complicated by Francis I's politics; this Catholic king, aware of the political necessity of opposing and counterbalancing the Hapsburgs, had entered into negotiations with the Turks as a preliminary to an actual alliance—the "impious league," as people called this association of a Catholic monarchy with the greatest enemy of the faith.

Charles V, as a condition of his participation in an anti-Turk league, demanded that Francis I be excommunicated and that the pope's troops fight against France on his side. Paul III, though indignant, would not allow the urgent and serious danger of the Turks to turn into a personal advantage for the emperor. Once more he managed to keep his precious neutrality, the only guarantee of peace for Italy. In 1537, however, the menace of an Ottoman invasion having in the meantime increased, it became necessary even for Charles V to face the problem of a joint expedition against the infidels, since so far the only measures taken had been local defenses of the Italian coasts. "Things are ready to explode," wrote a Venetian diplomat, depicting the situation in the bleakest way. Everyone seemed to have lost his head but the pope, who set off to inspect the fortresses of Civitavecchia, Ancona, Ostia, Terracina, and those on the coast of the Romagna. He imposed new taxes and tolls to finance the defense. If anyone complained, he answered gravely that to help the faith, good Christians should be ready to give the clothes off their backs, and that he himself was ready to spend his entire fortune and to give his life without

27

hesitation. As time went by, people's fear increased. Many Romans, heedless of the warning of the pope who, to set an example, had stated that he would never abandon Rome, evacuated the city. A bloody raid by the Turks in Puglia, followed by a massive attack on the Venetian garrison in Corfu, spread the conviction that only a strong European league could stop, or at least contain, the infidels' ruinous expansion west.

In that same year, 1538, a league, formed by Spain, Venice, and the Vatican, was solemnly proclaimed to the accompaniment of music, fireworks, and special Masses. The pope opened his arms as he always did when he was happy. He did not imagine then that his joy would soon turn into bitterness, that reciprocal distrust and antagonism was to turn negotiations about the aims, the expenses, and the number of troops each member was to contribute into a dreary and prolix matter. Meanwhile Suleiman rejoiced. Christian leagues, he repeated, are like old brooms which cannot sweep properly, because they fall apart.

The league represented much trouble for the pope. To begin with, it meant finding six thousand oarsmen for the thirty-two galleys he had agreed to contribute. Despite the fact that the fear of "those dogs," the Turks, was so strong, the ships would never have left the harbor if the papacy had not finally ordered compulsory recruitments. All through the Papal States men fit for service hid themselves. A Bolognese chronicler observed: "It was hilarious to see all those people holed up for fear of the galley." Bandits were offered amnesty in exchange for getting the ships out of the Ancona harbor, where they had been bobbing up and down for a long while. Finally, twenty-six galleys set sail, and the favorable wind that accompanied them was considered a good omen. Instead, it was ordained that, in the waters around Preves, a small town of western Greece, the first meeting between Christians and Turks should end in a retreat of forty thousand cowardly men "too frightened by the very mention of the Turks" to even try to engage them. The admiral,

Andrea Doria, the most famous seaman of the time, did not escape charges of cowardice, wickedness, indifference to Christendom, ill will toward the allies, and of having made secret agreements with the Turks. Everyone had his say, but charges and countercharges did not change the fact that the league had at least succeeded in deferring an imminent invasion of Italy.

Although the pope had failed against the infidels, he succeeded in another plan. He called an ecumenical council with the purpose of establishing order in the Church and Christianity. Of all the councils, this one was the most difficult, for during those years the Reformation, sustained by an inexhaustible polemic impulse—the Teutonic, plebeian violence of Martin Luther—had spread like a forest fire from Germany to the rest of northern Europe. In addition to England, Holland, Switzerland, and Denmark were won over by the new doctrine and became involved in that great spiritual revolution. Everywhere the religious dispute deepened, reason was overcome by emotions, justice by violence. In the name of Christ—now become a war cry—military expeditions overran France and Germany with the fury of hurricanes.

Most of the Catholic world was so pessimistic about the religious situation, its conflicting interests, and its deep-rooted passions, that it considered the council useless, if not absurd. Prominent people like Ferdinand, Charles V's brother, openly discredited the council even before it started, arguing that action should replace the many words of the council, and that action had to come from Rome to have any effect on Germany, for apparently "Rome set the example." As for the Protestants, they laughed at the council, saying that they would never be part of a gathering of men "who called themselves Their Holinesses."

What actually seemed to make the council almost impossible was the absence of a real, solid peace between the king of France and the emperor. The former was determined not to participate, and the latter was annoyed because, in the papal bull calling for the council, he had been put on the same level with Francis I, the Turks' ally, who, far from being worthy of the title of Catholic monarch, deserved excommunication. In short, the council was facing difficulties that were inevitable, considering the different goals of the participants, who disagreed even about the town in which they should meet. Only after interminable discussions about the suitability of Mantua, Piacenza, Bologna, or Cambrai, did they finally settle on Trent, because it was close enough to Germany to hope for the participation of the German cardinals. In small groups, the prelates (ashamed of being so few) arrived in Trent, where the population received them in an atmosphere of distrust.

Suspended and resumed several times, the Council of Trent was interrupted when Charles V, once again at war with France, asked for the help of the German Protestants in exchange for generous concessions in religious matters. In Rome, the pope stormed against the emperor for "involving himself with an enemy of Christ even worse than the Turks . . ." and for not being "able to excommunicate Francis I without excommunicating the emperor." The emperor was deaf to the pope's tirades. At that particular moment, Protestants were more than necessary, they were essential. What counted was seeing them line up beside him against Francis I, who had said he wanted to water his horse in the Rhine. The council was not mentioned again before the Treaty of Crépy—the fourth signed by the two kings. Now that the indulgence toward the Protestants had no more reason to exist and the animosities had cooled down, the council, after a few more starts, was officially opened in December, 1545. In this gathering, which represented for the Christian world a promise of divine grace, forgiveness, wisdom, and saintliness, Paul III, the last of the Renaissance popes, a man refined and cultivated to the point of paganism, invested all his passionate energy, his high moral authority. He died four years later, too soon to witness the spiritual rebirth of Catholicism, which did not blossom before the second half of the century, but in time to realize the importance of his own contribution. He had been a great pope, an exceptional man, with only one weakness, but one which gave him human dimension: his family.

"He is very much inclined to promote his relatives," Matteo Dandolo informed the Venetian town council. "It cannot be denied that His Holiness is the most considerate man in the world to his own blood." When Paul was elected pope, his son, nephews, and relatives all came to Rome. Paul was old, they reasoned, he might die at any moment, and there was no time to waste. Pier Luigi, the only survivor of his three sons, was the most brazen. The uniqueness of being the pope's only son seems to have gone to his head, for he ate alone at a small table, exactly as his father did. "Too mad for words," said the Romans.

The old pope, however, knew how to keep his greedy relatives from crowding the Vatican. To each one, and especially to Pier Luigi, he tirelessly recommended discretion and prudence, consideration for the family's name, but above all patience, for he would do his best to benefit all. He promised them wealth, authority, important marriages, and public offices that would lead them to even greater power. Only in one matter he did not wait: he appointed his two fifteen-year-old nephews, Alessandro, Pier Luigi's first-born, and Guido Ascanio, son of Costanza, his daughter, to the sacred college. The news of this act, which conferred great privileges, prebends, and various bishoprics on two children, created a great stir. But the pope defended himself, arguing that it had become a custom for newly elected popes to raise their nephews to high ranks. Hadn't Leo X, for example, bestowed the red hat on the cardinal of Portugal when the latter was still in the crib?

To Pier Luigi's other two sons the pope reserved equally important destinies. He sent one to Charles V, the other to Francis I, convinced that the presence of the little Farneses at both courts would be the best guarantee of his own political neutrality, the preservation of which inspired him to undertake a vast program of marriages meant to consolidate the difficult position of the Vatican in the great game of European diplomacy.

He started by planning the marriage of Pier Luigi's daughter, Vittoria, to some princeling of the French court. The French put forward such illustrious names as the Duke of Vendôme and the Duke of Guise, but negotiations failed mostly because of Charles V's antagonism, who saw in the marriage, if not an alliance, at least a rapprochement between the Vatican and France. Later, Vittoria, "a beautiful and good girl," found herself in the middle of a merry-go-round of eligible husbands. Among the candidates were Louis of Bavaria, the Duke of Braganza, the Prince of Benevento, the son of Ascanio Colonna, and even the young Marquis of Vasto, still a boy. In the end they were all turned down, partly because the pope kept looking for something better, partly because Vittoria now flattered herself that she was pursuing her own schemes, which would ensure her the highest patrician distinction. The greatness of the Farneses exalted her; she surveyed the marriage proposals with disdain, looking for a man about whom she had formed a vague but constant image. Better to end up with nothing, she said, than to accept a husband unworthy of her. Meanwhile, she tormented herself and, worse, had to endure the insolent mockery of Pasquino,* the voice of the satirical Roman spirit. Her saintly

* *Translator's note:* A mutilated, anonymous statue in Rome, to which in the fifteenth century it was customary to affix lampoons satirizing events and figures of the day.

mother, Gerolama, full of evangelical patience, wrote: "Every day Vittoria is plagued by all these husbands; she is crying her eyes out. No sooner do they propose one to her whom she likes, than something happens. They think of someone she cannot bear and the poor soul does not know in whom she can confide. . . ." Yearning for the supreme "investiture" of marriage, Vittoria eventually was more than happy, after so much heartache, to catch Guidobaldo della Rovere, Duke of Urbino, who, conveniently, had just become a widower.

To marry off Orazio, the second son of Pier Luigi, was less complicated. At first the pope thought of a daughter of the Duke of Mantua, but the Gonzagas, who resented the rise of the Farneses more than any other Italian house, had let it be known that they would rather give away the girl to an artisan than to the most important of the Farneses. They were crestfallen when the pope managed to engage young Orazio to Diane of Poitiers, the nine-year-old illegitimate daughter of the new king of France, Henry II. The news of the engagement was warmly welcomed in France, where Orazio, a pleasant and well-educated boy, was known and beloved. He met his fiancée before the entire court; everyone smiled, even the queen, Caterina de' Medici, who did not exactly adore her husband's bastard daughter. "At first the girl was a little shy and upset because someone had told her that *Messer Horatio* would take her away to Italy the next day, but then, when they told her it wasn't so, she brightened up and had a good time. She is truly a girl of great intelligence and quickness of mind, and as far as one can see, she shall become a woman of beautiful features and good skin. . . ."

This marriage, binding France to the Vatican, was arranged to counterbalance another marriage—a real master stroke of Farnese diplomacy—that of Ottavio, third-born of Pier Luigi, with Margherita, Charles V's illegitimate daughter. In Margherita, a rather big girl, one could already discern the arrogant woman she was to become. When only seventeen, she had become the widow of Alessandro de' Medici, who had been stabbed to death by his cousin Lorenzaccio. She wanted a new husband, so long as it was not Ottavio Farnese. She felt it would be only a makeshift marriage, and that she would be wasting herself after having been the first lady of Florence. Besides, she felt that her origins were distinguished enough to allow her to speak out, which she did with peremptory assurance, finding a hundred faults in the marriage contract, in the procedures, in the people in charge of the negotiations. She repeatedly declared that she was no shrinking violet but a grown woman, and independent enough to deserve the highest respect. At the end, however, she had to give in. She left Tuscany and made her appearance in Rome stiff-necked, affecting a half-arrogant, half-injured air, and all dressed in black. With her mourning attire Margherita wanted to indicate that, besides still considering herself Alessandro de' Medici's widow, she had "death in her heart" for having ended up "so basely married."

The pope paid no attention to her attire, embraced her almost in tears, and for days kept looking with loving eyes at the ill-mannered girl. She was the symbol of his highest ambitions, the beginning of the Farnese dynasty, the foundation of the future grandeur of the family. To favor the young couple, the pope had committed himself to creating a state worth 150,000 ducats a year in revenue: Camerino, a territory within the boundaries of the Marches province, purchased by the Papal States at a high price. But the pope was already planning something better for them, he said. Paul III respected money; even more, he respected the power gold has to defy time and to give prestige to a family.

Ottavio was two years younger than the bride. He was shy, clumsy, small, completely uneasy with this mustached, full-breasted, egocentric, and authoritarian girl who had become his wife. A certain hard, cold light in her eyes warned him to stay away from her, to beware of her, if he wanted to avoid being humiliated by her superior intelligence. Indeed, Margherita, who considered herself too clever for the mediocre husband she thought Ottavio, began to mistreat him from the start, looked at him without seeing him, and when she noticed him at all, it was always contemptuously, a prelude to insults and attacks. Margherita led her own life. Instead of living together, they met by chance here and there. For a while her attitude was tolerated in the Vatican, on account of Ottavio's young age, but after almost two years it become imperative that the marriage be consummated. Everyone, the pope, the emperor, public opinion, Pasquino, demanded it. But Margherita continued to persist in her *mala disposición* (she spoke Spanish), hoping perhaps with her irritating, ambiguous behavior to win time, to end up with an annulment and exchange the little Farnese for a pleasant and important (more important than pleasant, perhaps) husband. She would have liked Cosimo de' Medici, for example, the new Duke of Florence.

And so the story of this strange marriage became included among the political problems of those years, somewhere between the problem of the Counter Reformation and that of the Turkish threat. The more it was discussed the deeper it was plunged into ridicule. For months, every letter or dispatch sent from Rome contained a detailed report on the couple's intimacy. "She has not as yet taken him as her husband," the Spanish messengers repeated over and again, plying between Rome and Madrid with entreaties and chastisements for the recalcitrant bride. In the Vatican the pope continued to shower Margherita with kindness, fondled her, gave her jewels, tried in every way to create for the mustached girl an atmosphere of warmth and ease. Cardinal Alessandro, her brother-in-law, also tried to please her by organizing receptions in her honor. Half affectionate and half alarmed, he always kept an eye on her, as men usually do with intelligent women, and Margherita certainly was intelligent.

35

In the meantime Ottavio was growing, becoming a man, but he was still shy. "You don't have to be languorous and in love," the pope said to him. The only thing to do was to present Margherita with his rational desire for making children, "otherwise they will say that you are a worthless husband." This last argument impressed the young man, who was now preoccupied with maintaining his image. At night, excited and vexed at the same time, he resumed knocking at his wife's door. From inside, the unapproachable Margherita grumbled to be left alone because she had a headache. "I beg Your Majesty," she wrote to her father, "not to order me to do it for the moment, for I had rather drown myself."

Toward the end of 1539 people were dying of laughter. "Between the pope and Madama d'Austria there is bitterness and many harsh words." By now Paul III felt only reproach for Margherita. Suddenly a rumor was spread that the two had finally slept together. But the news was false, a belated April fools' joke. One can imagine the spirit with which the Vatican received the letters of congratulation that arrived from all over Europe. . . . The pope, indignant at having lost face with the emperor, thus negatively influencing the diplomatic relations between Spain and the Vatican, informed Charles V that if he, the emperor, did not see to it that the bride recover her senses, he would be forced to think that His Majesty tolerated his daughter's inconceivable obstinacy. The pope requested the immediate dismissal of Don Lope, Margherita's butler, and his wife, who influenced the princess with a lot of nonsense. "It's they who corrupt this lady," was the general opinion of the papal court.

Margherita agreed to dismiss the two Spaniards but not to sleep with her husband. She pleaded that he was a simpleton, that he smelled, had bad breath, and wet the bed. At that point the emperor decided to appoint a commission to examine the reasons the princess gave for wanting an annulment. The commission's declaring her case invalid, and the news that Cosimo de' Medici had married Eleonora of Toledo began to wear down Margherita's resistance. On the night of October 18, 1540, after two years of grumbling chastity, Ottavio, scrubbed for the occasion, slipped into the four-posted, silk-curtained bed, and Madama d'Austria resigned herself to her destiny of being a Farnese wife.

*

Margherita by no means was the most complex character in the family. This distinction belonged to her father-in-law, Pier Luigi. Titian portrayed him as he was—without inhibitions and full of sanguine vitality. His rich black beard—one of the few beards of the time—gave him a certain majesty and an almost barbaric magnificence. For his portrait, Pier Luigi insisted on posing encased in the heavy armor of a *condottiere,* or more precisely, of a *Gonfaloniere della Chiesa* [Standard-bearer of the Church], one of the first titles his father had obtained for him. His stance clearly suggests the kind of life he led, one without self-denial or difficulty, a life befitting a ruler and a soldier. At that time, all of Italy gossiped about his sodomitical habits which, on occasion, exceeded all limits and burst into criminal proportion, shaking even that early cinquecento, usually so tolerant of the sins of the flesh. Pier Luigi's prominent position and his early experience in public life had taught him the value of self-control as a political, but not as a moral, virtue. The pope's moral zeal did not spare his son, but Pier Luigi was not intimidated by his father's scoldings, as he demonstrated in the incident with Monsignor Cosimo Geri, the fair and gentle Bishop of Fano. The bishop died of shame and a broken heart at only twenty-four, after having endured the savage assaults of the *Gonfaloniere* while he was visiting Fano. The scandal made the rounds of all chancelleries in Europe, and the pope complained about it in a memorable letter to Pier Luigi, who couldn't care less and continued to "exceed," as they euphemistically said in Rome, almost as if he deliberately wanted to keep up-to-date his reputation of being an intemperate and ill-mannered man. His wife Gerolama said nothing; she never allowed herself a reproach, not even a sarcastic remark. She had an inimitable angelic streak and the patience of a woman who chose to be wise.

Except for his homosexuality, Pier Luigi was a man full of good qualities. He was intelligent, active, and had a humanistic education, as was the custom in that fierce but highly spiritual era. Although his father had entrusted him with several important appointments, both political and military, Pier Luigi owed his status to the duchy of Castro, a small, wooded estate near Lake Bolsena. Pride in being its ruler led him to administer it wisely and to try to improve its conditions. Annibal Caro, who hated Castro, described it as "a gipsy hovel so shabby and dirty one had to shut his eyes and hold his nose." But thanks to Pier Luigi's care, the town, planned by Antonio da Sangallo, turned into a "new Carthage," a comparison which fits, if nothing else, because one hundred years later the town was destroyed to its last stone.

Castro, a land doomed to mediocrity in spite of the most enthusiastic improvements, awakened in Pier Luigi the desire for a larger, more illustrious domain. His will needed to realize itself in great enterprises. Suddenly, he could no longer bear to be one of the many ambitious participants in the game of high politics who never reach the goal. The idea of getting hold of Parma and Piacenza—two cities he knew well since he had often fortified and defended them against local conflicts and against the Spanish and French troops ranged along the borders —became a cherished, greedy, secret project of his. He did not reveal his plan to his father, convinced that, in order to succeed

38

in the chaos of Italian politics, he had to plan a very subtle diplomatic operation. He got his example directly from the pope, his father, who was spending his life in a constant effort not to quarrel either with France or with Spain, while at the same time he was trying to foresee the movements of European politics, so much more disquieting in peacetime than in the clamor of war. From him Pier Luigi had learned that the first thing to do to prevent the two big powers from jeopardizing his project was to keep rigorously neutral.

From 1540 to 1545 Pier Luigi schemed incessantly; that is, he gave both kings testimonials of his allegiance. He was so engaged in his project that he did not mind being a slave to either master, or repressing his rather unorthodox habits. "Now he is all spiritual," Cardinal Gonzaga wrote of him. "Every day he attends High Mass and has St. Paul's Epistles read to him, to show how greatly changed his life is." If the cardinal could only have imagined that the "change" was part of a well-defined political calculation, he would have spared his irony.

Parma and Piacenza, as noted before, belonged to the Papal States; therefore, should the pope decide to give them to a member of his family, the emperor's legal consent was not necessary. Nonetheless, for the sake of peace and quiet, it would have been wiser for everyone to secure Charles V's approval, considering that the two cities had always been a temptation for him too.

At the beginning of 1545, something important happened: Margherita became pregnant. Pier Luigi felt immediately that his daughter-in-law's pregnancy ought to be exploited. The emperor would be soon a grandfather, and grandfathers always have a soft heart. Was there ever one insensitive to the flesh of his flesh? This grandson, this little Farnese could not have been announced at a better time. Margherita had given a hand to fortune, that famous Farnese fortune which for many years had excited the envy of so many people. They maliciously called it

39

la fortunazza paolina, Paul's damn good luck. People of the highest rank enviously cursed at the mere thought of this family that had everything—the papal tiara, the purple of cardinalship, wealth, authority, fame, kinship with the most important dynasties in Europe. And now, with the advent of this pregnancy, they possessed the key to considerably more good fortune: the mustached girl could not have chosen a better moment to get pregnant. Cardinal Gonzaga suffered bilious attacks from rage: "I have never seen anything more timely done than the blessed seed of Ottavio entering the venerable womb of Madama d'Austria. The ineffable luck of Pope Paul frightens everyone, and especially those to whom he has never shown too much friendship, such as we."

Pier Luigi built his plan on Margherita's pregnancy and feverishly entered the Parma-and-Piacenza competition. But he had to hurry. "What can be done today should never be postponed till tomorrow," he advised his secretary, the faithful Annibal Caro. All the more reason for the homily, since the pope's health was declining and his death approaching. As it always happened at the deaths of nepotistic popes, sons, nephews, and friends remained unprotected and were at the mercy of those who had been repressed for too long. Another reason to hurry was that Parma and Piacenza had to be his before the opening of the ecumenical council, among whose programs was that of putting an end to any sort of ecclesiastical favoritism. Thus the password was to hurry.

Paul III did not want, or at least was reluctant, to part with Parma and Piacenza. He was the first to realize the gravity of such a separation. When conversation began to touch on the two cities, he would speak only in very vague terms. Meanwhile, Pier Luigi was busy fortifying Piacenza as if it already belonged to him and he kept in contact with his two agents in Rome, Gambara and Filareto, with instructions that are models of ruthless, lucid political prose: "My dear Apollonio, don't miss the present occasion. Go, supplicate humbly, implore, constantly entreat and remind, and use all the diligence I trust you to have." Filareto reassured him that things were going well; in fact they were now moving by themselves, he had simply to give them a finishing touch at the right moment. In truth, all the caution, the whole evasive patience, the subtle ability of both agents were necessary to convince the old pope that it was not really a loss for him, just an exchange: Camerino and Nepi were to be given to the Papal States in return for Parma and Piacenza. The Holy See, insisted Filareto, could only gain from this exchange because, oddly enough, the incomes from Parma and Piacenza were smaller than the incomes from Camerino and Nepi. But the pope continued to be evasive; although "he was greedy," he understood very well that Parma and Piacenza had a political value enormously superior to the economic value of Camerino and Nepi. To give them away meant to cause an uproar and to harm the Vatican, even if Filareto was ready to talk for hours to demonstrate the contrary.

Days passed in uncertainty. Although Filareto pressed him relentlessly, the pope stalled, as he always did before making any decision. Parma and Piacenza, so isolated, Filareto said, from the rest of the Papal States, after Modena and Reggio had gone to the Estensi family, would be very difficult to defend in case of war. It would therefore be wise to entrust them to a vassal who had authority and military experience. And who was better suited than Pier Luigi to keep the towns safe for the Vatican? Paul III reflected awhile, then opened his arms in his typical gesture of satisfaction. There, finally, was a sensible argument, one which flattered his fatherly pride, dispelled any doubt, and offered him a solid case against the adversaries who already were raising their voices in protest. Filareto was right. Pier Luigi was the suitable person.

While the pope was already assuring Filareto that the Parma and Piacenza matter was as good as settled, two messengers from

Charles V unexpectedly appeared in the Vatican. The emperor, they said, was willing to give his consent to the investiture on the condition that the two cities go to Ottavio, the emperor's son-in-law. The chroniclers of the time record that the news, given to Paul when he was about to go to sleep, put him in a state of tremendous agitation. He was not a man who accepted orders, not even from the emperor. More than once, in the last years, threats had proven to have just the opposite effect on His Holiness. This time the effect was disastrous, for in a fit of anger he decided to submit the matter to the Consistory Court. The cardinals would decide about Parma and Piacenza —Pier Luigi would have to get them from the Consistory. And if not, so much the worse for him. No matter what, he had to teach a lesson to this emperor who interfered in his family business.

Needless to say, the pope's decision threw the Farneses into great anxiety. Margherita, in her seventh month, with the neurotic mood of pregnant women, staged fainting fits. She was by now openly backing her father-in-law's and her husband's interests; she wanted at all cost to become the Duchess of Parma and Piacenza. Annoyed, the pope avoided her. These were bad days for the Farneses, and even the cardinals loyal to them could not hide their embarrassment. Others, openly opposed, deserted the meetings with the excuse of having to attend religious exercises or make penitential visits to the churches of Rome. The French cardinals bristled at the very name of the two towns; not to mention the Spanish and the reformist cardinals, who expressed their opposition in the most fiery speeches. But all this disagreement stimulated the old pope. Outside the meetings he never tired of trying to win over the cardinals, echoing, over and again, Filareto's argument which had now become his own. But they were "badly digested arguments," said Ercole Gonzaga venomously, "and so weak it is a shame mentioning them." So, if the pope gave Parma and Piacenza up just because they were too far from the rest of the

Papal States' territories, he could, for that matter, get rid of Avignon, which is in France. And why not Bologna too, since it was a border town and cost a fortune to keep? The pope took no notice of the sarcasm. He doubled his efforts and, using all the subtleties of curial rhetoric, he kept going from cardinal to cardinal with admirable patience.

Eventually Paul III's patience was rewarded. On August 19, 1545, the Consistory Court turned Parma and Piacenza over to Pier Luigi and approved the restitution of Camerino and Nepi to the Papal States. Ottavio was compensated with the small duchy of Castro, which had belonged to his father, and with the rights of succession to the duchy of Parma and Piacenza for himself and his heirs.

The disappointment in what proved to be the greatest act of nepotism ever committed, and one destined to remain unsurpassed, was enormous. Charles V considered the new duke too greedy and capable of being politically dangerous, yet he preferred not to "undo what had already been done," first because he did not want an open break with the pope (whom he needed in the imminent war against the Turks) and second because Margherita had given birth to twins, and it would have been illogical to object to a provision ensuring the duchy to his grandchildren. The French were indignant; they insisted that Parma and Piacenza belonged to the state of Milan, the sovereignty of which they hoped one day to claim. They were also alarmed because the Consistory decree, to which Charles V had not really objected, would link the Farneses definitively with the emperor. The Italian states, too, were unhappy, for they saw the new duchy as a disturbing element in an already uncertain and humiliating political situation. The most unhappy of all—in fact, he was furious—was Cardinal Ercole Gonzaga, who gave voice to his resentment in a series of vehement letters. "We," he wrote to the Duke of Ferrara, "who have inherited land earned so arduously by our forefathers, and which we retain with so much effort and anguish, we think it is very strange to see a duke be made in one night, like a mushroom." And, "I am stunned by that damn luck of his [Paul III's]." He would not be surprised, he said, if one day Paul, considering that all he did turned out so well, found the way of making his son king of Spain, of France, of everything.

Fortune undoubtedly loved the Farneses, and if it sometimes abandoned them it always returned to lead them to even greater heights. "And I, fool that I am," Cardinal Gonzaga continued, "am here racking my brain, while the sweet little old man gloats most happily over his victory."

Perhaps Paul III did not gloat, but he certainly was very happy. In his euphoria, he ordered the engraver Grechetto to design a memorial coin with the Farnese lilies surmounted by a Ganymede leaning over Jove's eagle.

Pier Luigi was happy too. A joke went around that "he traded a Camerino [Italian for water-closet] for two beautiful chambers." Pier Luigi did not care. He smiled the scoffing smile of Fortune's darling. To reign was for him an exalting, intoxicating activity, the best way to assert his leadership. Wars, famines, increasing poverty, the continuous flow of foreign armies had brought the duchy almost to the verge of anarchy; yet, to Pier Luigi it was a promised land which would flourish under his wise administration. He immediately began to busy himself furiously, as if he had a premonition that his life would not last long and he wanted to live fully the little that was left. To think that an astrologer had once predicted he would die of dissipation at seventy-four! Pier Luigi believed in Machiavelli's concept of the state and the prince (he was very envious of Cesare Borgia, whom Machiavelli had taken as a model) and now his first concern was to be strong and respected. He set out, as did those who succeeded him, to revoke many of the nobility's privileges and to destroy any political power opposing his dictatorship.

The pope, to relieve his conscience toward the Church for what he had done for his son, had prudently limited Pier Luigi's jurisdictional rights. For months he cautioned him to be careful with the nobles, to gain their friendship with presents and favors. "They are more powerful than those from Ferrara," the pope wrote, "and are used to the Vatican's gentle rule." He advised the new duke how to treat his vassals in order to keep them faithful and to use them at his convenience, instead of alienating them, as he indeed was now doing.

Of course this advice remained unheeded. Incapable of moderation, Pier Luigi continued in his centralizing policy. Before too long, the vassals felt the strong authority that radiated from Piacenza, the chosen capital. The duchy was studded with fortresses and castles, and the lords who owned them were among the most fierce, independent, tyrannical men in Italy. The whole territory of Parma and Piacenza resembled an archipelago of island-communities where the papal administration had merely meandered. They were greedy, almost rapacious, and cruel to their serfs. They often forbade the latter, for example, to transport food to the city, so as to be able to export or smuggle it themselves. The zeal Pier Luigi showed in stopping these abuses brought him to affect a concern for the serfs which was not entirely sincere. But the poor people did not know that. Fascinated by the duke's personality, they saw in him only a father figure willing to take their misery upon himself. Who before him had ever cared for the "well-being of the poor"? Pier Luigi had only to stretch out his arm in a gesture of reassurance to make them feel protected and a little less poor.

Pier Luigi had undoubtedly a natural propensity for order. He surrounded himself with excellent assistants, diplomats, and public officers, whose very presence was a guarantee of the honesty and efficiency of the new administration; and he himself had apparently decided to lead a more wholesome life. His seeming moderation (if only a more discreet practice of his vices, it still appeared very similar to a real emotional stability) was in itself surprising for a man to whom all the vices of the century had been attributed. He had even asked his wife to join him in Piacenza. The excellent Girolama, a matron with little authority but great dignity, was incredulous and touched by this honor coming from a husband "who had never cared for her when she was young."

The almost virtuous behavior and the reforms were not the only thing about Pier Luigi that surprised the lords of Parma and Piacenza. They were unused to the Farnese pomp, the magnificent receptions, the carnivals and tournaments to which all the beautiful women of Piacenza were invited. New, too, was the fortress: Pier Luigi had a mania for fortresses. "The prince who fears his own people more than any foreigner," Machiavelli had cautioned, "has to build fortresses." And Pier Luigi, fearing especially local enemies, in addition to the many outside the duchy, had started immediately to build a formidable one in Piacenza, in order not to remain defenseless once the pope died. On May 15, 1547, with artillery booming and public celebration, the first stone was laid. The pope, having previously fixed the day and the hour, attended the ceremony by proxy, sending his blessings from Rome. His sign of the cross was all the support he gave to architect Domenico Giannelli's masterpiece. "Help yourself so that God will help you," the pope wrote to his son, promising him money that never arrived. Pier Luigi, who had no time to lose, complained to him in every letter.

In spite of financial difficulties, however, the construction of the fortress continued feverishly, employing thousands of workers from all over the province, and hundreds of oxen and carts provided by an exasperated nobility. "The duke thinks, talks, dreams of nothing but his damn castle." The fortress was almost completed when, tragically, one Ferrante Gonzaga, threatening for a moment to break the *fortunazza paolina,* cut short Pier Luigi's life.

This Don Ferrante was the son of Isabella d'Este, the famous Marchioness of Mantua, from whom he had inherited neither her political genius nor artistic sensibility, but only a certain measure of business intuition. He was governor of Milan, and to please Charles V, whose policy in Italy he passionately favored, he incited the emperor with elaborate schemes for the annexation of Italian territories and towns to the Spanish Empire. Don Ferrante, incidentally, was the brother of the same Cardinal Gonzaga who for years had annoyed the Farneses with his relentless sarcasm, and he too was spellbound by his brother's subtle and dangerously clever suggestions. The most active years of his life were dedicated to the Farneses' destruction. To organize political assassinations and conspiracies was his specialty—he had already proven his talents in Genoa and in Siena —the plot to liquidate Pier Luigi was to become his masterpiece. Even if Charles V should not reward him (all of Ferrante's conspiracies were designed to make money), the satisfaction of destroying the hated Farnese would be enough.

The emperor seemed quite interested. First of all, he had never officially recognized Pier Luigi as Duke of Parma and Piacenza and was thinking of confiscating the two towns himself as soon as the pope died. Secondly, the duke was provoking a number of irritating diplomatic incidents with his drastic measures against the lords. Finally, he was anxious to rid himself of an ambitious man who could turn against him at any moment. That Pier Luigi was his daughter's father-in-law was an insignificant detail in a big matter, as Parma and Piacenza undoubtedly were. "As long as his father lives," wrote Don Ferrante to Charles V—and perhaps it was Ercole who held the pen—"Pier Luigi leads a secure life and is not as careful as

47

he will be once he loses his shield. It is conceivable, therefore, that he will guard his land much more carefully than he does now." Most probably this was the argument that convinced the emperor to agree to the plot. He wanted no murder, though; it was enough for him that they capture Pier Luigi and keep him in prison until the Spanish troops had secured the duchy. Don Ferrante did not agree. "Once he is dead," he objected, "we won't have to bother with him any longer." But since the emperor insisted they be careful, Ferrante pretended to agree, for fear Charles should withdraw his permission. With no great difficulty Ferrante found in Piacenza the cooperation of some lords who had had enough of Pier Luigi, and these gentlemen added to the "contract" a tiny, apparently insignificant clause: "There shall be no mention made of, no questions asked about, any dead man or profit made on the side." Charles V signed it without realizing he had signed Pier Luigi's death sentence.

Chief among Ferrante's accomplices was Count Giovanni Anguissola, a prominent figure in Piacenza, a man of bold wickedness, courageous, violent, one of those men, according to Machiavelli, ideal in "matters of life and death." Many historians, *cherchant la femme* in this story, suggested that Pier Luigi had seduced Anguissola's wife. But the assumption is groundless, for the count later declared he had acted only on behalf of his mother country, so to speak. He was a born conspirator. He could not have better chosen the actors for this drama, cast the roles more cleverly, and played the protagonist with more aplomb.

Pier Luigi was killed in September. He was just back from an inspection of the fortress and was talking to his private physician, Doctor Coppalata, perhaps about his last fit of gout. Suddenly Count Anguissola, "the leader of the assault," followed by Agostino Landi, Camillo Pallavicini, and Gianluigi Confalonieri, attacked him with a dagger. Pier Luigi had just time to whisper "Lord," then he collapsed. His disfigured corpse was hung out of a window. A frightened crowd stood in front of the castle and stared in silence. Two days later, Don Ferrante Gonzaga occupied the town in the name of the emperor. He could not reach Parma, however, for troops faithful to Pier Luigi had concentrated there and held the town. In Piacenza the new masters found a somber and hostile atmosphere. It did not surprise them. The conspirators themselves had declared that "the townspeople are so determined to remain faithful to the duke that it is not wise to try to change their minds." In the confusion of the occupation Annibal Caro managed to escape, but Apollonio Filareto was imprisoned for three years, in a dungeon "too dark and damp even for an eel."

On the day they killed his son, Pope Paul, in an excellent mood, was giving audience to an ambassador. When they cautiously gave him the news, he made a tremendous effort to control his anguish. Even later, he constantly pretended that he considered politics too impersonal for personal grief, but as soon as he was alone, he cried desperately, inconsolably. His body hunched over, his wrinkles like thousand of scars, his mouth itself resembling a scar quivering with pain, he lived for two more years, each day a battle against the sorrow of knowing his son dead, of realizing the futility and the vanity of human ambitions. He never again was heard to say that the Farneses were lucky. Immediately after Pier Luigi's assassination, however, he started an intense diplomatic activity for the recovery of Piacenza. In spite of all his experience, it took him some time before realizing that Charles V, who promised that sooner or later the town would be returned, had no intention of doing so and was using the issue of Piacenza now as a threat, now as an enticement, depending on his political needs of the moment. In the end, Charles V declared that he not only would not return Piacenza but that he also wanted Parma. By way of compensation—a sign of his generosity, not of indemnity—the emperor offered the Farneses a small estate near Naples worth forty thousand ducats a year. Pope Paul staggered under this new blow. "If he does not die of grief now, he is immortal," the dignitaries whispered in the Vatican.

The pope did not die, and a contemporary biographer, almost sober and accurate in a time of rhetorical excess, said that Pope Farnese "had a Roman soul which would not bear insult." And indeed his pride made him seek a moral victory which turned out to be almost a defeat. He commanded the return of Parma and Piacenza to the Papal States. Ottavio was to become Duke of Castro, and Orazio, his brother, Duke of Camerino. At the same time, a member of the Orsini family faithful to the pope would occupy Parma in the name of the Holy See. This decision, which the pope thought the best answer to his defeat, distressed all the Farneses. With the eternal injustice that drives the young against the old, the grandchildren united against the pope in a palace plot. Ottavio and his brother Cardinal Alessandro were soon negotiating with Charles V and were even considering the murder of their father. Don Ferrante, in fact, had urged them for some time to take sides openly with the emperor, for only he was in the position to return—in one way or another, sooner or later—what their grandfather was now depriving them of. Terrified of ending up destitute and forgotten, which was worse than being killed, and ready to make any compromise in order to remain "someone" after the pope's death, which could not be far off, Ottavio secretly left Rome and set out for Parma. But there Camillo Orsini, obedient to the pope's orders, stopped him at the gates and forced him to retreat to the nearby castle of Torchiara.

Meanwhile, Ottavio's wife went about in a frenzy; she wanted to kneel with her child (the other twin had died) before the emperor her father or to kill herself in the presence of His

Holiness. But His Holiness did not bat an eye to her im-
plorations. None of his relatives could ever again make him
change his mind. He had always wished to live until the jubilee
year celebrations of 1550, but the open insubordination of his
family was fatal to him. He was eighty-three years old. When
he heard that Ottavio, "his idol," had run away, Paul was
swept by a terrible anger; he trampled on his skullcap, accused
his grandchildren of treason, shouted he would destroy them
as quickly as he had elevated them, and uttered "the worse
words on earth." The next morning, perhaps to relax, he went
to his vineyard on Monte Cavallo. The same evening, either
because of anger or of the cold weather, he got a stomach illness and he started to throw up, and, to the dismay of those
around him, he was taken by a high fever. "I beg you not to
cause the death of your illustrious grandfather," wrote one of
the pope's attendants to Ottavio, hoping his return to Rome
would postpone the inevitable. "Has Ottavio come back?" asked
the sick man between one retch and the other. Ottavio did not
come back; he remained at Torchiara, wavering between re-
pentance and obstinacy. The old Cardinal del Monte was
sent to convince him to return but came back alone and grieved,
"It is unheard of, ever since St. Peter, that a pope should send
an old and respectable cardinal to a prince—less than a king—
who does not even listen to the message." In any case, at that
point, not even Ottavio's return could have saved the pope.
"*Contra vim mortis*," pronounced the physicians, "*non est me-
dicamen fortis.*" Paul III was dying; in his agony he found a
serenity that had only a shade of sadness. "His Holiness is
still conscious and talks with feeling to Madama d'Austria,
and to Cardinal Alessandro especially he says kind and loving
words that would touch a stone." Around the deathbed there
came the whole family, that much beloved and pampered family of Paul III. In his last days he kept apologizing to God and

repeated the words of the Psalm: "My sin remains before my eyes; if it had not dominated me, I would not deserve so much penance." One day before his death, he entered into a coma and felt nothing more. He did not realize that Cardinal Alessandro was extorting from him one last concession: a papal bull with which Parma and Piacenza were to be given to Ottavio. On November 10, 1549, a time of rain and chrysanthemums, of flowers for the dead, Paul expired. Everyone thought he had died of anguish and anger. The autopsy revealed "very healthy organs which could have lasted for years; but in his heart there were three drops of congealed blood thought to have been caused by his fit of anger."

The pope's body was exhibited in St. Peter's, and the Romans went en masse to kiss his foot, "pitying him for having been killed by the very people he had loved so much." Everyone understood that an exceptional man had died. Only at the court of Spain was his death celebrated "with undescribable gaiety." Pasquino was silent, not one malicious verse appeared either in Latin or Italian—the sincerest homage Paul could have wished. Guglielmo della Porta designed a splendid tomb for him.

Ottavio returned to Parma with the papal bull countersigned by the college of cardinals but was driven back once again. Camillo Orsini declared that the bull had been extorted from a dying man and that the sacred college, when the papal see was vacant, had no authority to transfer papal possessions. He must therefore wait for the new pope's decision.

The new pope, Julius II, was elected after a very long conclave. He confirmed the Farneses' ownership of Parma. Piacenza was still in the hands of the emperor. When the papal court reproached Julius II for giving away Parma instead of keeping it for himself or his relatives, the new pope, who owed his election mostly to Cardinal Alessandro Farnese, answered that he preferred to be poor and a gentleman rather than to be rich and falsehearted.

Ottavio solemnly entered Parma at the end of February, 1550. The *fortunazza paolina* had been kind to him, and he had a premonition it would not leave him for a long time.

*

Good luck indeed did not desert Ottavio. It was there to protect the first years of his conspiracy-threatened administration. For months "he had to be cautious, he could not leave the house or venture to go out too far, and he was always accompanied by a well-armed escort." For Parma was an incubator of conspiracies. Among the lords there was more than one who offered himself to kill Ottavio. And there was Ferrante Gonzaga, who still wanted to cut any Farnese to pieces and who wrote to Charles V apologizing in advance for anything he might undertake against the Farnese family, for, he said, "I would judge myself too much a coward if I did not try something against them."

Good fortune also remained with Ottavio later in his career, when, for complicated political reasons, he was forced to ally himself with France against Spain, whose siege of Parma almost ravaged the duchy. Philip II of Spain and Ottavio concluded the war with the Treaty of Ghent, in which Piacenza was returned to the Farneses.

Eight years had passed since the assassination of Pier Luigi. A clause in the treaty bound Ottavio to pardon his vassals any political crime, to treat his father's murderers with equanimity, and to protect their life and property. If any of them wanted to leave the duchy, he had to let him go after buying his property at a fair price. Ottavio did more. During his long administration, he adopted toward his vassals—eternal thorn in the side of every ruler of the time—a policy quite different from that of his descendants, one of moderation. He sought their favor

53

with gifts and rewards; he entertained them magnificently and encouraged them to compete with each other in the fineness of clothes, in the luxury and inventiveness of tournaments and hunting parties, thinking he could thereby transform those quarrelsome and anarchic country squires into disciplined courtiers. But his project was only partly successful; the restless lords, bound by their aggressive pride and dreams of power, remained essentially unchanged.

Once the initial threat of war was over, Ottavio's administration was peaceful, constructive, and moderate. In the tiny duchy everything had to be redone—from juridical reform to street-paving, from census-taking to agrarian improvement, supervision of bridges and canals, and reorganization of the army and the towns, especially the capital, Parma, "a jungle of noise, theft, and murder," as an ambassador had described it some years before. Finally there were Parma's ugly and inadequate buildings to improve, and the construction of a palace for Ottavio, who was temporarily housed in the bishop's residence. There were public holidays to organize, new coins to mint. Work had to be done to encourage printers to produce new and accurate editions of the classics; to promote music, patronize architects, writers, painters. And all had to be done in the style that had given the Farneses a reputation throughout Europe. In short, Ottavio attempted to achieve a delicate balance between humaneness and magnificence, leisure and industry, which would make it possible to equal other European courts where the art of good living had reached perfection.

Beside a passion for leadership, Ottavio had inherited from his father a strong sensuality. His conduct with women was curt, and with a patriarchal indifference for morals, he had love affairs that were all fruitful—a flock of illegitimate daughters all splendidly married off to the best families in the duchy. His marriage with Margherita had long since stopped being a marriage; it had turned into a chaste political alliance. They

54

saw each other so infrequently that at times Ottavio had to make an effort to remember her face. At the beginning, caught in the euphoria of ruling the new duchy, Margherita had promised to join Ottavio in Parma "with the firm intention of never to quarrel again but to live happily together." It was an excellent resolution, and one which she never kept, for she continued to live apart from her husband and insisted on her right to an independent life. In 1559 her stepbrother, Philip II of Spain, entrusted her with the administration of Flanders, a task she handled brilliantly, mastering the rebellious country with great shrewdness. When she returned to Italy eight years later, worn out by gout and fatigue, with the excuse that the air was too heavy in Parma she settled in the mountain town of L'Aquila, where Philip had made her governor. There, in those often snowy mountains, she lived in a rustic seclusion that made her ladies-in-waiting yearn for the pleasures of society and for less cruel winters. Ottavio rarely visited her; by now they treated each other with fraternal tolerance. Madama had become matronly; her face, covered with a web of wrinkles, spoke of a life both full and uneasy. It was one of those faces that improve with age, although she still had a mustache. Her court was simple and it expressed her instinct for moderation and frugality. Ottavio's visits were brief, listless. After a few days, Madama was alone again with her bored courtiers grumbling because of the wind, the long winters, the inadequate fireplaces. And the duke returned to the plain, to his life of a semi-bachelor ruler free to devote himself to an exuberant and promiscuous sensual life. He had never felt any tenderness for Margherita; and it took him years to forget the time she had locked him out of their bedroom. But now that a great part of their stormy life had passed, he felt grateful to her. A strange woman, Margherita—hard, motherly, and masculine all at once. One would not have thought, when she so savagely refused herself to her

55

husband, that one day she would do so much, and with so much devotion, in the interest of the dynasty.

Another person who dedicated his entire life to the upkeep of the family name and on whom Ottavio could always depend, was his brother Alessandro. For many years Alessandro had pursued the dream of becoming pope—the only thing he never obtained, and that because of the enmity of Cardinals d'Este and de' Medici. Philip II, intolerant of the elevation of any Italian family, had forced Alessandro to renounce forever the papal tiara in exchange for the privilege of personally choosing every pope. In little less than twenty-five years Alessandro created six popes—a bittersweet satisfaction, but one that made of him in Rome a king without crown, with immense power both in Italy and abroad in the highest spheres of European politics.

Alessandro also succeeded in linking his name to a whole artistic and cultural era; his villa at Caprarola, near Rome, became a center of Italian Renaissance. He was rich and loved to display his opulence; his court numbered more than three hundred people and he lived sumptuously, as had his grand-father, Pope Paul, who had instilled a sense of family grandeur in all his sons, nephews, and grandsons since their childhood. An aesthete and an intellectual, educated in the polished and ornate sixteenth-century taste, an amateur in the best hu-manistic sense, Cardinal Alessandro received the approbation of the most illustrious men in Italy. His guests were scholars, politicians, artists. Philologists and bibliophiles came from all over Europe to examine reverently the incunabula, the Greek codes, the rare manuscripts of the famous Farnese library. Scholars who had been favored by the cardinal and had enjoyed his friendship and protection did their utmost to find rare editions and other literary and artistic treasures for him. Many bequeathed to him their books, and others scouted all over Italy to buy him original Greek texts, at that time already difficult to find. His secretary and friend, Annibal Caro, who had devoted most of his life to the Farnese family, literally scoured the remotest monasteries for precious volumes. In Rome, Alessandro had settled in the Palazzo della Cancelleria; he never really inhabited Palazzo Farnese, whose upper stories at the time were still unfinished. But there, in the big family house, Alessandro displayed his immense art collection: armors, statues, antiques, medals, books, precious stones, paintings. All his life, in this palace which is still one of the most beautiful, perhaps the most beautiful, in Rome, Alessandro collected masterpieces, savoring the most refined cultural experiences. Which does not mean he did not enjoy other, less spiritual pleasures. "I wish Your Lordship weren't studying so much," a friend wrote to him playfully. "Take example from me, be happy. And if there aren't enough attractive women over there, Your Lordship should give me permission to bring you one so beautiful that all the Greek and Latin philosophers you have around you will leave their books to dance and make love with her." The cardinal did not need any encouragement; his charm his trips and diplomatic missions were combined with gallant escapades. Any of the portraits Titian made of him show how fascinating he must have been. The velvet tricorn crowns a handsome, dark head, and the face would be almost too perfect if it were not for a touch of irony barely discernible in his magnificent eyes and at the corners of his too-delicate mouth. Everyone thought him extraordinarily affable, which perhaps somewhat harmed the statesman but added charm to the man of the world. Pope Paul often complained about this grandson who so often "sailed for Cythera," that is, embarked on ephemeral, though genuine and enthusiastic, love affairs. Public opinion judged these adventures to be signs of an immense vitality that had to be accepted if not praised.

In the second part of his life, however, Alessandro gave up women and dedicated himself, with remarkable seriousness, to religion. He founded schools of theology, canon law, and science, and promoted many enterprises of Counter Reformation propaganda, making of Rome an intellectual and religious center more important than ever. He became dean of the sacred college, protector of the newly founded Society of Jesus, friend of such saintly men as Philip Neri and Francis Borgia. He now built churches as magnificent as the *palazzi* he had built before, but without giving up his refined and wise epicureanism. "Rome is the world's stage," wrote one of his friends, "and Your Lordship is a portrait of all the beauty there is in Rome."

When Alessandro died of a stroke at sixty-nine, three years after his brother Ottavio had died, the grief was enormous. "The whole of Rome grieves over his death," said a dispatch from the court of Mantua, usually so hostile to the Farneses. "The only light in the papal court and the sacred college has gone out. The father of charitable institutions, who spent forty thousand scudi each year to feed the poor, orphans, artists, widows, spinsters, and who during famines always held out his generous hand, has gone. He was a great man, the grandson of a pope; he was cardinal for fifty-four years, helped the Church in many ways, subsidized other cardinals and princes with thousands of scudi, constructed many buildings both sacred and profane. He was buried in the Chiesa del Gesù and rose to Heaven. . . ."

II

Alessandro Farnese

At the end of 1592, a messenger from Flanders reported to the court of Parma the death of Duke Alessandro. The news was not unexpected. For months, the health of the third Duke of Parma had been discussed, and his son Ranuccio, who acted as regent, was kept informed of it by letters so detailed that, on their basis alone, it is possible to outline the history of his sickness, or better, sicknesses. Some of these were mysterious and incurable; others were quite well defined. Gout, kidney infection, stones, vapors, melancholia, roaming cramps, a little tertian fever, perhaps a touch of syphilis—an intricate pathological tangle which made it impossible to understand what was actually killing him.

Like night birds, the physicians in their black velvet coats gathered around Alessandro's bed in endless and futile consultations, made learnedly ignorant reports in Latin, and exonerated each other of any responsibility. What tormented Alessandro most was hydropsy, caused, so the doctors thought, partly by his drinking water instead of wine (a measure which should have cured his gout), and partly by the many years he had spent in humid and unhealthy places—during battle he often had been knee-deep in water. This had "frozen his stomach and loosened him up." His spleen, too, gave him pain. There is still a letter of his to Ranuccio asking him to inquire in Naples about ways of curing it, for he had heard that they had found a remedy there. And finally, his legs also troubled him; often they swelled so much that he could wear only slippers and had to be brought to the field on a litter. His many doctors had tried to cure him with simplistic zeal, fruitless good intentions, and a variety of medicines: plasters, rhubarb potions, kermes infusions. But each time one of these remedies seemed to work, a new crisis thrust him back almost to the edge of the grave.

Alessandro, however, had never let himself go, and he had taken constant care not to damage his public image. Indeed, the more he felt his life pulse slowing down, the more he took care of his appearance. He showed himself in public each time he found the strength, always magnificently dressed and accompanied by his retinue. Deathly pale, prematurely old at forty-seven, he insisted on mounting his horse and somehow found the energy to stay on, though two footmen had to walk on either side to support him when he weakened. He certainly did his best to maintain a stance—he used up a hat a day to answer his soldiers' salutes—and only his closest friends saw the mortal sadness that possessed him. He now thought only about death, and how time slowly consumed him. Anything he did was with the knowledge that it hastened his death. His words had a sepulchral serenity; months passed quickly, and around him was the atmosphere of termination.

Alessandro Farnese died on a cold winter night in the Abbey of St. Vedasto, in Arras, as a good Christian but regretting that he, a soldier, should die slowly in a bed rather than gloriously on a battlefield. In Brussels he received the most sumptuous funeral ever held for a *condottiere*. Around his coffin, soldiers of various countries fought for precedence in honoring the beloved *capitano*. In the light of five hundred candles they stared worshipfully at those features so worn out by pain, self-sacrifice, and sense of duty as to acquire the rigidity and purity of a symbol. Many touched his hands and feet as if to honor a saint. That day, more than one old mercenary cried the only tears of his life. In Rome, Clement VIII paid regal homage to his memory and had his statue placed in the Palazzo dei Conservatori on the Campidoglio.

Embalmed, clad in a Franciscan habit, a rosary in his interlocked fingers, Alessandro's body arrived in Parma on March 15, 1593, where the exequies were repeated with equal solemnity in the presence of the people and the aristocracy. The youngest among the lords had almost never seen him; the older ones remembered him as a boy, when he had been sent to Madrid by his father to thank Philip II for returning Piacenza to the Farneses and to assure him of his devotion to Spain. They remembered him as a young man of about twenty, with a goatee that gave him a hard look in contrast to the warmth of his gaze. He had come back from Spain married to a wife eight years older than himself, who had been imposed on him by considerations of state.

Maria Daviz, the bride, was discreet and ladylike, but not pretty. To this day, her large, protruding, somewhat desolate eyes look out from the beautiful portrait by Pourbus. They tell the story of a neglected wife. Discarding a niece of Pope Pius IV, a princess d'Este, and a daughter of the emperor of Austria (one of the many unattractive girls Ferdinand II was marrying off without dowry to various Italian rulers), Philip II had chosen for Alessandro this anemic, quiet, reasonable Maria of Portugal. When he saw her, Alessandro made a wry face. The bride was undoubtedly loaded with solid virtues but she had all the faults resulting from the excess of these virtues. The engraver had done miracles but could not hide, on the medallion, those bulging sad eyes. Alessandro yielded to the immense authority of his uncle but hoped the ship that carried the bride would sink into the ocean. And it must have been a powerful wish, for in the Bay of Biscay, caught in a storm, the Portuguese galleon almost went to the bottom together with the armada escorting it.

The wedding was celebrated in Brussels. "The bride," wrote Captain Francesco Marchi from Alessandro's suite, "is much better than we thought. She is well brought up and looks not older than twenty-three." She was in fact twenty-eight. Everyone agreed that Maria was one of those types who, when warmed up by feelings, could be more pleasing, more valuable than a real beauty. She too, like Alessandro, had accepted the marriage docilely, without qualifications; she knew all along it would not be a love match—something unheard of among members of ruling families—and expected nothing from her life with Alessandro.

Unexpectedly, the marriage turned out to be a long hell for Maria. Armed with chastity, determined never to yield to the disorder of sensuality, Maria developed a burning passion for her husband; she suffered from jealousy and the humiliation of being given children but not love. Her life was marked by secret throbs, rejected advances. It was hard for her to accept the reality of her failure: that Alessandro was a ladies' man, that he preferred other women to a wife whom he treated with an absent-minded courtesy which bad humor often turned into a yawning indifference. "His Excellency," wrote Alessandro's secretary, Luisino, "is not in love with the princess as she is with him and has already given signs of dissatisfaction when Her Excellency stays up too long at night when they go together to some reception. . . ." And more: "The princess is wise, still she shows her displeasure when His Excellency treats those young attractive ladies of Parma and Piacenza so familiarly. . . ." "His Excellency does not know how to make a show of affection, as some people do." He certainly did not, at least not with his wife. "But with other women," Marchi noticed, "I can tell you how shrewd he is in the love game." Maria Daviz suffered, passively, resigned to her fate. Each new mistress of her husband gave her occasion to flaunt her own impeccable manners. She became pregnant with commendable frequency and in the role of mother she found the strength to play that of wife.

All the while Alessandro was making love to the girls of Parma and Piacenza, he longed for glory, to make war—a very noble profession in those days, a sanguinary but pleasant affair. Reluctant to accept the dullness of a subordinate position and believing only in his own resources, he dreamed of a position worthy of his name and at the same time independent from his father's. Duke Ottavio, however, never tired of advising him that it was much better, or at least wiser, to avoid as many responsibilities as possible. Why all that hurry to become a captain of fortune? "These things bring only scandal and bad name to our house," the duke would say, his face darkening in irritated refusal.

Madama d'Austria agreed with her husband but was more flexible. "Our son," she would say with the wise old smile of a mother, "is not the first who, once grown up, does not want to follow his father's advice." Personally, she found Alessandro handsome, intelligent—a good man. If she hadn't been such a well-balanced woman, she would have been guilty of pride. Alessandro never wearied of expounding his cause, and when he could not do it in person, he wrote letters: "My lord, I have neither land of my own nor power in this world nor, except to take care of my honor and reputation, an occupation to busy myself with. Apart from the duties of my rank, I owe nothing to anyone in this world in the matter of honor. And, for modesty's sake, I shall say no more."

At this point, usually, Ottavio would rebuke him for minding only his own interests and neglecting the dynasty's, to which

Alessandro invariably answered that no one could censure him for wanting to fulfill his aspirations, and since he had decided to put his sword at the Farneses' service, his father should not complain if he was looking for something that could make of him a "useful" soldier. He felt he was cut out to be a captain, born to make war. Every now and then his anxiety found relief in the love for one of those Parma girls who could, as he used to say, make a rogue of a saint. But it was only an expedient, perhaps the most pleasant one, to forget that time was passing without giving him the chance to prove himself. In Spain, where he had spent his adolescence, none of the great captains of the time, the Duke of Alba, Granvela, Ruy-Gomez, not even his uncle Philip had yet entrusted him with a military assignment; he had to release his tension in the narrow limits of the gymnasium playing ball, hunting, practicing with arms. With the enthusiasm that always moved him at the mere thought of a fight, he would say to Giovan Pietro, the renowned Mantuan fencing master, "Do not play with me gently, Master; I do not like it. Hit me if you can, for I shall do the same to you." And Giovan Pietro did indeed hit him hard. "Today the prince has trained at the bar," meticulously reported Francesco Marchi, "and has come to blows with Messer Marcello. He has broken four pikes and six rapiers. He fights with a strength and a rapidity that puts everyone to shame." And obsequiously, in a tone which sounds already commemorative: "No one looks better than he in battle dress. He is really a very skillful prince, a true friend to friends, and he will be a fighting man."

But in Parma, where his father held him by a leash, there was nothing to fight for; after fifty years of continuous conflict, Italy was finally enjoying a solid peace. Alessandro yearned for a war, a skirmish, anything that could shake off that respectable boredom, and, consumed by ennui, he continued to joust and hunt. "His Lordship goes hunting six times a week and takes no heed of the most inclement weather."

Suddenly he discovered that a small war was being fought in Spain against the Moors of Granada. "A toy war," but better than nothing, it was perhaps the great occasion that would prevent him from sinking into mediocrity. He was about to leave when the ridiculous little war became even more ridiculous by quickly getting settled. Alessandro set aside his armor, dismissed the knights, suppressed an incipient nervous breakdown, and started waiting again.

Finally, after four years, a more serious war, this one between Turks and Christians, loomed on the horizon. Alessandro heard of it, got ready, and left at full speed. He did not inform his father nor his uncle of it for fear of being stopped; the only person he confided in was his mother: "I want you to know that, having been denied any opportunity to fight in the service of His Majesty my king, especially now that Granada and all other places are peaceful, I could not possibly miss this war against the Turks without doing damage to my honor. Should His Majesty decide to take part in it, I shall be glad to serve him, but should he abstain, I shall have to go out on my own. I find myself at twenty-five having seen nothing, experienced nothing, and one has to practice this kind of work in order to know about it. And this to better serve His Majesty when it will please him to give me orders, as I have mentioned to Your Highness."

Alessandro could not imagine then that he would breathe war all his life and that one day, launched toward impossible goals, he would be crushed by battles and weapons, and that he would, with aching but vain desire, yearn for his peaceful little duchy.

Madama d'Austria disapproved of his project, and Philip II ordered him to stay home and restrain himself, for he considered it unworthy of Alessandro's name to serve under a foreign flag. Another year passed before events took a better turn for the young prince. In 1571 Philip II entered into an alliance with the pope and Venice, declaring war on the Ottomans, and Ottavio granted his son the much-longed-for permission. Alessandro left with three hundred soldiers and eighty-two knights chosen from the best families of Parma and Piacenza.

It was a sheer miracle that he did not die at the Battle of Lepanto, "the most terrible, memorable, glorious day of all." Five hours of fighting, the sea bristling with masts, the sun obscured by gun smoke, thirty thousand dead in one day . . . it was one of the biggest sea battles in history. The whole of Europe had joined against the common enemy, the Turks. The chief of the expedition was the famous Don Juan of Austria, Charles V's illegitimate son, who on the deck of the flagship danced the galliard before his officers and troops all ranged in battle formation, lifting their morale before they attacked the Turks. Waving his dagger and shouting oaths mixed with energetically obscene invocations, Alessandro mowed down dozens of Janizaries, finally tasting war for the first time in his life. Now he, too, thought to have bewitched good fortune.

From the military point of view the Battle of Lepanto became Alessandro's visiting card. In 1577, when he was already famous, he was called to Flanders by Don Juan, the young uncle who loved him like a brother. Shortly after, Juan died in his arms of typhoid fever. On the verge of death, he entrusted Alessandro with the command of his army.

✳

The present kingdoms of Netherlands and Belgium correspond only very approximately to the region which in the sixteenth century was called Flanders. It then included several parts of Prussia, a large section of northern France, a strip of Alsace-Lorraine—altogether seventeen regions extremely different from

66

one another in size, structure, and history. United under the
Hapsburg rule by means of a long series of wars, treaties, shrewd
marriages, and inheritances, Flanders was a splendid land, extremely rich, populous, full of rivers and towns; it was one of
the most precious gems of the Spanish crown. No wonder Spain
endured eighty years of fierce war in order to keep it.

When Alessandro arrived in Flanders, only two of the seventeen regions—the duchy of Limburg and the county of Naumur
—recognized Spain's authority. Rebellion was spreading among
all the others, and the major cities, Brussels, Liège, and Ghent,
were in the hands of William of Orange, the soul of the anti-
Spanish revolt. Alessandro was too clever to accept lightheartedly
the task entrusted to him by his dying uncle and confirmed by
Philip II. Alessandro's restrained, disciplined character was
emerging. He loved wars, battles, and weapons, but to put
Flanders in order was a task to make anyone's blood run cold.
The enthusiasm of command did not blind him to the enormous
difficulties at hand nor make him unaware of the danger his
reputation as a soldier would be exposed to.

The situation in Flanders was in fact worse than desperate,
and in many letters written at that crucial moment of his life
Alessandro repeated over and again that any improvement would
have to be regarded as a miracle. "The situation here is such,"
he informed his mother, "that any reasonable man would refuse
to take command, if he could do so honorably." And to his
uncle the cardinal: "I'd be satisfied if the world knew how deeply
I am in this sea of trouble. Whatever I undertake I shall do
it as a duty and not out of choice. Nevertheless, I beg Your
Lordship to be certain that all these troubles, dangers, vexations,
and lack of means do not frighten me at all; as a matter of fact
they give me courage, for I know that in times like these men
should show firmness and not fail to employ all possible remedies,
and even try the impossible."

And, indeed, Alessandro more than once achieved the impossible. In addition to personal courage, the strategic ability of a truly great general, generosity—very rare in those days—and a typically Italian equanimity, he had common sense and a humaneness that helped him to accomplish that at which everyone before him had failed: to rule Flanders in the name of the hated king of Spain. Alessandro was the first general of the Spanish army to enter into negotiations and reasonable discussions with the rebels. His treaties with the Walloons, his laws, his efforts to relieve the population from the suffering of war, his efforts to improve agriculture, the trade he encouraged between conquered provinces and rebellious ones—all this is part of Flanders' history. To study it in depth would be to explain the subtle political sagacity of the Duke of Parma; and it also would considerably mitigate the only stain on his spotless career: the consent, albeit reluctant, he gave to Philip's project to assassinate William of Orange. While Alessandro, as an individual, was responsible for his own good qualities, his era was responsible for his crime. It was the century of the Massacre of St. Bartholomew, of the murders of the Duke of Guise, Mary Stuart, Henry III. It was the century in which the British Parliament voted the death penalty for anyone who heard Mass, while on the piazzas of Europe, Catholic and reformist stakes blazed incessantly.

The fifteen years Alessandro spent in Flanders comprised a long series of sieges and battles which, since they were almost always successful, made of him the greatest *condottiere* of the century and the most notable exponent of the Hispano-Italian military school that had cast off old-fashioned strategies and opened the way to modern warfare. Alessandro soon became famous for several things: for the great care he gave to the artillery, for developing the cavalry—"the apple of any army's eye," as he called it—for the large number of mines he used, for the fortifications he himself designed and sometimes constructed in a few hours, and for the ingenuity with which he made use of hydraulic devices. In an era when rivers and water-ways were the main lines of communication and bridges had the strategic importance of today's railroad stations, Alessandro was so skillful in deflecting rivers, digging canals, draining ditches and building bridges that he became a hero to writers of trea-tises on military history.

Alessandro had a natural flair for authority. He could do whatever he wished with his soldiers, whom he treated with benevolence, indulgence, or severity as the occasion demanded, but always with a subtleness and demagoguery comparable to that of Napoleon. He visited wounded soldiers and saw to it that each one received proper care. He shared the risks of his men; he ate the same food they ate; slept in the trenches which he had helped to dig, and operated the cannons. Above all, he never risked their lives uselessly. On the other hand, he could be inflexible. He was once seen, sword drawn, driving out soldiers who were looting a village. The Duke of Pastrana, Philip's natural son, was put under arrest for violating an order, and many officers were executed for insubordination. Discipline was very difficult to maintain, even among the highest ranks. The Spanish and the Flemish officers hated each other; the first were proud of the king's favor, and the latter were conscious of their local power and the high price of their loyalty to Spain in a fratricidal war. But Alessandro treated them all with great amiability, tact, and patience. He covered these gentlemen with honors, decorations, praise; often he presented those who had distinguished themselves on the battlefield with beautiful weapons, jewels, even with clothes, all of which they treasured like relics. He listened to their opinions—though later he usually had his own way, sometimes exactly the opposite of their sug-gestions—giving them the impression that the conduct of the war depended upon their advice. His physical strength and his personality exercised irresistible charm. A woman who had spread the rumor that Alessandro had been defeated was put in the pillory by his soldiers, for whom "to slander His Excellency the Duke of Parma is to slander Jesus Christ."

Alessandro had one weakness only, pride in his control over his emotions. He loved to exhibit his calmness. During the siege of Oudenarde, a cannon shot swept away three officers dining with him in his tent. Without batting an eye, he ordered the removal of the tablecloth and the bloodstained dishes, and resumed his meal. He knew his value, yet he was modest; gone was the arrogance of his childhood in Madrid, where his tutors had brought him up with a Spanish haughtiness of language, habits, and manners. He was also sincerely religious; he preferred, he said, thirty God-fearing soldiers to ten thousand infidels, believing that only faith could hold together an army of men of different nationalities. Thanks to his ability to deal with all kinds of people, there were never incidents due to national jealousy or to excessive *esprit de corps*. Alessandro was an expert on mercenary troops. His secret was that he requested from them only what they could do best. He knew, for example, that Germans were excellent in defending strongholds and "had little inclination for scandal" but had the fault (very serious for those times) of not being a good investment if they did not receive their pay punctually. The Walloons, less expensive than the Germans, were also good, but Alessandro's favorites were the Spaniards. While Don Juan of Austria and many other *condottieri* preferred the Swiss to the Italians, Alessandro enlisted the latter willingly, for they seemed "able to do anything."

Italian mercenaries, however, had many faults. They were quarrelsome, something which enraged Alessandro because he could not tolerate that his country should have cause to be criticized, or "have other countries believe that Italians don't get along among themselves." Generally, though, Italian troops in Alessandro's service behaved well and contributed to improve Italy's reputation which, in those days, was rather low.

The siege of Antwerp was Alessandro's masterpiece. His natural reserve, his moderation, always prevented him from speaking about himself and his abilities, but he was so satisfied with the siege of Antwerp that he could not restrain himself from praising it—modestly, of course—to the king of Spain: "The exploit of Antwerp is so great and heroic that to describe it I would have to speak longer than the fear of boring Your Majesty allows me."

Antwerp, on the left bank of the river Schelde, to which the town owed most of its rich trade, was hardly less large and populous than it is today. And it was the heart of the Flemish revolt. Protected on one side by the river, on the other, Antwerp had ten bastions—high and thick walls supported by huge ramparts—as well as moats, 150 feet wide, fortified with counterscarps and filled with water drawn from the Schelde by ingeniously conceived machines. At the southern end of this imposing fortification, built by a group of Italian engineers, there was a famous fortress, still in existence today, deservedly called the Queen of All Citadels. The garrison included a strong regiment of British infantry, a cavalry squadron, and twenty thousand soldiers very effectively commanded by eight colonels and trained by veterans who had literally spent their lives on battlefields.

"To attempt to take Antwerp is pure folly," said Alessandro's officers. And yet Alessandro took Antwerp, by starving it out, or rather by constructing a solid bridge that blocked the river, thereby preventing the besieged town from receiving supplies from the sea. In the nearby village of Calloo—comprising four houses, ten trees, one church with storks nesting on the roof— Alessandro set up a shipyard where he summoned all the blacksmiths, carpenters, boatsmen, calkers, masons, and arms makers of Flanders and Brabant. For months the once tranquil village resounded with the noise of saws, hammers, axes, and planes, with the clang of machines and the shouts of sentries. There was a shortage of tools, of engineers, and especially of money;

but Alessandro, by paying regularly, kept the work going. On February 25, 1585, the bridge was ready. Seven hundred and twenty yards long, it had at the center thirty-two boats sixty feet long and twelve feet wide, tied together by a fourfold series of chains and ropes. At the extremities, near the embankments, there were several piles secured to the river bed, held together by other piles placed horizontally. The boats were covered with beams flanked by musketproof parapets made of wood and pressed soil. The boats were kept in place by two anchors, one at the prow and the other at the stern, with a device for shortening or lengthening the ropes according to the tides. Each boat could hold thirty soldiers, four sailors, and two cannons. On both ends of the bridge was a stronghold with fifteen cannons. The center, weaker than the extremities, was additionally fortified by a number of barges in groups of three, tied together by chains and ropes, which pointed toward the enemy 154 stakes, extending to approximately four hundred yards on each side. More iron stakes protected the piles. Finally, two squads of twenty galleons, with twelve men on each side and a cannon on the prow, constantly patrolled the bridge.

"The bridge is so strong," Alessandro said, "that according to the experts it would hold even if the whole of the Netherland and Zeeland were to attack it. The boats are filled with the best officers and soldiers. If the enemy comes, he will be defeated." An Antwerp spy caught prying near the bridge was released, so that the enemy could be informed about the strength of the bridge. Philip II, in Madrid, contributed his prayers, and his daughter, her shirt: she vowed she would not take it off as long as the siege of Antwerp lasted. And God certainly threw in His protection, for apparently all the incendiary barges sent down the river by the besieged were smashed against the embankments or sunk by Alessandro's guns before they could reach their goal.

It so happened that Antwerp was being defended by another

[1] Pope Paul III. Titian. Museo Nazionale, Naples. PHOTOGRAPH BY ALINARI.

[2]   Pier Luigi Farnese, first Duke of Parma and Piacenza. Titian. Museo
Nazionale, Naples. PHOTOGRAPH BY ALINARI.

[3]   Pope Paul III with Cardinal Alessandro Farnese and Ottavio Farnese.
Titian. Museo Nazionale, Naples. PHOTOGRAPH BY ALINARI.

[4] Cardinal Alessandro Farnese. Titian. Museo Nazionale, Naples. PHOTOGRAPH BY ALINARI.

[5] *Below:* Ottavio Farnese, second Duke of Parma and Piacenza. Artist unknown. Ordine Costantiniano di San Giorgio, Parma. PHOTOGRAPH BY VAGHI.

Italian, Federico Gianibelli from Mantua, one of the many Italians who left their country in search of adventure. No historian could ever tell with accuracy whether Gianibelli joined the Flemish rebels because of frustrated ambitions, because of Philip's indifference, or simply because he happened to be one of the few supporters Luther managed to recruit in Italy. Shut up in the stronghold on the Schelde, this obscure Mantuan was busy inventing devices to destroy Alessandro's bridge and, with the bridge, the drama of starvation. His last, most ingenious invention consisted of four barges reinforced with plaster and loaded with gunpowder and big bombs hidden under logs covered with sulfur and tar, the whole joined together and provided with long fuses and flints. Baptized "Speranza" [Hope], it was sent down the river, accompanied by the prayers of the citizens of Antwerp.

The moment this infernal machine reached its destination, Alessandro's big bridge, the result of eight months of labor, blew sky-high. The waters of the Schelde mounted so high as to expose the river bed and, overflowing the dams, flooded the countryside and dragged away embankments, fences, blockhouses, batteries. The night lit up, and all the stones, sword blades, nails, millstones, tombstones, chains, and iron bars Gianibelli had had heaped in the craft were hurled in the air by the explosives; all the windows in nearby Ghent were shattered to pieces. Almost eight hundred officers and soldiers, said the chronicle of that terrible night, died instantly. Alessandro himself fainted, and seeing him unconscious and lifeless, his men thought him dead and were paralyzed by terror. But suddenly Alessandro recovered, invoked Saint Leocardia, patroness of Toledo and protectress of the Spanish army, and resumed command. He himself said later: "I do not wish to speak of what happened and what I did that night, because modesty does not allow me."

Alessandro's plan was to repair the bridge in a few hours, or at least to seem to have repaired it in order to deceive the enemy, "to trick them all." And indeed in a few hours, during which the trumpets covered the noise of the reconstruction, the bridge looked its usual self. In the uncertain light of dawn it appeared almost untouched to the scouts of Antwerp, who kept at a respectful distance. In failing to see the real condition of the bridge they lost the only chance the town had to lift the blockade.

Gianibelli was stunned at the bad news, and the furious citizens almost lynched him. Presently the town capitulated to an attack which astounded the whole of Europe. Gianibelli, "the Archimedes of Antwerp," as Friedrich Schiller called him two hundred years later, mysteriously disappeared and most probably ended badly.

Philip II allowed himself one of his rare pale smiles. On the now famous bridge, flowers and garlands replaced the cannons, and the soldiers were drunk for three days. The king's daughter finally changed her shirt; the old one was yellow, with shades of amber, which immediately became a fashionable color under the name of "Isabella."

The war went on, and for the first time Alessandro began to have enough of it. But sieges and battles had to continue, and so did the enervating requests to Madrid for the money necessary for those sieges and battles. Every letter Alessandro wrote to Philip referred to his financial problems: "The million you promised me," he wrote in 1586, "arrived piecemeal and with so much ceremony that I haven't ten crowns at my disposal. I myself cannot understand how I managed to keep even this handful of soldiers—yes, the army is reduced to such miserable proportions that Your Majesty would be astounded. And the million has all gone." Sometimes, always because of lack of money, the situation became so desperate that Alessandro gave it up for lost, "unless God gives us a holy hand." And God, eventually, in one way or another, gave Alessandro a hand, so that he cheered up and repeated one of his favorite sayings: "In this world there is a remedy to everything but death."

That same year came the news of Ottavio's death. Bent under the weight of sorrow, Alessandro mourned the memory of his father, but Philip II, the pitiless master of his life, did not allow him to leave the field. He had not allowed it in 1577, when Alessandro's wife had died, nor in 1581 for his daughter's wedding, and not now that he was becoming Duke of Parma. So, from then on, Alessandro had to rule his duchy by correspondence, because the regent, his son Ranuccio, was too young and inexperienced to know where to start. Ranuccio wrote to his father: "What do you wish me to do with these two cities of Parma and Piacenza and their lords?" And Alessandro, between battles, answered: "Follow the style of our late duke, of blessed memory, and give the lords honors, tickle them, give them all the satisfaction you can in keeping with your position." This did not satisfy the young regent; he was greatly perplexed: "How shall I proceed with the Italian rulers and in particular with the governor of Milan, especially if he wants, as it happened recently, to recruit men in our state?" Alessandro sighed and wrote again: "Regarding the governor of Milan, remember that, if there is anything the king my lord needs, the order is to assist and to help him in every way. As for the rulers, deal with them with the greatest caution and courtesy."

Would Ranuccio be able to keep up with the duchy? In truth, Ranuccio was less naïve than his questions would suggest. As a matter of fact, he secretly hoped to take over completely, and then he would rule without a thought to the lords, the governor of Milan, or anybody else. Alessandro, pent up in Flanders, did not suspect this. He hardly knew his son at all. And now he felt homesick and wished he could go back home and be young again. He thought of his life, yearned for the skies of Parma, the sunny plain, the winter fogs that covered it like a soft blanket. He dreamed of a life made up of little habits, of days all alike, of a peaceful life in the little provincial capital with its little problems, its petulance and hidden sweetness. He dreamed of a quiet and merciful reign, of raising his children and spending year after year of sweet boredom beside his gently fading wife. The memory of Maria Daviz was now always with him, like his conscience, a relentless, affectionate persecution deepened by a feeling of guilt, which he nourished almost voluptuously, for not having loved her when he could have. The sexy Flemish blondes his grandfather Charles V had liked so much, and who now enlivened the evenings of his own officers, no longer appealed to him. He now avoided them through indifference, and not because he wished to enter history, as he in fact did, for having been, among other things, one of the few great nobles of his era who did not leave behind a trail of natural children—a singular example of continence during a time when, in noble families, illegitimate offspring often outnumbered the legitimate.

Maria Daviz had given birth to three children, two boys and a girl. Then, exhausted by a series of miscarriages, she had died in an attempt to give to the Farneses yet another heir. The memory of her touched Alessandro, especially since Philip had taken into his head the idea of marrying his nephew to Mary Stuart of Scotland, in order to make him king of that faraway country. Mary was a frail, proud woman, a femme fatale over whose Gothic charm many men had gone mad. One such, an Italian, had been killed at her feet. She lived in Edinburgh, a town hirsute with dark spires, surrounded by a mob of lawless Scottish lords. Alessandro had no intention of going mad over her but, in conformity with the sublime and degrading devotion that linked him to Philip, he would have married her.

The king of Spain had plotted this marriage in order better to take revenge on Elizabeth of England, who had openly taken sides with the Flemish rebels, and in order to lay the groundwork for a future invasion of the hated Protestant country.

Philip's plans, however, went awry. Alessandro did not marry Mary Stuart, who ended under the executioner's ax, and the Invincible Armada, the invasion fleet bound for the conquest of England, was defeated by a stormy sea and Drake's ships. Dismasted, smashed, and almost completely destroyed, the Spanish ships were dispersed in the English Channel, and only half of the 132 vessels managed to reach Spanish ports. Philip's ambitious dream was crushed.

The basic plan of the enterprise belonged to the Duke of Parma, and it was a clever, competent scheme. Alessandro insisted, above all, on mounting the expedition in the Netherlands because of its proximity to the English coast. Secondly, he suggested taking along only men and weapons, leaving aside horses and food supplies, which could be easily appropriated on enemy soil. For this reason he suggested that the attack be launched in October, when crops were ripe and the harvest completed. For the landing of Philip's forces he chose the heavily forested coast between Dover and Margate, the closest to Flanders, a perfect terrain for the landing of the infantry. As for the ships, the best thing was to use light and speedy boats rather than battleships. Finally, he advised that they take a large supply of money to avoid mutinies once on English soil. The essential condition for success, however, was absolute secrecy, and for that it was necessary to gather troops quietly in Flanders, build the boats between Dunkerque and Nieuwport, store up weapons and ammunition and, most importantly, do without allies ("for every alliance soon becomes public") and confide only in oneself.

These practical and modest suggestions, which perhaps held some hope of success, did not suit Philip's pride, and eventually the expedition, planned and discussed in endless meetings at the Escorial, was completely transformed from the Duke of Parma's original project. Rather than in Flanders and in secret, the Invincible Armada was built in the harbors of Spain, Portugal, Naples, and Sicily, and with such publicity that London could hardly miss it. Not even at Lepanto had a Catholic country prepared such a huge naval effort: 132 battleships to be loaded with soldiers, among them the representatives of the best Spanish families, and, in addition, six hundred priests to convert the English population.

The commander-in-chief was the Duke of Medina-Sidonia, "an inexperienced young man who has never sailed before and suffers from seasickness." Touching his stomach in a gesture of respectful and allusive discouragement, the duke had asked the king to exempt him, but Philip, convinced that wars were decided in heaven and that there was a special secretariat for Spanish affairs up there, reminded the duke that God was the real admiral of the Armada, and dismissed his request.

Setting out from Lisbon, the Armada was supposed to be joined on the Dutch coast by Alessandro, who was gathering an army of thirty thousand men. Although the cream of the Spanish, Italian, and Catholic German youth had answered his appeal, Alessandro was tormented by misgivings. He did not trust that huge expedition which more and more differed from the one he had originally conceived. At the same time, Queen Elizabeth's privateers ceaselessly cruised the Channel, and the Flemish rebels watched the coasts with ships ready not merely to harass, but to prevent the troops from embarking. Furthermore, while waiting for the Spanish fleet—which took an unduly long time to arrive because of the difficulties created by distance—Alessandro's troops were troubled by dreadful illnesses. The Italians died; the Spaniards filled up the hospitals; the others were in a pitiful condition. Eventually, Alessandro's troops were reduced to half their original strength. At the beginning, when the plan was to invade England by surprise, the number of soldiers needed had been fixed at thirty thousand. Now that Elizabeth was on guard and had to be fought both by land and sea, fifty thousand would not have been sufficient. "Four warships could sink all my boats. Nonetheless"—and here, as usual, Alessandro's blind devotion to Spain got the upper hand—"if Your Majesty seriously expects me to break through, I shall do it, even if I have to do it alone in a skiff."

Such an extreme fortunately was not necessary. Toward the end of May, 1588, the Invincible Armada, the result of three years of labor, set sail. In the Channel, in front of Plymouth, the sailors of Elizabeth, "the Jezebel of the North," were waiting. Among them were legendary men: John Hawkins, the former slave-dealer who had become so rich and powerful in trading slaves for spices as to obtain the title of Treasurer of the Fleet; the privateer Francis Drake, mythical, idolized by his crew, capable, if ship discipline required it, of sentencing an officer to death and playing cards with him to the last minute.

The Duke of Medina-Sidonia intended, after the strategy of the time, to transform the naval battle into hand-to-hand combat as quickly as possible, and his soldiers were ready with grappling irons for the boarding of the English ships. But the fleet of Hawkins and Drake took an unexpected formation, sailing away in single file beyond reach of the Spanish artillery but close enough to use effectively their cannons on the Spaniards. The Armada was harassed, harried, and vexed by the elusive English boats, without ever being able to engage them in a regular battle. The Spaniards lost seven ships in a few days.

Alessandro was still waiting, between Dunkerque and Nieuwport. Informed that the Armada was about to arrive, he had ordered the embarkation of his men. On the boats, however, they were "so tightly pressed," said an eyewitness, "that they looked not like soldiers but rather like piled-up sacks on a merchant boat." But the Armada still did not appear, nor could Alessandro try to sail and meet it in the open sea because his boats, meant only for the transport of goods, would have been unable to compete with the Flemish rebel ships still cruising off-shore.

On August 6, the Armada cast anchor in front of Calais, twenty-five miles from Dunkerque. It was the beginning of the end. How right Alessandro had been in requiring a large and protected harbor which could, in case of bad weather, accommodate the entire fleet, and in insisting that the infantry be safely aboard the ships. Unfortunately Philip had denied him permission to besiege Vlissingen, the only town with adequate harbor facilities, and now the Armada was paying for that thoughtless refusal. On the night of August 7, the English directed fire ships loaded with gunpowder and pitch against the moored fleet. The actual damage was negligible, but the panic was incalculable. In a few minutes chaos spread throughout the entire Armada. Some of the sailors cut the anchor lines, some hoisted the sails, others ran to the oars. The ships smashed into one another, the masts intertwisted and broke, while the sea was rising, white with foam in the stormy dawn. By midmorning, tossed by the waves and the winds, chased by the enemy, the fleet was dispersed. Some of the ships tried to reach Catholic Ireland but were wrecked against the rocky coasts, stranded on the beaches, or bombarded by the English. In such a manner, half of the Armada was destroyed.

When he was informed of the catastrophe, Philip stiffened, anguished. He demanded to know why it had happened. As often happens in such cases, everyone was anxious to rid himself of the responsibility for the disaster and began to accuse others. But that they should choose the Duke of Parma as the scapegoat, this Alessandro did not expect, and his sorrow undoubtedly contributed to shortening his life. On the other hand, it was to be expected that such a man should sooner or later become the victim of intrigues and plots which, in the Spanish court, were a daily hazard. The wreck of the Armada was a good opportunity for Alessandro's many rivals to damage his reputation. The invasion of England had failed, they said, because *il Farnese,* through bad timing or miscalculation, had not succeeded in joining the main body of the fleet. As a consequence, the Inquisition brought him to secret trial—later suspended for insufficient evidence—as a suspected Lutheran.

The accusations, of course, reached Philip's ears. Locked in the huge palace that served him as a royal mansion, monastery, prison, shrine, and mausoleum, Philip had become more and more misanthropic with age. His natural suspiciousness, aggravated by the courtiers' insinuations, made him doubt even Alessandro. He forgot his nephew's loyalty to Spain and suddenly feared that, counting on the popularity which Alessandro had won in Flanders by his valor, mildness, religious tolerance, and authority with the army—in short in virtue of the fact that his rule was the opposite of that of his predecessors—Alessandro was trying to become king of Flanders. Others, in those fraudulent, lawless times, might have tried it, but Alessandro thought only of retiring to a monastery: "I am getting so disillusioned by the world that the best thing for my soul and body would be to serve God." But, in the end, he stayed, committed to his role of *condottiere* by an almost masochistic desire for self-sacrifice. His uncle, Cardinal Alessandro, also wanted him to come home: "As long as I see you in that country, I will not be at peace. Not because I fear for your reputation, for it is well known that you were not at fault for a defeat which you foresaw and warned against a long time ago, but because I wish to see you free from trouble. I see you are left to the mercy of fortune and have no way, in this world, of solving anything without money or trustworthy men or the loyalty of a country. I would give thanks if you returned, so that together we would begin something good for our family. . . ."

It was impossible to return. Probably around this time, an English emissary was sent to invite Alessandro to take over the administration of Flanders. The emissary guaranteed the unreserved approval and support of Queen Elizabeth. Alessandro reportedly had him thrown out. Philip, thus reassured about his nephew's absolute loyalty, decided to entrust him with still another mission. Fearing a Protestant victory in the religious war that was driving France to anarchy, Philip sent Alessandro to the aid of the Catholic League with the task of freeing Paris from Henry of Navarre's siege. Alessandro, as usual, obeyed but complained to the king who, as usual, had not given him enough money. "It hurts me to see Your Majesty order me to do the impossible, for only God can perform miracles. How can Your Majesty believe I will satisfy all the soldiers enlisted in these provinces, appease the mutinous Spaniards and Germans—obviously, if I am going to use them in the expedition, I have at least to satisfy them—pay Mayenne [brother of the third Duke of Guise, Henri I of Lorraine] and the Parisians, pay salaries to the German cavalry protecting these provinces and the coastal strongholds? The poverty, the discontent, the desperation of this unlucky country have been so often described to Your Majesty that I have nothing new to add. I reached the point where I must sentence my veterans to the gallows and to prison simply because they rebel for want of salary and not because they are criminals. In these conditions I have to march to France with twenty thousand soldiers—the minimum necessary to hope for any success at all. I am confused, perplexed; the whole world rails at me that if I leave Flanders, which had been entrusted to me, the country will be irremediably lost. On the other hand, the French people cry that if Paris and with it the entire Catholic cause in France is wrecked it is only because of me."

And yet Alessandro obeyed. He would have never dared to deprive Spain of the only sword and brain capable of confronting with any success the Huguenots' Valois king. Besides, in his total disillusion, he had the bitter vanity of wanting to compete with the only *condottiere* whose fame equaled his:

Henry of Navarre, the future Henry IV of France. Henry was an honorable adversary, resembling Alessandro in many ways. He was magnanimous, courageous, frugal, good-humored, tolerant, and realistic. He always knew how to say the right thing at the right moment. He had one fault: he smelled, but it was such a common fault that nobody, except his mistress, made any account of it. He was not very religious; twice the stormy politics of his time forced him to renounce the Catholic faith, and twice the Huguenot one. But in spite of his proneness to abjuration, Henry's concern was to be a good Christian, and he had a clear sense of good and evil. He, too, was curious, and he wanted to face Alessandro. "The king," wrote an ambassador, "has no other ambition than to fight for one day against the Duke of Parma, so that he can take pride in having fought against the most famous man-at-arms of Christendom." Surely he did not expect them to find in the legendary *capitano* a most unpredictable adversary, someone who would hold him at bay with feints worthy of an extraordinary duelist, and who would conquer Paris by a series of ingenious stratagems. In addition, making Henry believe he would any moment engage in an open battle, Alessandro reconquered Flanders without having once entered the field, and finally disappeared, leaving Henry utterly confused.

Two years later the two great generals met again, when Philip forced Alessandro into another expedition to France, where Alessandro was defeated by Henry's restored forces. After a retreat that Henry himself called "more glorious than two victories," Alessandro returned exhausted to Flanders. He was ill, suffering from jaundice, with his right arm pierced by a musket bullet that stuck in the bone of his hand and threatened an amputation. The Duke of Mayenne, who had taken command in Alessandro's absence, was sick, too, but of an illness "less honorable than the one afflicting the Duke of Parma."

Around Alessandro the situation was rapidly worsening. The

Flemish rebels, taking advantage of his second expedition to France to reorganize themselves, resumed attack under the command of Maurice of Nassau. The Spanish troops rioted; the unpaid garrisons mutinied; the state treasury was unable even to find "credit for twenty-five thousand scudi"; in Bruges, the Spanish soldiers were literally begging for food. The structure, painfully built up by fourteen years of effort, was collapsing. Philip now more than ever listened to Alessandro's opponents, and his suspicion aroused him to a point where the removal of Alessandro from command seemed inevitable. In the last letter Alessandro wrote to the king, he lamented: "What is most hard for me is to see Your Majesty listening to these accusations without investigating them, although they involve my honor and reputation, and not giving my past service the attention it deserves. People, in this world, take more account of these accusations than of my deeds. I regret that, after so much hard work and so many dangers in the service of Your Majesty, now that I am barely hanging on to life and am about to die away from my children, home, and friends, I should be thus treated, instead of being honored and respected and allowed to leave my sons something more precious than all the riches a king can grant: an honorable name."

When Alessandro wrote that he was "barely hanging on to life" he was not exaggerating. He prepared himself bravely to die, and he was finally freed of Philip on the night of December 2, 1592.

III

Margherita Farnese

At the time he succeeded Alessandro as Duke of Parma, Ranuccio Farnese was no longer the handsome, sturdy youth with large eyes, fresh complexion, and melon-shaped pantaloons who can be admired in the portrait by a pupil of Parmigianino. At twenty-three he had already begun to show the tyrannical, devious character of a professional ruler. Lacking finesse and affability, Ranuccio was irascible, always ill-tempered, obsessed with being the victim of imaginary abuses. He certainly did not resemble his father. From his mother, Maria Daviz, he had inherited a gloomy nature, and in time he would reach the depths of paranoia and come to see the world as one vast conspiracy against him.

Ranuccio saw enemies in people, objects, events, in the phantoms of his sleepless nights. His greatest enemy of all, or so he thought, was Vincenzo Gonzaga, the future Duke of Mantua. Indeed, the hostility between the Farneses and the Gonzagas was not a product of Ranuccio's hallucinations; it was an old story. It had all started in 1549 when the nobles of Piacenza, under the efficient direction of Ferrante Gonzaga, had hung Pier Luigi,

85

Ranuccio's great-grandfather, out of a window of his own castle. The Farneses had chosen a refined, bloodless revenge; they simply handled things in such a way as to prevent Cardinal Ercole Gonzaga from becoming pope, Ercole's dearest ambition in the world. For the Gonzagas, this had been worse than ten murdered great-grandfathers. The rivalry between the two families was not of the kind that is forgotten with the protagonists' death. Ranuccio, a man capable of lasting resentments, now offended by the increasing prestige of the Gonzagas, seemed born to rekindle the embers of that rivalry.

There had been, however, a moment when hostilities seemed on the point of subsiding. During Ottavio's administration, in order to strengthen a pact signed by Parma, Turin, Mantua, and Ferrara, it had been decided that Margherita, Ranuccio's sister, should marry the young Vincenzo Gonzaga. The hope was that the Farnese girl would succeed in filling the gap gouged out between Mantua and Parma by half a century of enmity. Besides, it was a convenient marriage. "The more I think of this arrangement," wrote Alessandro, Margherita's father, "the more I approve of it, since we cannot hope to marry her off to Savoy or Florence. I don't think we could place her more conveniently."

The negotiations were extremely long, partly due to the Gonzagas' demands, partly to the Farneses' avarice. Ottavio found the manners of the Duke of Mantua "such that they would nauseate a saint." But in the end they agreed: "With God's blessing we have established this kinship." Still, it was a great undertaking in those days to marry off a prince's daughter; and one of the complications here was that Ottavio was closefisted— "constipated," said the Gonzagas. Only with great trouble was he finally convinced that it was better to have one daughter less than hundred ducats more. Once the contract was signed, it became necessary to scrape together the dowry, to make loans from Jewish merchants, to increase taxes, to sell properties, to borrow from the lords, and to beg the rich authoritarian grandmother,

Margherita, for cash. Hunchbacked Guglielmo Gonzaga, tapping his long forefinger, had insisted that the 300,000 gold scudi of the dowry be all from the best coinage of the Parma mint. Ottavio, for his part, insisted that the contract fixed the number of scudi, not their weight, and that even if he wanted, he could not find so many scudi of the same coinage. This problem solved, the one of the counter-dowry was raised. Ottavio, by now resigned to loosening his purse strings, decided to rely on Guglielmo's generosity. But the old Gonzaga drew an obscene symbol on the paper the Parma ambassador had given him to indicate the sum he would agree to pay. Evidently thinking he was dealing with "a twisted mind," Ottavio cut off negotiations and agreed to give away his granddaughter without a counter-dowry. On November 25, 1580, the marriage oath was signed, and everyone drew an almost palpable sigh of relief.

Margherita Farnese was, at that time, a girl of only thirteen. Docile, lazy, open to affection and life's simplest joys, she was incapable of expressing any idea, for she as yet had none. Without this marriage she would have become a serene and frivolous woman with an easy and banal life. Her face was round, her features still undecided, her complexion poor. "She is not pretty by nature," observed a contemporary, "and a terrible case of measles has stolen from her the freshness of youth."

Vincenzo Gonzaga took little notice of his bride, and a few days after the wedding in Piacenza, though apparently engaged in a very active honeymoon, he was already flirting with Hippolita Torricella, Polissena Gonzaga, and Barbara di Sanseverino, all available and most obliging ladies, and reducing his marriage to a Boccaccioesque farce. His libertine lungs thrived in that rustling, perfumed air which surrounded the court ladies.

The Mantuan emissary to Parma, ordered to describe Margherita in detail, mentioned her absolute ignorance in spite of her knowledge of the first book of *The Aeneid*. The weakest points of her faulty education were Latin, logic, and religion, about which she confessed herself to know nothing. On the whole, however, there was little of which to complain; she would make a good wife. When she had been introduced to the Gonzaga delegation, Margherita had found a wall of eyes which examined her from head to foot, pitilessly calculating the breadth of her hips, the capacity of her womb, the fullness of her breast. At the end they all had voted. Will she produce children, Guglielmo Gonzaga insistently asked. To all appearances, the emissary reassured him, she was of the kind who has half a dozen at least. After all, her mother, Maria Daviz, had been very prolific, though not all her children had lived.

Vincenzo Gonzaga was known as the handsomest of the Italian princes. He was blond, charmingly masculine, gregarious, and given to a certain ironic detachment with just a hint of vanity— everything about him was seductive. And it would be unfair not to mention that he was rather tall in an era when height represented a rare virile quality. Girls loved him passionately, mature women tenderly—he was one of those men whom women never forget. His wife, too, was madly in love with him, but her marriage had a humiliating destiny.

Ranuccio was twelve years old when his sister was declared unfit not only for motherhood but even for marriage. Her husband, it was rumored, was incapable of "taking her maidenhood." Margherita emerged pale and exhausted from her nuptial nights. She sobbed and choked with shame, while her ladies in waiting scolded her: had there ever been a more cowardly bride? "I'll try again," said the poor girl, holding back her tears. After a while, hoping there would be some cure, surgeons, obstetricians, midwives were called to examine her. In no time, the secret of her malformation was on everybody's lips, made the rounds of the courts, was discussed in diplomatic reports and ironically commented upon everywhere. But for Margherita, even to be dragged most loudly into the limelight was an acceptable humiliation if it helped her to become normal. She still hoped that time, perhaps, would set things right. After all, she was fifteen, the age of miracles.

After one year Guglielmo Gonzaga, preoccupied by the delayed succession, began to say that the Farneses had made a fool of him. Parma answered that the bride was all right, but that Vincenzo was sexually inadequate as a result of his intemperance. Old Guglielmo would not swallow this insult and asked for an annulment of the marriage. The Farneses then proposed surgery for Margherita, and if physicians chosen by both families were to declare the operation successful, Vincenzo would have to keep his wife with no further right to protest. The Duke of Mantua, however, did not agree on this point and after long consideration informed Parma that he wanted to break the contract, since the law was on his side and "the succession of our dynasty seems by now hopeless." "If he cares for his succession," Ottavio replied scornfully, "I care for my reputation." And he immediately called his granddaughter back home, with the excuse that Mantua's humidity gave her colds. Upon which Guglielmo Gonzaga asked for a refund of the wedding expenses, a request which Parma found "most impertinent."

Once she was back, Margherita eventually yielded to the iron logic of Saint Charles Borromeo, a person one hardly imagines involved in this "carnal" story. Fearing, and rightly so, that this unlucky marriage might cause an open hostility between the two families, thus breaking the balance and the peace of the Italian states, Pope Gregory XIII had asked the famous saint of Milan to arbitrate this delicate question. And Borromeo, an upright, resolute man, though not used to this kind of investigation, intervened with a logic rendered so sharp and ruthless by his Catholic pessimism that Margherita was soon convinced of that which neither her grandfather nor her father had been able to persuade her: that a woman with her kind of physical handicap was born for the solitude of the cloister.

Madama d'Austria had been the first to sum up the complicated matter: "I say you should, with discretion and strength, make up your mind not to become your own executioner with remedies that are violent and dangerous," she wrote to Margherita. "And since God chose to give you this impediment, you should voluntarily say that, not being suitable for marriage, you are resolved to serve the Lord in a convent, and to carry out this plan without delay. . . ." Margherita finally understood that those were not cruel words, only the bitter truth: the cloister was the best place for someone like herself. With saintly obstinacy Cardinal Borromeo insisted over and again that nothing was more noble than her sacrifice, her magnificent self-denial. For a while she almost managed to believe him. On October 30, 1583, convinced of the need to cut short all uncertainties and doubts, Margherita took the veil in the convent of San Paolo, with the name of Maura Lucenia. Her face whiter than her veil, bewildered and distracted, she looked like a victim led to the sacrifice. They cut her hair, they undressed her, redressed her, and all the time she perceived nothing; during the whole ceremony she kept her eyes on Borromeo's big nose, while he recited the service.

The convent of San Paolo was the most aristocratic in Parma, and since the time of the famous Abbess Giovanna it had enjoyed autonomy and many privileges. The nuns were not completely isolated; they divided their time between gossip and prayers and indulged in little sins of vanity, as was the custom in the convents in those days. They dressed with almost worldly elegance, they used perfumes, silk stockings, ribbons in their shoes. The most daring ones curled their hair and wore it half out of their bonnets.

The cell reserved for Maura Lucenia was frescoed with the

chaste myth of Diana, the only mythological allusion not embarrassing to her situation. The ladies of the city were allowed
to pay her visits, but at the court it was preferable not to
mention her; the Farneses seemed eager to forget the whole
unpleasant business. Only Ranuccio brooded over it, interpret-
ing the episode as a clear sign of fate: the Farneses could not,
and should not, be friends with the Gonzagas.

It was then that Maura Lucenia fell in love with Giulino. He
had been given this diminutive perhaps because he was delicate
and short. His real name was Giulio Cima, and he was a
pleasant-looking youth of about twenty, with a beautiful voice.
As a court employee, Giulino earned nine gold scudi a month.
His salary was regularly collected by his father, for the young
man was a spendthrift. In 1585 Giulino was teaching music
to Ranuccio. Margherita had once been his pupil too, and now,
locked behind those unyielding walls, the memory of the young
teacher and his lessons brought back something of her lost
youth and invited her to dream. The only men Maura Lucenia
had occasion to meet in San Paolo were priests; Rome had not
yet issued the order forbidding them to visit nuns. Why not have
Giulino come in the convent's parlor, or better, in the more
intimate, less echoing *Audenzino*. Unfortunately, Giulino had no
reason to justify his visits to the convent—which did not prevent
him eventually from becoming a *monachino,* as the admirers
of the nuns were called.

One night Giulino lingered under a window of the convent
and sang one of his best love songs, accompanying himself on
a lute. He gazed up in the darkness with an expression of
desperate tenderness. The bars at her window made of Maura
Lucenia forbidden fruit. That song was the appeal of a lover
who would like to say more but restrains himself in the hope
that his feelings will be guessed. Maura Lucenia guessed right
away. Ripe for a new encounter, feeling a confused desire to
love, her heart was caught in the serenade like a butterfly in a

web. She confided in Sister Alessandra and Sister Veronica and, with the help of an old servant, she sent for Giulino.

The first time the young teacher appeared at the convent, Maura Lucenia had a headache. She said to him: "I sent for you because I don't feel well. I'd feel better if we sing one of those songs we used to sing together." And they intoned an aria from Ariosto's *Olimpia,* which begins with the words: "Dhe, Vita mia, non vi mettete affanno per Dio di così lieve cosa!" And another: "Rugiero, qual sempe fui tale esser voglio!"* Spellbound, they kept singing, not knowing what they were doing but compelled to do it. They sat on the hard benches in the *Audenzino,* hardly touching each other, like respectful but no less passionate sweethearts. And after each meeting came a tender, desperate good-bye, for what is more heart-rending and intoxicating than a love with no future?

The scandal broke in June, 1585. Secretly informed, perhaps by a nun, the vicar ran to the governor of Parma asking him to put Giulino in prison because "he, personally, had found him in San Paolo talking to a nun." The vicar had already given Giulino a scolding but he suggested that the governor inform His Highness of what was going on in the convent.

This vicar was burning with a zeal for reform and was well-known in town for his moralistic tirades. Once, complained a harassed cleric, "he harassed the priests of the diocese because of their frocks and their tonsures, and forbade them to wear white shoes, to urinate in the streets, and a thousand other silly things." And this was nothing compared to "sending the gendarmes to the priests' houses to investigate if their housekeepers were real housekeepers and of the right age, something that greatly displeased the whole town." Sometimes the impulsive prelate regretted his too-strict and unpopular measures, which

* *Translator's note:* "Oh, love of my life, do not worry my God for so little a matter!" "Rugiero, I want to be the same as I always was."

almost always led to denunciations and arrests. Also in Giulino's case, when he wanted to make amends, it was too late: Giulino was already in prison, although the authorities, after a long interrogation, seemed convinced that "nothing but words" had passed between the teacher and the princess.

Days passed, full of tension. The convent echoed with bead-telling and prayers. The nuns were terrified that the town would "talk maliciously about the convent." Maura Lucenia already thought that death, inevitable in all great love stories, was about to tear Giulino from her arms and desperately sent him word "to stand firm." But if Giulino got away without being tortured it was not so much because of the princess's influence as in order not to compromise her. To put that weak thoughtless boy on the rack, to dislocate his bones, would have made him confess to things he probably did not even know about. "We think it best not to investigate any further," pronounced the governor of Parma. All the same, Giulino remained in prison meditating on the dangers of playing music in a convent.

For the wretched Maura Lucenia, locked in her frescoed cell, life was not easy. Followed by spies, ignored by the nuns, neglected by her family, with no visitors, no Giulino, no lute, her days stood still and she felt herself the most unhappy of women. A year passed, and during that year the situation apparently was not much improved, since Father Pietro Consoli, a prominent prelate of Parma, had to write to Alessandro to leave Flanders for at least a fortnight in order to settle things at home that only he could handle. "I'll mention to Your Highness only three facts," he wrote to Alessandro, "which you, as a good judge, should consider and ponder over with great care. First, there are people here who can harm more than only the prince's soul. Second, the same will I say of Your Highness's daughter in San Paolo. And third, the same again of those who administer justice. And if Your Highness will not take care of these three disorders, they will turn not only into injuries but into disgraces. . . ."

Too much involved in the war, Alessandro found no time to "ponder over" Father Consoli's warnings nor to descend from Flanders to rescue the Farnese reputation endangered by his "most eccentric daughter." When he became duke in 1587, he simply wrote to Ranuccio, the regent, to increase Margherita's isolation. Only the nun's close relatives were allowed, once a year, to enter San Paolo's parlor. Three lashes were to be administered to anybody found there unlawfully. In the face of Ranuccio's harassment, Maura Lucenia did not turn a hair. She had become shrewd and watchful, capable of controlling any feeling and hiding her tears. In only one year she had become a skillful dissimulator. Premature wrinkles covered her young but decrepit face; rings circled her foxy eyes and one could no longer read them as an open book. Incapable of finding relief in tears, her grief had turned into anger. But to Cardinal Alessandro, who had shown her some affection, Margherita wrote touching letters through which the broad lines of this complicated story have been reconstructed.

At Alessandro's death, Ranuccio became duke. Confronted by her brother's authority, Margherita, who had bowed to her grandfather's and later to her father's will, found again the energy and the obstinacy she had shown at the time of her marriage, when she had endured the gynecologists' polemics, the impatience of the Gonzagas, and her own family's pressures. Ranuccio was not easily softened by her outbursts; the few times he met Margherita he merely stared at her with unforgiving eyes. He was irritated rather than touched by her pitiful fate, and he associated the wretched little nun with his hatred for the Gonzagas, since both were guilty of interfering with the Farneses' grandeur. Thus, he continued to torment Maura Lucenia, and with such perversity that the other brother, the young Cardinal Odoardo, grew disgusted by it. From Rome he urged Ranuccio to moderate his absurd resentment, reminding him that Margherita, who was "born a princess and had tasted a life of distinction only to end up in a convent," deserved, especially from her brothers, much compassion. "And do not forget," he wrote, "that her nature and temperament are such that she is more easily won by gentleness than by the so-called iron rod. Therefore, we beg you, for the love and respect we owe to the memory of our beloved father and mother, and for God's sake, to treat her with the kindness she certainly will appreciate and which will induce her to do whatever Your Highness shall order her to do." But Ranuccio still burned with humiliation, and his brother's words only increased his stubbornness.

Finally the pope, to whom Margherita secretly sent heart-breaking "pleas not to allow her soul to be damned, expressing the wretchedness of her situation better than any orator in the world," intervened once more. "Be careful that our sister," wrote Odoardo from Rome, greatly upset, "does not have cause to send so many complaints here, for a soul as upset and dis-tressed as hers (not to say desperate) might do something rash, the danger being that His Holiness might decide to put her in a convent in Rome where it will be decided if she actually deserves to be treated as she is by Your Highness." In which case, no need to say, he added, "how unpleasant for us and how sullied our reputation would be."

This last argument finally convinced Ranuccio that it was not wise to alienate the pope for a family matter. Maura Lucenia got a better life, she stopped writing to the pope, and her name disappeared from the chronicles. Only in 1593 was it mentioned when she was transferred from San Paolo to Santo Alessandro, where she remained fifty-one years and was elected abbess ten times. The acquisition of such solid authority means that, in time, she had learned to turn to religion for help. Silently nursing her resignation, she came to consider her pain as a sign of God's favor. Naturally, she never busied herself again with music. The mere thought of plucking a lute string reminded her of Giulino still locked in the Rocchetta, Parma's sinister prison.

One day Giulino somehow escaped and entered Vincenzo Gonzaga's service (everyone compelled to leave Parma by the Farneses' disfavor was welcomed by the Gonzagas). Ranuccio never resigned himself to Giulino's escape. After years of ambushes, his henchmen—*i farinelli,* as they were called—managed one day to capture Giulino on his way to a rendezvous in Cremona. It was his destiny that women should ruin his life. He was sent back to the Rocchetta, this time forever. Mangled by torture, reduced to a pitiful condition, his very guardians wondered if it wasn't too cruel to torture a poor devil so much.

From the convent, Maura Lucenia prayed for him. Then, perhaps, she forgot him. Life had burned her deeply, making her a wise, patient woman whose soul was pure, with no joy nor wish for it. She had encased herself in an armor of self-defense; her only affection was for the illegitimate daughters of the duke, her brother: Maria, Isabellina, and Margherita, good girls who lived with her in the convent, which had become a sort of ducal orphanage. Her relations with her family were reduced to impersonal notes at Christmas and Easter, congratulations, condolences. She died at seventy-six, having outlived her father, her husband, all of her brothers, and Giulino. She had been so virtuous and so exemplary a nun for so long that, if it had not been for the affair of the lute, the Farneses would doubtlessly have tried to have her canonized, in order to have in the family, in addition to a great pope and a famous *condottiere,* also a saint.

IV

Ranuccio Farnese

In 1592, when he became duke at his father's death, Ranuccio was about twenty years old. It had not taken him long to substitute, for the brilliant atmosphere that had surrounded first Ottavio and then Alessandro, a wearisome etiquette on the pattern of the Spanish court, where expressions of obedience and homage to the king had become rigidly choreographed. Introspective, already inclined to despotism, Ranuccio lived a life complicated by uncertainties, grudges, disillusions, and maniacal dislikes, tormented by pessimism and a monstrous distrust for his fellow men whom he saw as problem-ridden phantoms wavering between sin and madness. Brought up to be strong, but ultimately very little convinced of being so, he demanded constant homage to reassure his self-esteem, and, haunted by the memory of Pier Luigi left to dangle from the castle window, he anticipated an enemy in every vassal. Under his administration the tribunals of the duchy were stricter than in most Italian states, and the frequent pilloryings, beatings, whippings, and hangings advised the citizens that the young duke sought their fear rather than their love.

Ranuccio was indeed a singular mixture of the most disparate characteristics. He was intelligent, yet he believed in spells and black magic with the same faith with which he accepted religious dogmas. On one hand, his credulity compelled him to persecute anyone suspected of witchcraft; on the other, he made alchemy the great passion of his life.

To be sure, it was a very reasonable passion. Alchemy in those days was considered a very noble art, and it was widely practiced. Sovereigns, especially, were fascinated by it; many of them had, in addition to a personal physician and a confessor, a personal alchemist. Elizabeth of England herself had reputedly helped to transmute several pounds of quicksilver into gold and had ordered a medal struck in memory of that divine metamorphosis. And Rudolf of Hapsburg was so infatuated with similar processes as to prefer being an alchemist to being an emperor, and he had accepted the latter calling only because of an atavistic sense of duty. At his court in Prague, ambassadors were kept waiting for days, while alchemists of every nationality were received with great ardor.

In 1610, a strange fellow by the name of Oliviero Olivieri da Todi sent word to Ranuccio that he had mastered "several secret methods of how to distill water, make gold drinkable, transmute base metals into silver and gold" and that he knew how to manufacture the philosophers' stone and could make gold and silver multiply in great quantities.

Ranuccio chose the multiplication of gold—twenty-eight pounds for every original pound—and signed a contract right away. The alchemist swore he would use his powers only for the duke's benefit; he offered to go into his service under the obligation of multiplying three hundred sequins every twenty months, with a net profit of 150,000 gold scudi each time. Ranuccio, in exchange, promised to make him a count and to give him estates, in addition to 3 per cent of the profits and an income of three thousand scudi a year.

Surrounding himself with mystery, Oliviero installed his laboratory in the Casino di Santa Croce. Ranuccio provided him with all the paraphernalia he needed: alembics, pots, mortars, bellows, grills, jars, phials, vases full of quicksilver, ammonia, vitriol, saltpeter, "and other devilries." Not to mention the several hundred gold sequins, gold and silver bars, for the alchemist said he could not start working without a great deal of raw material. Occasionally Ranuccio, driven by impatience and curiosity, entered Oliviero's smoky laboratory and, after witnessing "coagulations, purifications, alterations, sublimations, desiccations, mixing, cooling, filters, and the use of the biggest imaginable stoves," left again, fascinated and horrified. Oliviero worked slowly, but Ranuccio found no fault with him. There are things, he thought, with which one has to proceed very cautiously. *Lege, lege, relege, ora, labora et invenis,* was the saying preferred by the alchemists: read, read, reread, pray, work and you shall find. Hadn't Saint Thomas Aquinas himself said that the preparation of the philosophers' stone was the most difficult of all undertakings? Ranuccio's hopes had put on wings when Oliviero, in a first lucky experiment, had succeeded in producing, from twenty-four silver ducats, twenty-eight pounds of the same metal. This experiment dispelled Ranuccio's doubts, convincing him it was absurd to doubt someone who could present him with excellent silver "resistant to any test, comparison, and hammer."

Days went by, and from the laboratory's chimney floated a greenish, smelly, quite promising smoke. Oliviero appeared at court only to ask for acids and containers, each time complaining with professional asperity about the inferior quality of this or that. Between one mishap and another, the alchemist managed to hold the duke at bay, spying his moods and anticipating his possible disappointments with excuses that, if the gold hadn't percolated from the alembic, et cetera, the blame rested on one or another trivial accident, some imponderable technical inaccuracy. He thus succeeded in "delaying his promises with several pretenses, explaining why, for one reason or another, he could not produce what he had promised."

Months passed by, and Ranuccio was patient. By night he dreamed about the multiplication of gold; by day he thought of nothing else. One morning the Casino di Santa Croce was found crammed with evil-smelling potsherds; in the fireplace languished a small, dejected-looking fire, in a corner a black cat purred, on the window sill an owl deloused itself. There was no sign of Oliviero. He had left with eight hundred sequins and several pounds of silver. Someone later remembered having seen him riding, with much speed, in the direction of Reggio Emilia.

Ranuccio was not, as one might believe, humiliated or made desperate by this. Nothing could destroy his naïveté or shake his faith in alchemy. If the fellow from Todi had chosen to run away, it was not because of professional incapacity but because he meant to break the contract and work on his own. It is understandable, therefore, that Ranuccio continued to attract impostors and charlatans—true confidence men who, for the entire duration of his administration, enchanted him with ever more astonishing projects. In 1608, for example, he gave audience to someone who maintained he was able to transform fire into water. Sometime after, he gave order to contact and negotiate with someone who knew "a secret of how to put sentries to sleep."

These promises, these useless expectations, were among the few things capable of stimulating Ranuccio's colorless days and helping to keep him alive. He enjoyed himself very rarely. He preferred to work; in fact, his inclination and capacity for work were prodigious, for work meant to him a continuous flight from sadness. His extraordinary endurance, so out of proportion to his poor health, was not shaken even by his epilepsy attacks, after which he seemed merely a bit more gloomy than usual. His tendency to depression increased with the years and finally bordered on that arbitrary and nebulous zone where normality ends and pathology begins. Sometimes, when his depression coincided with some real adversity, the world seemed ready to collapse on him. Then his will for recovery reached an incredible intensity. He slept little and badly; on moonlit nights especially, he heard sinister tinklings coming from the tapestries, saw tiny little birds, heard the ghosts and the souls in purgatory moan. At other times he listened to silence, for which he said he had a sharp ear, or he stared at the gray stream of sand in the sandglass, horrified by the relentlessness of a flow he could not control. Then he went back to work, and the yellow circle of light on his desk became the only steady spot in the sea of hostile darkness.

With so much work it seems impossible that he should have been able also to find time for women. When this did happen, the courtiers said: "His Highness is in heat," and they had to find someone to quench it. This does not mean Ranuccio particularly liked women, but in his own way he could not do without them; he was driven by a coarse sensuality complicated, among other things, by strange fears. His mistress on one side and his confessor on the other held in his life the pans of a scale which could drop indifferently to one side or the other. He could not conceive of women without anguish, without relating everything back to the original sin. This metaphysical fear made his escapades all the more guilt-laden and sorrowful. His affairs therefore were brief and squalid, with no sentimental participation. They ended badly, some very badly indeed. Claudia Colla, for example, was done away with and buried alive in the Gragnano castle, under the charge of practicing witchcraft against the duke's family.

The only exception in this bevy of ill-treated mistresses was Briseide Ceretoli. Perhaps Ranuccio really loved her. He began to like her at the time when Briseide's father, a nobleman from Parma, served with Alessandro in Flanders, where he died bravely. They met at various receptions "but always innocently," specify the chronicles, "without the slightest reason for scandal." Later, as it happens, they lost their heads and "had occasion to know each other carnally," and in 1598, on a December night, a son was born to them. The following evening a ducal carriage stopped in front of the Ceretoli house; from it emerged Bartolomeo Riva—the prime minister—and Count Alessandro Sforza, who took the child and had him baptized under the name of Ottavio, the name of Ranuccio's grandfather and Briseide's late father. Weakened by the recent childbirth, Briseide parted from her baby with a heartbreaking smile: she knew she would never see him again.

A year later, reasons of state induced Ranuccio to marry Margherita Aldobrandini, a niece of Clement VIII. Since he abhorred the idea of long-term affairs, and since he was convinced that decency and respectability demanded fidelity in an honest man, he forced Briseide also to marry. He himself chose the husband for her: Alessandro Carissimi, a learned advocate and fairly good scholar. Later Briseide was taken ill with one of those mysterious diseases in those days classified generally as a "broken heart," and shortly afterward she died of it. Ranuccio honored her memory by exercising benevolence on behalf of her widower who, having entered the clergy, with the duke's help eventually became Bishop of Castro.

Maria Aldobrandini, a princess who used to say of herself, "I belong to God," was a thorough, Spanish-style Catholic, and she contributed to making Parma one of the most clerical cities of Italy. She was "better qualified for the Church than to be a good duchess," was the judgment of Ippolito Calandrini, a historian of the time. Maria was ignorant, and since culture inspired in her a mysterious awe, she was never tempted to improve her mind. Her style as a duchess was sedate, rather dowdy, and scrupulously formal. Yet, underlying all was a deep sensuality, as shown in certain letters she wrote that reveal how demanding she was regarding intimacy with her husband. She was unattractive and had a plain face with the thin mouth of a money box, and deep black eyes. With middle age she became obese, which in itself would not be too important except that this characteristic was inherited by the following generations, and it probably was an important factor in the final extinction of the Farnese dynasty.

The idea of marrying a pope's niece, a union "of greater profit, splendor and security" than any other, was a product of that political perspicacity which made of Ranuccio a most determined and shrewd statesman. There was nothing more strategically important for him than a matrimonial connection with the pope, of whom he was a vassal and from whom he could hope to obtain, in addition to the title of *Gonfaloniere della Chiesa* [Standard-bearer of the Church], the final recognition of the hereditary authority of the still young Farnese dynasty. Politically, however, Ranuccio was more committed to Spain than to the pope, and by tradition and belief he remained unalterably loyal to Spain—although the ingratitude with which King Philip had repaid Alessandro's devotion left Ranuccio deeply discontented. That resentment, concealed during Ranuccio's lifetime, burst out in the rabidly Francophile (i.e., anti-Spanish) politics of his immediate successor. For the time being, however, the official relations between the Hapsburgs of Madrid and the Farneses were marked by the greatest obsequiousness on the part of the latter. In 1601, as the pope's emissary, Ranuccio even went to Valladolid for the baptism of the daughter of Philip III, Philip II's successor, and on that occasion received the Order of the Golden Fleece and a yearly pension of fifteen thousand ducats. Behind the courtesy, of course, both Philip III and Ranuccio strove to best one another in "secrecy, reserve, and dissimulation," the three basic qualities for a good seventeenth-century ruler.

Unfortunately, in Italy, these courteous exchanges lost value each time Ranuccio had to deal with the Spanish governor in Lombardy. At the beginning of the seventeenth century there arrived in Milan, as His Catholic Majesty's representative, a man who for years would frustrate Ranuccio's political ambitions. This man was the Duke of Fuentes, a grand old man of imposing soldierly pride, the last real *capitano* of Spain, and so influential a nobleman that even the Duke of Lerma, Philip's favorite, was jealous of him. The Duke of Fuentes came to Milan at the age of seventy, strong as a man of forty, and for ten years he lorded over Milan and the neighboring states, declaring that Philip ruled in Madrid, but that in Milan Fuentes was the only master. Some years before, after Alessandro's death, he had been sent to Flanders and tried in vain to rival Alessandro's successes. He felt, therefore, quite resentful toward the Farneses and, through spite, he repeatedly caused difficulties with the family notwithstanding his government's instructions to the contrary. For example, when a famine struck the duchy of Parma, he prevented Milan from supplying its neighbor with much-needed wheat; and shortly after he held up the shipment of more wheat from Piedmont, thereby causing great distress in Parma.

Don Julio Fuentes indulged himself in the dream of turning Italy into an enormous province of Spain. Accordingly, in order to protect Milan, which he considered a strategic stronghold of the Spanish possessions in Italy, he proceeded to make a number of territorial annexations: Correggio, Mirandola, part of Lunigiana, Soncino, Castiglione, and Novara. Many years earlier, Charles V had ceded Novara to Pier Luigi—officially as a gracious present, in truth at the price of 225,000 scudi—and had reserved to his own successors in the duchy of Milan the right of buying the town back for the same price. Novara was not particularly rich, but for more than half a century it had given the Farneses a prestige that Ranuccio treasured more than any financial advantage. To deprive him of the place was to shorten his life ten years, a consideration which did not prevent the Duke of Fuentes, in 1606, from installing a Spanish mayor in Novara.

Ranuccio's frantic intrigues proved useless, as did the pope's intervention, the recommendations of Philip III's confessor, and even the favorable disposition of the Spanish sovereigns. Don Julio, indifferent to everyone, occupied Novara, setting an example to the future Spanish governors in Italy, whose autonomy in the seventeenth century greatly weakened the central government. In the last years of his life, he became so menacing that Parma lived in the constant fear that an invasion would sooner or later follow one of the frequent border controversies between Milan and the Farnese territory.

Ranuccio lit candles and prayed for the death of the terrible governor; and when finally the news came that the governor had died (at well over eighty) he could not believe it. "If it is true," he wrote, distrustfully as usual, to his brother Odoardo, "God forbid that someone worse than he should come, since things always seem to get worse." Despite all of this, as soon as the king of Spain needed any military help Ranuccio professed himself "more than ready to give not only his land but his life."

Not yet disillusioned by "the rigid and offensive attitude" with which Spain repaid his services, Ranuccio held with great perseverance to his various dreams: to become governor of Milan, commander-in-chief of the Spanish troops in Italy, king of the Balkans, leader of a war against the Turks. But that "damned luck" of Paul III had not been transmitted to Ranuccio. That unfortunate story of Portugal, for example, still hurt him after many years. It happened when he was twelve years old. Don Sebastiano, king of Portugal, had died without children, leaving behind only his uncle, a very old, deaf, arterio-sclerotic cardinal, who was duly crowned. Since he obviously was not going to live much longer, many candidates to the throne stepped forward: Antony, the illegitimate son of John III of Braganza's brother; Emmanuel Philibert of Savoy, Caterina de' Medici, Philip II of Spain, and also Alessandro Farnese who, having married Maria Daviz, a Portuguese royal princess, asked the succession for his son Ranuccio. Ranuccio, as it happened, was the favorite of the Portuguese people, who hoped to educate the boy in their customs; also, as grandson of Pope Paul, he could guarantee the support of the Church.

At this point, the old cardinal-king, confused by dozens of advisors, each one supplying him with different advice, suddenly decided to go his own way and solemnly announced that he had asked for a papal dispensation, for he wanted to marry and give Portugal an heir. The whole of Europe laughed. Some-one suggested that he drink unicorn powder dissolved in water; others recommended the bezoar stone, famous for its aph-rodisiac qualities; others still, suggested that he marry a preg-nant woman. In the middle of that insolent bantering, the old king died, and the struggle for the succession accelerated.

If young Ranuccio was the most convenient candidate, Philip II was the most dangerously powerful. Pope Gregory XIII, who dreaded an increase in Spanish influence, advised Philip to be moderate and prudent. Knowing the king's passion for relics, he presented him with half of the body of a child mas-sacred in the Slaughter of the Innocents. But, for once, Philip was not impressed by the pope's rare present. A few days after the cardinal-king's death, Philip ordered his troops to invade Portugal, while seventy-two Spanish galleons "tall as castles, terrible to look at" sailed toward the mouth of the Tagus River. Ranuccio, already eager at thirteen to emulate his father, buried his first dream of glory under a fit of melancholia. Later, having entered an uneventful adolescence, he continued to envision his life as glorious, and he longed to exchange the ducal diadem for a royal crown. If he had failed with Portugal, perhaps he would succeed in Albania, he thought, where so many unlucky infidels were waiting to be converted. And why not also try in England, which Elizabeth, because of her inclination to play the role of maiden queen, was going to leave without an heir? At once exalted and oppressed by the glory of the Farnese dynasty, his awareness of belonging to one of the most prominent families in Italy was becoming pathological. He could not for a moment forget he was the great-grandson of a pope who had kept in check men like Charles V and Francis I, the grand-nephew of Cardinal Alessandro, the creator of six popes, close to the tiara himself and for decades considered the most power-ful man in Rome, and the son of Alessandro, whom the Romans had honored with a statue in the Campidoglio.

Thus regarding himself as the natural heir of the power and prestige of the Farneses, Ranuccio was inevitably prone to be dissatisfied with his small duchy to which, however, he pas-sionately dedicated himself. Ranuccio's administration was one of intense public service. In 1594 he effectively reorganized the duchy by means of a constitution that remained the basis of the Farnese regime. A glance through the statutes and the articles, or through any document of the Parma administration of those years, is sufficient to make one feel the presence of a very capable man, inclined to understand and solve particularly difficult problems. The patron of the Accademia degli Innocenti, the reorganizer of the university, the creator of the Collegio dei Nobili (which became the most renowned and exclusive board-ing school in Europe), the founder of a botanical garden praised by Ulisse Aldrovandi, Ranuccio showed in these efforts a real interest in improving public education. He was also fascinated by science, as were many princes in those days, and he greatly admired, for example, Pompilio Tagliaferri, the distinguished Bolognese surgeon to whom he gave the chair of medicine at the university.

Under Ranuccio, life in the duchy was regulated by laws governing the upkeep of the roads, the sewerage system, the disposal of garbage, ordinances for "good and quiet living" that controlled beggary, forbade work and card playing on holidays, and punished blasphemers and criminals. Nor did Ranuccio's firmness fail in the most critical circumstances of his administration, as for instance during the famine of 1607, which the duchy survived with little damage thanks to a series of judicious measures on Ranuccio's part.

The population, especially the rural part of it, was exposed to the feudal lords' irrational rule and lived in lamentable social and human conditions. This was a perennial problem in the duchy and, although interested in agricultural issues, Ranuccio barely managed not to worsen the peasants' situation. On the other hand, social forces were fermenting in the two cities, especially in the more enterprising Piacenza. There, the middle class was growing richer through commerce and government contracts and was developing into a professional class, which then bought titles from the court and, faithful to the duke, began to take over the offices previously reserved to the old aristocracy.

The clergy, too, unlike the feudatories, were devoted to Ranuccio, although ecclesiastical immunities, especially the fiscal ones, sometimes gave origin to controversies between the civil government and Church authorities. Because of financial difficulties in the duchy, Ranuccio often had to disregard his religious sentiments and force the clergy to pay taxes like everyone else.

The duke exercised constant and total control over all his subjects. On matters ranging from the private enterprises of his courtiers to women's hairdos, he did not spare advice, prohibitions, and interventions, all of which he mistook for foresighted political wisdom. "Prepare yourself," he once ordered Count

Teodoro Scotti, "to go on a trip as His Highness's representative. You'll need the following wardrobe: a city suit, decent and fine, black or any color Your Lordship prefers, but if it is black it would be advisable to have at least a vest of gold material or gold-embroidered, a gilded sword, colored stockings, a jeweled hat, a beautiful chain, and, if Your Lordship wishes, gold buttons." Thus attired, the count was sent to pay homage to the new governor of Milan.

Also decided at court were the appointments of abbots and priors, Lenten preachers, nuns' habits and their admission to convents, and also attendance at religious ceremonies and cat- echism classes. Fortunately, the duchy was free from religious ferment at a time when new doctrines kept the Inquisition busy in many Italian cities. As his predecessors had been, Ranuccio was deeply committed to the Church and supported to an amazing degree what could be called "legal confessionalism," that is, the translation of religious precepts into legal norms. For instance, physicians called at sickbeds had to prescribe, first of all, a confession, "as if it were the most important and beneficial medicine of all." Ranuccio's totalitarian Catholicism made itself felt in the economic and private lives of the citizens and mortified their proud, outgoing, enterprising nature. On the other hand, it did lead them to a more orderly, quiet, lawful existence. His dictatorship extended to the aristocracy—an un- usual situation in Italy, where most rulers were never allowed to forget that the old feudal families were practically their equals. The reason was that, unlike other princely families, most of whom had reached a dominant position through the support of one or more local factions, the Farneses, from the beginning, had obtained power from the outside, through a direct in- vestiture from the pope. They owed nothing to the local lords, and therefore they could afford to order them about as they did the other citizens.

With Ranuccio, absolutism reached its apex. He even shook

the guilds to their roots, reducing them to mere departments of his administrative body. He dismissed everyone who had had any importance under Alessandro, a name he obsessively associated with the limitation of power in his own youth. The aristocracy was irritated by such restraints. Kept in gilded deprivation, pressed by leisure's hard labor, the young gentlemen of Parma cursed the flatness of their lives and spent the days looking for anything that could dispel their boredom.

As a result, the Spanish-like servility of court protocol was balanced by the courtiers' outbursts of violent passion, blusterings, duels, quixotic rebellions. Their lives seemed to swing between conformity and scorn of convention, between discipline and disorder, with an ever present yearning for the unusual, the novel. And so they engaged in sophomoric tricks and pranks. For a while there was the fad of stealing each other's flower pots. Count Gianbattista Masi one day took some from Guido Torelli's garden. Torelli was very angry and complained so much that he got the duke to have Count Masi confined to his home. Like a child put in a corner, the count, "his blood boiling," could not find peace "that he alone should be treated that way for such a bagatelle" as a flower-pot game, which, incidentally, other people of quality continued to play undisturbed, for everyone was convinced that "a few flowers did not deserve so much noise." From a Parma nunnery, for instance, twenty-eight pots had disappeared in one night, and no one had said a word. Yet Count Masi's confinement lasted several months. The truth was that Ranuccio saw in the exuberant count one of those potentially dangerous young men who made him dread the future. In his letters to his fiancée, which three centuries later were discovered in a dusty corner of an archive, Gianbattista Masi grieved for his honor: "I would thank Our Lord for the gift of sufficient courage to take the duke's life should he try to take my honor, which is the best part of me, even if they tear me to pieces. This prince would not be alive if everyone thought as I do." Meanwhile, Masi had to stay home, and his mother had personally to humble herself before the duke and ask forgiveness for her son, who got back his freedom on the condition that he give satisfaction as "an honorable gentleman" to the owner of the pots.

Ranuccio equally divided his interest between Parma and Piacenza, thus creating a very strong rivalry between the two cities. He often went to Piacenza—Parma called her *Piacenza la brutta* [Piacenza the ugly]—for he felt comfortable there; he loved her fragrant old churches, their shades and silence, the ancient buildings clustered around the piazza, the patrician houses. He liked the tenacity and reserve of the townspeople, their attachment to the Farneses in honor of whom they later dedicated two equestrian statues, one of Ranuccio, the other of his father. Despite the opinion of Massimo d'Azeglio, who a few centuries later was to compare the manes to snakes and macaroni, the statues are splendid jewels of the Italian baroque.

Parma was more cheerful than Piacenza but less distinguished architecturally. The town itself has changed a good deal in modern times, but the people were essentially the same as those of today: lucid, sensible, enterprising. They were, and still are, industrious, courteous people who view the world with optimism. But Parma's public buildings and palaces of that period—most of them gray and soberly decorated—reflected more Ranuccio's personality than the citizens' traditional amiability.

La Pilotta, where Ranuccio lived, is perhaps the starkest of Italian princely residences. Looking at it one feels that the man who chose it regarded hugeness as the highest expression of beauty. Lady Morgan, an intellectual gentlewoman who traveled in Italy at the beginning of the nineteenth century, judged it "a heavy assemblage of ill-assorted buildings with no style, old without being antique, with many rooms and dark, uncomfortable corridors." Had she seen it at the time of Ranuccio, her judgment would have perhaps been more sympathetic, for the palace, with its three courtyards enlivened by a brilliant band of courtiers, must have had a certain splendor.

Ranuccio decided to expand La Pilotta when he heard that the Grand Duke of Tuscany would pass through Parma on his way to Milan. The temptation to show off to a person who was an expert in luxury obsessed him; he bought the adjoining buildings and equipped them to quarter comfortably up to six princes at one time, with their retinues, as many as three hundred people all together. In 1602, in addition to these renovations, new buildings, judged necessary to a ruler's residence, were put up. The most famous painters of the Bologna school were called to decorate them, and there is proof that even the ovens and the laundry rooms were frescoed.

Later Ranuccio was overcome by the desire to own also a country villa, so as to emulate the famous residences of the d'Este and Gonzaga families. For this purpose he restored and enlarged—wanting it to be both stately and cheerful—a palace across the Po, called Palazzo del Giardino, which his grandfather had thought of transforming, together with the landscape, into a country house. Many times remodeled, this palace has now lost its original aspect, retaining only in the central part something of its sixteenth-century elegance. The fountain, the pride of Parma's citizens, who used to say, "The fountains of Caprarola are nothing compared to ours," stands no longer in front of it. The frescoes also have been destroyed: the "Venus with Adonis," by Paolo Veronese; a famous Correggio; twelve emperors in chiaroscuro by Titian; a series of Raphaels; several portraits by Parmigianino, Giulio Romano, and Andrea del Sarto. Almost nothing is left of the "naked women, so difficult to paint," by Agostino Carracci, Ranuccio's favorite painter, whom Ranuccio, against the will of his brother Alessandro, had sent for from Rome, where the painter was working at the Palazzo Farnese. Carracci died in Parma at the age of forty, leaving unfinished an oval in one of the halls he had frescoed with cherubs. Ranuccio ordered that the oval be left blank and had a plaque immured there in the artist's honor with an inscription by the court poet.

The ducal garden had enough shade and coolness to be one of those lovely, gossipy Italian parks with people strolling to and fro at sundown. There were fishponds and rare plants, and a wood of big *melagoli* trees, which in the winter the gardeners surrounded with live charcoals to keep them from freezing.

Like all the rulers of his time, many of whom left us splendid private legacies and miserable public ones, Ranuccio meant to prove himself a prince also through art and architecture. His patronage was part of the Farnese tradition and dictated by personal ambition as well. And so, in the years of transition from the splendors of the cinquecento to the pompousness of the baroque, Ranuccio conceived the famous Teatro Farnesiano, a remarkable example of the classical theater destined to welcome the melodrama, the last creation of the Renaissance. The architect, Gian Battista Aleotti, had been inspired by Palladio, who a few years earlier in Vicenza had revived the classical theater, the celebrated Teatro Olimpico, in the Vitruvian tradition.

Until recently, in the gloomy atmosphere of the Parma palace, the deserted theater was the most squalid of places; time had added to it only the stench of years, the grayness of dust and decay. Dozens of famous visitors wandered about this hall, under a ceiling broken through in many places, among gray mutilated statues. The famous Montesquieu, when he saw the theater, said it seemed to him too big for a small prince who had nothing to make it famous. In 1628, however, a performance that would have intoxicated Ranuccio, had he been alive, took place in the Teatro Farnesiano with enormous success. The performance, celebrating the wedding of Ranuccio's son Odoardo to Margherita de' Medici, involved bringing water up to the second floor of the theater and building suitable tanks hidden from the audience in order to flood the stage by surprise—not only a problem of hydraulics but a true hazard for the building. Suddenly, when no one expected it, the stage turned into a small sea, with sea monsters and a floating island clustered with nymphs. Simultaneously the "sky" of the stage opened wide, revealing the gods of Olympus seated in a semicircle amidst a bevy of round-cheeked cupids. At a certain moment Jupiter effected a reconciliation between Mars and Mercury, appealed to Peace, and hurled Discord and the Furies into the sea beneath.

In the early seventeenth century Ranuccio looked very much like the equestrian statue Francesco Mochi had made of him for the Piazza Cavalli in Piacenza; and as a living monument, he intimidated the citizens with his very presence. Physically, between the ailments he actually suffered, those he felt would come with old age, and a few imaginary ones, he was not in very good shape. He was heavy, his hair was thin on top though still thick at the temples; he had a beard neatly divided in the middle, a short mustache, tumid, flabby lips, slightly swollen eyelids, and black-ringed eyes that could not smile. Common sense suggested to him that it was ridiculous to worry about such inevitable things as the passing of years. Yet getting old was for Ranuccio as distressing as an actual illness. The threshold of the forties suddenly revealed to him the slippery abyss of self-pity and old age (three centuries ago a man was already old at forty) rather than serenity. In addition to this, he had no

heirs and he continuously brooded over the misery of his in-
completeness as a ruler and as a man, dreaming of a family
tree made luxuriant by his great deeds and those of his many
descendants. Of the children born to his mistresses many had
died at birth. Three daughters, "fruits of human frailty," as they
used to say in those days, were entrusted to Ranuccio's sister,
Abbess Maura Lucenia, who raised them in her monastery.
Sometimes they turned up at the court under the Duchess
Margherita's cold but tolerant eyes; illegitimate children were
treated most humanely and politely. And yet the dynasty needed
legitimate heirs, not bastards, however handsome. Ranuccio
yearned for them and, in the constant hope of getting them, he
exhausted himself "in frequent and immoderate embraces" with
his wife. Ten years passed, and the court gossips said that
there was no hope.

The Aldobrandina was not sterile; as a matter of fact she
was almost constantly pregnant. But her children either were
stillborn or else died after a few hours. The duke, in any case,
did not blame her; he never reproached her, gracefully tolerat-
ing her sadness and her miscarriages, convinced that she had
been given the evil eye. To obliterate this curse, Ranuccio in-
defatigably consulted monks expert in exorcism, distributed
money to pregnant women, to the Capuchins of the Abbey of
Fontevivo, to the Santa Croce di Loreto, and to the many
churches in Parma, as his brother, Cardinal Odoardo, suggested.
Nothing helped, and Ranuccio sadly repeated that no illness
is more incurable than that of a childless ruler.

The nightmare of dying without an heir, and the love he felt
for Ottavio, the son of Briseide Ceretoli, drove Ranuccio to
endow him officially with all the rights of a legitimate son.
Ottavio was to succeed him, except in the event that God
should grant him a legitimate heir. In an outburst of fatherly
love, he severed the towns of Borgo San Donnino and Firenzuola and the entire Val di Nure from Parma and Piacenza's

jurisdiction, creating an estate for Ottavio and his descendants, with rights of primogeniture. Not satisfied yet, he made all the cannons and weapons and war machines in every stronghold of the duchy Ottavio's property, and transferred to him the seigniory of the towns of Ortona, Leonessa, Città Ducale, Altamura, Castellamare, and the rest of the southern estates the Farneses had inherited from Madama d'Austria. Finally, he recommended the boy to the pope, to the emperor, and to the king of Spain, entrusting him to their protection.

Ottavio was clever, alert and very ambitious. At twelve he already had his own courtiers, his pages, a rich wardrobe, carriages and horses. Certain of the duke's affection, he behaved with the authority of a hereditary prince. Everyone regarded him as the future duke—until, on September 5, 1610, the Aldobrandina gave birth to a boy, Alessandro. In the latter's honor there were prayers, cheers, alms, amnesties. The duchess had finally succeeded. The baby had survived. He would grow like a beautiful plant, wise as his father, brave as his grandfather. But after a few months it became clear that the heir could only bellow: he was mute, and also deaf. There was an experiment: a gentleman shot a pistol three feet from the crib, but the baby was not even startled. Deaf and doomed to the darkness of madness, he would never rule.

Such mishaps, very frequent in royal families and the causes of which people desperately questioned, are easily explained nowadays. The descendants of noble families almost always suffered the consequences of syphilis that was transmitted generation after generation. Or else, the offspring of marriages among a small number of families, too rarely invigorated by fresh blood, became debilitated, the victims of excessive consaguinity.

Naturally, Alessandro was not considered ill but only bewitched, as is shown in several letters of people who offered, as anti-witch remedy, miraculous ropes, relics, and detailed information about Saint Burchard, first Bishop of Vienna, over whose grave two mute boys had recovered the use of speech. Some people wrote that Alessandro's sickness was the deed of Jews, notoriously expert in witchcraft. Others optimistically offered to cure him "in three months at the most." A certain Brother Girolamo from Bologna arrived with one of the Little Innocents' skulls he had borrowed in Venice with special permission of the doge, "from the shrine where it had been preserved for seven hundred years." "You ought to place it over His Highness's head every time the Holy Spirit commands you to do so, with complete faith that God, in virtue of this holy skull, shall heal the child's sick skull."

When Alessandro grew a little older, Ranuccio decided to have him exorcised in Loreto and entrusted him to Father Pietro da Sardegna, a Capuchin monk expert in demonology. With the excuse of freeing him from the devil, the monk beat up the boy, making him cry desperately. There was, of course, no improvement. From Loreto, Alessandro was taken everywhere the Madonna had performed miracles: to Langhirano, Salso-maggiore, Reggio Emilia, and later to Assisi and Orvieto, where other brutal Capuchins repeated their useless attempts and from where the boy returned more deaf-mute and retarded than ever.

Finally Ranuccio lost faith in the exorcisms and turned to medicine for help. Physicians prescribed various prune-laxatives, molasses, and syrups. At the Farnese palace in Caprarola, where Cardinal Odoardo lived, there was held a consultation of Italy's foremost doctors, who declared the little prince not bewitched but really deaf and dumb and also epileptic. "The prince's sickness is caused by epilepsy which he developed in his mother's womb, the cause being humidity inherited from his mother and father who are both affected by humidity. Thus the child, having absorbed the above-mentioned humidity, now suffers from epilepsy; that is, he has always needed medical help, has never spoken nor shown any rationality, and his every act and gesture are those of a mute and a thorough idiot." This diagnosis sealed by the authority of science reduced everyone to silence. Brought back to Parma, Alessandro was finally left alone with no medicines to swallow, "for the less medicine one takes the better it is for one's stomach and vital spirit." He lived quietly in a little villa built for him in a corner of the duke's garden, and finally died at twenty.

All this time, Ottavio, healthy offspring of free love, had remained Ranuccio's and his subjects' favorite. Ottavio personified the naïve, prefabricated dream of popular imagination; he had the perfect physique for the role his destiny had chosen him for, or for the role which everyone would have liked him to play. People found him handsome, amiable, generous, and so different from his father that the ovations at his passing showed a popularity close to real affection. He would certainly have become duke if in April, 1612, the Duchess Margherita had not given birth to another boy, big and healthy this time, who was called Odoardo.

It is hard to say how Ottavio accepted the arrival of this stepbrother, who was taking from him a legacy he had considered his own. It is conceivable, though, that he was still too young or too proud and unconcerned to resign himself. Shortly before Odoardo's birth, in June, 1612, for three consecutive days, Ottavio had held in the cathedral a special seminar on "rational, natural, and human" philosophy. Ranuccio had ordered the famous Viotti printing house to publish the dialogue in book form. With the title page decorated with allegorical figures by Malosso, the work was dedicated to Pius V and was sent as a gift to the courts of Rome, Florence, and Urbino, to show to relatives and friends that, if Pico della Mirandola had waited eighteen years before presenting himself to an audience, Ottavio Farnese had accomplished this at a much younger age. Moreover Ranuccio continued to assign him missions of some importance, the arrangement of public ceremonies, receptions, and hunting parties. Once, during his absence, he even entrusted Ottavio with the administration of the state to the point of empowering him with the privilege of dispensing justice and mercy—one of the highest prerogatives of a ruler.

In time, however, with the tenacious ambition of a true Farnese, Ottavio began to realize that all that was not enough for him. He began to think of the future; Odoardo, the fat, lymphatic boy, one day would undermine him and ultimately usurp him in Ranuccio's affection. He anticipated being demoted to his original position, that of a bastard son with no future. In reality Ottavio did not want much—he did not have enough imagination for it. He craved power simply to be able to make war; like his grandfather, he yearned to "gain reputation" amidst the rumble of harquebuses and fluttering pennants, for he was convinced that a prince's prestige was unthinkable without military glory. "Woe to those who get caught in the slimy net of everyday routine," said Ottavio; "men have to look for something better and nobler." His restlessness expressed itself in dreams of battles and cavalry charges, while Ranuccio pitilessly nailed him down to studies of logic, philosophy, foreign languages, and canon law. "And do not brood over ideas," Ranuccio dryly ordered, "that are not relevant to your studies." The famous Giambattista Trotti, called Malosso, gave him drawing lessons; Gian Francesco Brandolo took care of his writing style and calligraphy. As for his military education, Ranuccio assigned him an instructor, Captain Gherardo Vicini, to teach him "the theory and practice of forming squadrons," but nothing else. And, for God's sake, "he should not give the boy any fiddle-faddle," that is, premature dreams of glory; such initiatives might compromise the Farneses' foreign policy which, at that time, was aimed at maintaining a scrupulous neutrality. It was up to the duke to choose the right moment for Ottavio to go to war with all the honors due his rank; but for the time being that meaningless strutting about was decidedly a silly idea, indicative of a growing desire for independence that had to be cooled off.

At twenty, Ottavio was still dreaming of smoky battlefields, and Ranuccio realized that after having dominated his son for so long, Ottavio had begun to escape him and to resist his orders. As a consequence, Marquis Pozzo was appointed to follow the young man everywhere and to report his every word to the duke. As time passed, father and son grew more and more estranged; Ottavio, feeling isolated, complained he was going mad. Indeed he was incapable of speaking frankly to his father, for Ranuccio was one of those fathers who do not discuss matters with their children, and even if he had, it would have been useless, because Ranuccio, constantly alarmed by possible threats to his position, was the kind of man who decided before-hand when to conclude a dialogue. Often Ottavio had difficulty recalling when and how he had offended his father. In one moment of self-examination, he found only two possible faults with himself: he had not ridden his horse through the city as His Highness had ordered him, and he had missed confession and Holy Communion on a certain religious holiday. For these faults he apologized in a detailed letter. He had not ridden only because, at that particular moment, he "did not have a fancy for it" and not because he wanted to defy His Highness. As for the Communion, His Highness should not judge him a bad Christian for having missed it once, because Holy Communion "is something one does not take merely to please others."

Thus wrote Ottavio. But after a while he would again rave that his father was driving him mad with humiliation, that he would kill himself, as men who have lost their honor must. Naturally, he did not kill himself. Instead, he began to think of escaping from the court, which now seemed to him but a sad parody of the Escorial. The attempt, promptly discovered by

[6]   Alessandro Farnese, third Duke of Parma and Piacenza. Pourbus the
Elder. Galleria Nazionale, Parma. PHOTOGRAPH BY TOSI.

[7]   Maria Daviz of Portugal, wife of Alessandro Farnese. Pourbus the
Younger. Galleria Nazionale, Parma. PHOTOGRAPH BY VAGHI.

[8]   Ranuccio I Farnese, fourth Duke of Parma and Piacenza. Artist unknown; copy by Cesare Aretusi. Galleria Nazionale, Parma. PHOTOGRAPH BY VAGHI.

[9] Margherita Aldobrandini, wife of Ranuccio I Farnese. Artist unknown. Galleria Nazionale, Parma. PHOTOGRAPH BY VAGHI.

Marquis Pozzo, cost Ottavio a temporary confinement in the palace; and for Captain Vicini, the instructor who had assisted in Ottavio's secret negotiations for a military assignment abroad, it meant life imprisonment in the darkest cell of the Rocchetta.

After a while Ranuccio calmed down, and when the possibility appeared of a marriage to Polissena, only daughter of the powerful Count Federico Landi, Ottavio fantasized that his luck had finally taken a turn. The *fortunazza paolina* had remembered him. He would be flattered to have Polissena at his side, to hold her in his arms; it would be balm to his wounds. A marriage with Polissena, the sole heiress of a large estate in the duchy, the envy of many Italian and foreign lords, would have been a splendid solution both for Count Landi (his daughter, once married, would not have to leave his beloved estate) and for Ranuccio, who would thus put an end to his old quarrels with the count, a troublemaker, and at the same time provide for his restless bastard son. In the end, however, the marriage did not take place. Ranuccio could not bring himself to forget that Polissena's father was a descendant of that Landi who had helped to hang Pier Luigi out of a window, and the count kept eating his heart out because the Farneses had deprived his ancestors of the estate of Borgotaro. These two considerations protracted the negotiations for months and finally interrupted them forever the day Ranuccio demanded from Landi, as an essential condition, an oath of total obedience, while Landi demanded the immediate restitution of Borgotaro.

Meanwhile Odoardo was growing, and the ducal pair, after so late a beginning, continued to have children. After Odoardo, in the space of three years, a boy and two girls were born. Fatter than ever, Margherita had finally become the fecund mother Ranuccio had always yearned for.

It was at this point that Ranuccio decided to start Ottavio on an ecclesiastical career. About that time the office of assistant judge in the Chamber of Rome, and that of treasurer to the

Holy See had become vacant. "Should you enter one of the above-mentioned offices," Ranuccio wrote to his son, "you need have no doubt, nay, you may be absolutely certain, that you will be made cardinal, if not by this pope, by the next, as it has been demonstrated in the past. Therefore, my brother the cardinal and I have thought to try by prudent negotiation and with the help of all our friends—since these offices can be bought—to obtain one of them for you by offering up to fifty thousand scudi. And since the opportunity is so good that, if we let it pass, God knows when there will be another, I wish you to tell me honestly if you are interested. However, I warn you to consider the matter most carefully for, should you lose this opportunity, you will have only yourself to blame, and I shall forever regret seeing my beloved son go to ruin for not listening to his loving father. In no other way will you ever attain so great a position, nor anything near it. May Our Lord and the Holy Virgin inspire you for the best. . . ."

Ottavio received no inspiration, and he did not care for the red hat. He said No. After this episode, things got worse, and Ottavio realized he was now alone.

Odoardo, at the age of fifteen, became engaged to a young lady of the Medici family. This compelled Ranuccio to withdraw the estates he had given to Ottavio, because the Grand Duke of Tuscany's condition to his daughter's marrying the future Duke of Parma was that the groom be the undisputed master of all the Farnese possessions. Once definitively sacrificed to his stepbrother's welfare, Ottavio lost all restraint; he acted irresponsibly and resumed secret negotiations with Count Landi, proposing to become his heir by marrying Polissena, then rescue Borgotaro and put himself under Spain's protection. In 1620 he also tried, unsuccessfully, another flight from the duchy. One year later, he was finally permitted to go off to the wars in Germany, except that the much-longed-for permission coincided with the discovery of compromising negotiations Ottavio had started with some enemies of the Farneses.

Ranuccio, proclaiming to act on God's behalf for the sake of the duchy and his subjects, and explaining to the ministers that his blood ties with Ottavio spurred him to even greater severity, ordered his son imprisoned in the Rocchetta. There Ottavio languished for years, forgotten by everyone as though he had never existed, until his tragically obscure death in 1643.

Public opinion was not unduly aroused by Ottavio's incarceration. As for Ranuccio, this drastic order was typical of his schizophrenia, that strange mixture of apparently incompatible qualities capable of coexisting without interfering with one another. He treated the aristocracy with the same arbitrariness; he loved a small group of patricians almost deliriously—Alessandro Anguissola of Piacenza, Nicolò Cesis, the Ceretolis of Parma, and a few others—but against the rest he harbored a grudge which in time turned to a deep hatred. He went to sleep thinking of them, he started the day with the same thought, and perhaps he even dreamed of them. His hostility eventually exploded in a tyrannical, sensational, and cruel affair—the trial of 1612—instituted against some of the most important families in the duchy.

In reviewing the fifty years that had seen Pier Luigi's assassination, Ottavio's narrow escape from several conspiracies, and the dispossession of the Pallavicinos ordered by Alessandro, one understands how, historically, Ranuccio was almost compelled to antagonize the aristocracy. Only by their destruction could the Farnese autocracy survive. The decline of the aristocracy had begun under Alessandro, but only Ranuccio openly acted against them. The *Constitutiones* compiled in 1594 were, in fact, the synopsis of Ranuccio's campaign against his nobles and of his effort toward jurisdictional unity and centralized authority in the state. The endless list of penalties and confiscations for disloyalty and minor offenses against the most prominent lords reveals how the duke, from the very beginning, had started to besiege their position relentlessly. Every month there was at least one incident designed to mortify and to undermine them. One day it was the turn of Alberto Scotti, called to answer to the ducal tribunal for abuses against some peasants; another day the Count of Santa Fiora was compelled to indemnify a group of farmers for alleged injustices and overbearing actions. Another judgment, this one affecting the dearest of their privileges, reserved to the duke the exclusive right to the use of the hunting grounds between the river Enza and the Via Emilia, including the woods of Sala and Collecchio. And finally, causing great indignation, came the renewal of an old statute enacted by Pier Luigi, which prohibited the lords from leaving the state without a valid reason and called for the confiscation of the property of anyone who did not re-enter the town within two months after his departure.

This latter law had been reactivated because the lords, neglecting their lands, often joined foreign courts with military or diplomatic appointments to try their luck with wars, politics, or both which, though their loyalty to their duke was implicit, often put them in the position of serving one of his enemies. But even those lords who remained quietly in their castles and were apparently without such ambitions could be treacherous to the duke. The experience of many Italian princes had taught Ranuccio that the lords who stayed put in one place might easily be inflamed by jealousy and desire to rule what was, by full right, their own land; and these, if they were shrewd, could become more dangerous than the ones who went abroad. And so, having yet to decide which kind of noble was more harmful to the peace of the state, Ranuccio preferred to keep them all at home under constant surveillance.

Indeed, the nobles of this era were often fanatically ambitious, and combined an irresistible desire to break laws with an incredible love of litigation. Thousands of disputes kept the law courts busy, and the judgments created discord among villages, caused riots, petitions, prosecutions. Protected by several immunities, educated in that great, unscrupulous school of life that was Italy at the end of the sixteenth century, the lords were, everything considered, very difficult to deal with. And, in the years we are concerned with, their relations with the duke had assumed an aspect of repressed yet unmistakable hostility

V

Lady with a Scorpion

The Countess of Sanseverino, herself an extraordinary woman, was no exception among this set of splendid, impudent aristocrats. Had she been painted as often as she has been celebrated in poems, Italian museums would be filled with portraits of her, and she would now be enjoying a little of the popularity she so much sought in her lifetime. Good portraits have saved many people from oblivion, or at least have contributed to preserving their memory. Time, on the contrary, has kept this woman, whose name will forever be tied to one of the darkest pages of Farnese history, behind the scenes.

Loved by princes and great lords, admired by poets and scholars, Barbara di Sanseverino made use of all her natural gifts—beauty, intelligence, wit, and courage—to play brilliantly a major role on the Italian stage of the late sixteenth century. She belonged to a fascinating generation of women who, toward the end of that luminous and corrupt era, chose with a boldness close to defiance to live an emancipated life.

Of Barbara di Sanseverino are left only two portraits. One is a tiny murky painting in the castle of Fontanellato. One has to go through immense halls and corridors packed with dozens of dark portraits before finding hers, no less dark, hanging in a room called "nuptial," near a carved bed black as a coffin. From this portrait Barbara looks down with a Leonardesque smile. She has large eyes and a vaguely ironic, amused look, which was undoubtedly a factor in the secret of her celebrated beauty. The neck is long, aristocratic; the face is framed by a tiaralike hairdo, and on the forehead rests a shiny, lacteous drop: a large pear-shaped pearl. The dress, of which only the geometry of the laces is visible and which probably was stiffened by whalebones, is emphatic and decorative, one of the many dresses from her boldly elegant wardrobe. But the smile is still the focus of her charm; it is a smile about to vanish or to begin, harboring perhaps such opposite impulses as tenderness and cruelty, passion and indifference, candor and perversity, generosity and absolute selfishness. Only one thing is explicit: she was a stunning beauty. The second portrait confirms that. In this one she wears a large Spanish-style ruff; a simple hairdo leaves her forehead free from baroque curls and ornaments. She was regal, her hair was her crown—as Torquato Tasso said in one of his adulatory sonnets—and she was blonde, in compliance with the ideal of femininity which, celebrated by the troubadours and later elaborated by Poliziano and Firenzuola, in the late sixteenth century required that beautiful women be blonde.

One would think that Colorno, the village that belonged to Barbara and in which she lived, would have kept something of her presence, as often happens to certain places evoking at each step memories of former times and people. Yet, here, time has eradicated any trace of the Countess of Sanseverino. No one remembers her. Today Colorno is one of many small towns scattered about the Po Valley, a flat town surrounded by fields cultivated to perfection by centuries of care, under a sky which in winter hugs the earth closely, heavy with fog, and in summer becomes vast and luminous. One senses the presence of the river flowing nearby. In that particular stretch, with the woods crowning the coves like painted backdrops, the rows of poplars on the embankments alternating with small beaches and thick lawns, the river exercises an unforgettable charm.

The castle of Barbara di Sanseverino (perhaps then more a fortress than a castle) rises in the middle of the village, on the bank of the river Lorno. It has changed since she lived there at the head of her brilliant little court. The Farneses were the first, after her death, to enlarge it and make of it, for more than a century, their favorite summer residence. The Bourbons, who succeeded the Farneses in 1731, altered it even further. Under them, Colorno knew a glorious era, having become that family's permanent residence, thanks to its double attraction of fishing and hunting. With the Bourbons the castle received its definitive look; the façade was capped by four square towers connected by an elegant balustrade. French gardeners transformed the park into a baroque feast. "The Versailles of the Duke of Parma," it was called, for it now had groves of oranges and pomegranates, greenhouses of hydrangeas, magnolias, lilacs, and also fountains, statues, miniature waterfalls, ingenious waterworks, and little Arcadian temples.

The interior of the castle was no less magnificent. The preciousness and the luxury of its refined eighteenth-century decorations, and a theater as beautiful as that of the Petit Trianon, made of Colorno one of the richest, most harmonious, and comfortable palaces of the century.

After a succession of many male owners, the memory of *la Sanseverina,* as Barbara was called, was already very distant when in the house that had been hers arrived another woman, Marie Louise of Austria, the second wife of Napoleon. When, after Napoleon's exile to Elba, Marie Louise became Duchess of Parma, Piacenza, and Guastalla, she brought to Colorno a homey atmosphere, the soft, mannered Biedermeier style much more becoming to her than the severe, neoclassical ambience in which she had lived her difficult imperial interlude. Under her direction the gardens also changed; they became less geometric, more "mystical," with weeping willows and swan lakes. Marie Louise loved this place; it fascinated her; and when she traveled incognito she chose for herself the title of Countess of Colorno.

In *The Charterhouse of Parma*, Stendhal refers to Colorno only in passing, but he more than once admitted to have been inspired by a chronicler of the Bourbon court of Parma during the time it resided at Colorno. Thus, Colorno, given the dignity of a memorable literary landscape, may be considered the ideal center of Stendhal's novel. Yet a very sad fate befell Colorno. This palace, which should have been respected as a shrine, today shelters the most squalid, most desolate of mental hospitals. Of the garden almost nothing is left, save a wild mass of trees, very green and leafy, as trees are in humid regions. In the little piazza in front of the building, on market days farmers discuss crops and cattle. Not far from there, between steep embankments, flows the Lorno; from the little bridge that crosses it are visible rows of poplars mapping out roads and pathways.

To see Colorno now, with cottages breaking up the flat monotony of the countryside, it is difficult to imagine it at the time when there was nothing but the Lorno flowing into the Po (for that reason later called Capo Lorno, hence Colorno), a sandy, deserted region, too susceptible of flooding by the Po to be inhabited.

In the Middle Ages, reticent, fearful shepherds had arrived first. Then, perhaps, the religious feeling of some Lombards who followed them inspired the building of a church on that desolate spot. A village was founded around the church, one of the many obscure villages threatened by the river which, at that time surrounded by woods and marshy tracts, did not even have a definite bed. Slowly, in the following centuries, a transformation occurred. Pastures replaced the shrubs and marshes, cultivated fields invaded the pastures. With its small houses clustered around the church, Colorno found itself at the center of a fertile region, although its people still preserved their ancient, stubborn distrust for the river, which still, once in a while, overflowed and carried away houses and animals and inundated the fields.

The first lords of Colorno were the Bishops of Parma, who became rich landowners under the Franks and the Lombards. Some of the bishops were good and honest, but most of them exploited their ecclesiastical privileges. Colorno eventually was enlarged and fortified, its walls attesting to the prominence it had attained in the valley. In the fourteenth century the town became involved in the feud between Guelphs and Ghibellines and was besieged and ravaged, then rebuilt and refortified. Yet the vicissitudes of war could not destroy the richness of the soil, constantly nourished by its friend-enemy, the Po. Indeed, in the first half of the fifteenth century, Colorno had reached such agricultural importance that the *condottiere* Francesco Sforza, who had become its owner, only reluctantly decided to concede it to his nephew Roberto di Sanseverino. Roberto had helped Francesco to take the duchy of Milan from the Visconti family and had fought beside him to establish one of the most powerful seigniories in Italy. That kind of devotion in those not-very-loyal times deserved a reward.

Roberto di Sanseverino, Count of Caiazzo, Barbara's great-grandfather, had come from southern Italy. His ancestors had been lords of San Severino, a small estate near Naples whose name they had adopted as their family name. Roberto's military talents later earned him other estates in Lombardy, but Colorno was his favorite. Accustomed to the sunny but poor-soiled south, this place near the river appeared to him immensely fertile and rich, if perhaps a little gloomy. His descendants also loved it, and in the time of his grandson, Gianfrancesco, Colorno had become desirable even to the Duke of Parma.

When Ottavio had just succeeded Pier Luigi and had had to face a new plot against his family, Gianfrancesco di Sanseverino was one of the conspirators. But Ottavio did not believe in violent revenge. Instead of having Sanseverino killed, as it would have been customary in his father's time, he sent for him with great courtesy. Unsuspecting, "he came to Parma and went to see the duke," relates a contemporary diary, "and the duke, pretending to take a walk with him, entered the fortress and told him: 'Your Lordship will stay here,' upon which the count was kept there with four servants. Later, the duke ordered the confiscation of Colorno." This happened in January, 1551. In the following months everything was set right again; Philip II, the successor of Charles V, returned Piacenza to Ottavio and induced him—how, it is not known—to pardon Gianfrancesco and to give him back his property. In a gentlemanly fashion, Ottavio forgot the old grudges, and Gianfrancesco, touched by such generosity, did so much to earn the duke's trust that in time he became his sincere friend and was frequently entrusted with important state missions. In 1564 Ottavio sealed the friendship with a decree allowing Gianfrancesco, in spite of a municipal law that forbade it, to bequeath Colorno to his two daughters, making them two of the most eligible girls in the duchy.

Barbara di Sanseverino was born in Milan. Her birth date, although impossible to establish solely from the parish registers, can be fixed as 1551, for it is recorded that "she was about twenty-seven or twenty-eight" at the time of a trial she was involved in during 1579. She was fifteen when her father decided to marry her off to Giberto Sanvitale.

Along with the Pallavicino family, the Sanvitale was the most prominent clan in the duchy. It had two branches: Fontanellato and Sala. Giberto was Count of Sala. There are no portraits of him that we know of, but we do know that he was a melancholic, aristocratically distant person, afraid of life and convinced he was destined to lifetime unhappiness. While still very young, impelled by a strong religious sense and the need for an ascetic life, he had taken up an ecclesiastical career. When the future Pope Paul III, Alessandro Farnese, was still Bishop of Parma, Giberto was appointed his private secretary. Paul loved him and certainly would have taken him to Rome, if in 1553 Giberto, whose brothers had died without children, had not been compelled to marry in order to save his illustrious family from extinction. He shed his vestments, searched for a wife, and accepted the one he found as an act of penitence. That Livia da Barbiano was a beautiful woman was not enough to sweeten for him the bitter pill of marriage. To conjugal life Giberto brought an open nostalgia for ecclesiastical habits, especially meditation and long prayers, and also for abstinence —in disconcerting contrast to other Renaissance prelates renowned for their incontinence. He lived frugally, in a sort of genteel poverty, spending the Sanvitale fortune only to build new chapels and to restore old ones, consecrating them all to his favorite saints, the martyrs Lorenzo and Stefano. Parmigianino worked for him for years, and Enea Vico, engraver and famous humanist, professed a great friendship for him. In fact, Giberto associated only with scholars and had a great liking for nuns and monks. His very religiosity smacked of the cloister: he loved to mull over Church dogmas and went into ecstasy listening to arcane ecclesiastical texts recited in a musical voice.

It is not known how Livia da Barbiano reacted to her husband's habits. Most probably she accepted Giberto as he was, reasoning that a husband obsessed by religion was preferable to one obsessed by women. In any case, after eight years, Livia died leaving one daughter, Eleonora. For Giberto it meant the embarrassment of a second marriage and the obligation of producing a male heir.

Torquato Tasso had not yet written of Barbara di Sanseverino that she seemed *non di mortal mano opra terrena* [unlike any mortal], but everybody could see how breathtakingly beautiful she was the day Giberto Sanvitale emerged with her from the church of Colorno in September of 1564. The gentle colors of autumn illuminated the countryside, and important guests had come—even Duke Ottavio, eager to emphasize his friendship with the Sanseverinos. The bride was radiant, for she took to marriage like a ship to the sea. She expected novelty, even notoriety—which is why she did not mind her husband being so much older, a former priest and a widower, the personification of the anti-Prince Charming.

Giberto, on the contrary, was anxious about the future. With contained apprehension, he scrutinized his bride, whom he still found it difficult to classify. First of all she seemed so young, not so much because she was fifteen but because of the difference in their ages. Certainly there are elderly husbands who treat young wives in a fatherly way, but Giberto had not enough tenderness in him to put aside his suspicion of her. Besides, "the little Sanseverina" was anything but little; tall, well built, she did not lend herself to pet names. Too young, too attractive, with that habit of lifting her face as if it were a trophy, Barbara had nothing of the placid charm of Livia, to whom Giberto had somehow grown accustomed. Too young, too attractive, and above all too proud to submit to conjugal discipline, Barbara had what three centuries later would be called sex appeal—more than enough of it to confound a man like Giberto who, after ten years of marriage, was still ill at ease with women. He also found her complicated, prone to irony, and too witty for a man with no sense of humor like himself. He sensed that sooner or later the determination, the stubborn desire for power he saw in her eyes, would be turned against him.

Gianfrancesco Sanvitale had given his daughters the best education available to girls of noble birth. Barbara, even more than her sister, was her tutors' delight. This somehow justified her father's pedagogical snobbery in having her rooms frescoed with scenes from the lives of famous Roman matrons. Barbara was precocious; she loved books, spoke Latin flawlessly, quoted from the classics, and mythological figures were her old friends. People said she was devout, too, and that would have pleased Giberto, if he had not realized how superficial her devotion was.

They settled down in Parma, at the Sanvitale palace. With unerring theatrical instinct, Barbara immediately found a way to make use of a religious ceremony for her sensational social debut. And she chose well, for a church was, at that time, a stage before which gathered, not always for devotional reasons, the entire population. During Lent, 1565, a Dominican monk from Siena, Brother Sisto, preached in the cathedral and "harvested a large crop of souls." On April 20 he invited fourteen converted prostitutes into the church and asked the congregation for funds to allow the women to live in chaste retirement. From the back of the church marched la Sanseverina, followed by the courtesans with eyes lowered. Barbara, watched and admired, walked among the congregation with a silver tray upon which coins, rings, gold chains, and earrings quickly piled up. It was her first social success. She renewed it on April 29, as an anonymous chronicler informs us, when, at the head of a group of ladies, she accompanied to the convent of San Tiburzio the famous courtesan Veronica di Casalmaggiore, who had decided to become a nun.

Reports concerning la Sanseverina and her husband end with the report of that sensational conversion. We shall never know when and how their life together began to deteriorate; there is no information about what kind of disharmony froze them into the insurmountable silence that destroys any hope for understanding and accepting one another. Most probably the main reason for it was that la Sanseverina no longer liked the idea of marriage, for basically she was too lazy and too egocentric to accept that kind of responsibility. At twenty-seven she decided to obtain a divorce.

Divorce, a word then abhorred by upright people, occurred only in rare and very serious cases. Only some prince, or duke, forced by considerations of state or dynasty, sometimes divorced, and even then scandal could not be avoided. But the young Countess of Sala—quite unlike Giberto who, like all extremely well-bred people, disliked public attention—loved to provoke scandals, to be the center of gossip.

In an age when a man of forty was considered to have reached his peak, Giberto was an old man. Gray-haired, melancholic, he lived in seclusion in the castle of Sala, where he tried to calm his religious disquiet by a highly moral life and austere religious practices. Needless to say, la Sanseverina was bored, and she was away as often as she could be, leaving Giberto to his books and to the company of his fellow theologians. In 1567, Girolamo, the much-longed-for heir, was born. He was followed, in 1572, by Barberina, a petulant, unbearable *enfant prodige*. La Sanseverina, however, was not a woman to be tied down by children. She remained in the castle of Sala until 1577, but when the old Sanseverinos died and she became Marchioness of Colorno, she decided to settle down there on the outskirts of Parma. Her behavior soon provoked indiscreet queries: was it true that her lovers never entered her bed twice? That the old duke, Ottavio, was in love with her, and Alessandro no less than his father? Or was it true that she played with her admirers a teasing, perverse game without ever satisfying them?

Concerned for his reputation, Giberto protested to her—but not too energetically. He was not even taken by surprise the day his wife first uttered the dread word "divorce" and demanded the restitution of her dowry. Personally, he had nothing for which to reproach himself. The marriage had been consummated, his virility had been proven by the birth of the two children, and the whole of Parma knew him to be an honest and reasonable husband incapable of what one day would be called mental cruelty. A few weeks after abandoning Giberto, Barbara informed him that, because of a blood relationship between them, they would have to dissolve their marriage, an illicit union, she said, in which they had already lived too long.

Barbara had a relative, an ancient nun in the convent of Sant'Agostino, who was a stubborn little creature with a talent for family gossip. It was she who told Barbara that Giberto's first wife had among her ancestors a Caterina Visconti, whose sister was Barbara's great-great-grandmother. Having unearthed this entangled genealogy, Barbara immediately declared that her marriage was incestuous. Bewildered and terrified by the already spreading gossip, Giberto would have done anything to bring Barbara back home. He felt he had the patience and the energy to rebuild his marriage. Cardinal Gambara and Marquis Giulio Pallavicino offered themselves as mediators in the affair, but, in the face of Barbara's obstinacy, they had to retreat.

The legal process, then as now, seemed to take forever; finally, since it fell within the competence of canon law, it came to the attention of Pope Gregory XIII. His Holiness ordered the Bishop of Parma to investigate and report to him. Once translated into juridical terms and into the heavy Latin of the court, this marriage became a case suitable for the pedantic judges of the Church's highest marriage court, the Sacra Rota. On December 3, 1584, the Bishop of Parma ordered the couple to give, within three days, the reasons for their illegal separation. Giberto answered that he was willing to forget everything and take back his wife; but la Sanseverina protested that she was too devout a Catholic to continue a sinful relationship. Gregory XIII then declared the case for annulment to be open and authorized the Bishop of Parma to isolate Barbara in a convent until the settlement of the dispute.

The idea of the cloister did not displease Barbara; it was customary among the gentlewomen of the time periodically to "purify" themselves with the prayers, meditation, and spiritual atmosphere of a convent—making certain, of course, that it was a comfortable, rich convent and one that allowed them to receive visits and enjoy a restful vacation. The only thing la Sanseverina feared was that the suit might last too long, forcing her to stay in the convent more than was convenient. Giberto himself, however, resolved her difficulty. He died, tired, ill, and pious, on December 31, 1585.

✳

A new life began at Colorno. La Sanseverina was one of those people, perhaps enviable, who set out daily to conquer happiness and for whom life was a gift to be enjoyed in the best possible way. She had a superficial but quite impressive culture, and there was no discussion about literature, art, philosophy, heraldry, or rhetoric which caught her completely unprepared. A brilliant conversationalist, her reasoning suggested a superior intelligence in which sensations, feelings, and memories were blended harmoniously—not stifled by culture but rather made more personable and agreeable because of it. At the same time, she was a master of that society argot which is so useful in getting and maintaining worldly success. Like most ladies of her time, Barbara cultivated poetry as a hobby, though she doubtless preferred to inspire a poem than read one. She liked no one better than a poet who wished to dedicate his verse to her; and indeed there was no lack of obsequious poets about, for servility was included among the artist's requisites. Inevitably, she became involved in the world of the academies, the mania of the century, a kind of mild obsession of Italian intellectuals; there was no city which did not claim at least two academies.

As a reaction to that politically disastrous period, intellectuals (from the genius to the hack writer) felt the need to collaborate in order to establish at least an intellectual unity amidst the chaos of Italy, and the various academies answered that need. The tasks of these academies were diverse; some dedicated themselves to the improvement of the language; some specialized in philosophy; others published ancient manuscripts, compiled dictionaries, and amended texts. Some worked seriously; others held fruitless debates on grammar and aesthetics. Everyone was eager to make some contribution, large or small, to Italian culture.

The academies usually had sarcastically laudatory or disparaging names. Ferrara was the seat of the *Oziosi* [the Lazy Ones], the *Sonnacchiosi* [the Sleepy Ones], and the *Storditi* [the Absent-minded Ones]. In Tuscany, twenty-three academies out of forty-two flourished in Siena, among them the *Intronati* [the Stunned Ones]. Pauda exhibited the *Infiammati* [the Inflamed Ones], Venice the *Incurabili* [the Incurables] and the *Industriosi* [the Industrious Ones]. Rome had one too: *Notti Vaticane* [Vatican Nights], so-called because of the time and place of the meetings. Charles Borromeo, the future saint, who was its sponsor, had chosen for himself the name of Chaos. Parma, envious of the success of the *Ortolani* [the Gardeners] of Piacenza, promptly founded the *Innominati* [the Unnamed Ones]. The Gardeners, "so pleasant and mischievous at the same time," had Priapus's sickle as their emblem. It is a very active academy, wrote Doni; "they do many beautiful things, and every academician produces so many love poems, comedies, dialogues about the spiritual love of nuns, and various compositions in Latin and in vernacular, that Pegasus could not carry them all had he a mule's pack." In turn, their rivals of Parma, the *Innominati,* succeeded in securing the works of Duke Ottavio and his son Ranuccio, the latter with the name of Immutabile. As for the *Amorevoli* [the Loving Ones], sponsored by Barbara, their ambitions are not known, but certainly they were more entertaining than didactic, with absolute priority in matters of love.

When there were no academicians and friends to entertain, la Sanseverina recruited them outside of Colorno, in the nearby princely courts. In her literary symposia the place of honor was always reserved for Torquato Tasso. She loved his grand, solemn, slightly melancholic poems; they made her breathe an atmosphere of voluptuousness and passion, of religious ecstasy and chivalric heroism. Tasso was a man whom women adored. This charming stutterer, who stopped stuttering when he recited poetry, gratified their maternal instincts. There was no woman who had not, for a moment, felt she loved him; all wished at least to protect him, so myopic and in need of affection was he, and possessed by the daemon of poetry.

Not only Tasso but all the most intelligent, brilliant men in Italy were Barbara's friends. The young Ferrante Gonzaga, lord of Guastalla, for example, learned in theology, philosophy, mathematics, and the author of a pastoral tale unknown today but then the marvel of his contemporaries, found in her admiration the best incentive for persevering in his humanistic efforts. Because of him, his town, Guastalla, was nicknamed the "Muses' Vessel." Bernardino Baldi, mathematician, poet, and polyglot, was another admirer. He despised everything that was not intellectual and even studied while he ate, and got up in the middle of the night for more reading. Only Barbara's bubbling laughter was able to smooth his brow.

From a fashion initiated by Tasso, poets and scholars had taken up the practice of submitting their still-unpublished work to other scholars in order to obtain criticism and suggestions, a fashion born of the desire for both perfection and admiration. La Sanseverina, though not a scholar, had a reputation for intelligence, and she was often invited to express her critical opinion. Experts attributed to her an unusual intuition, a great aesthetic sensibility. She was capable of destroying solid literary reputations with one or two cruel remarks, but she could also make the fortune of unknown authors, for people who disagreed with her feared to be thought fools—or worse, old-fashioned. Curzio Gonzaga, one of the many lords of Mantua's ruling family, had given her his *Fidamante* to read, and immediately the rumor spread that it was even better than the *Orlando Furioso*. She made a better guess in 1582, during a sojourn in Guastalla, when she foretold the success of *Il Pastor Fido,* which the author, Battista Guarini, read to his friends at a symposium. Guarini was so grateful to her that the following year, putting aside for once his bad temper, his poor health, and his family troubles, he went as far as Colorno to join the *Amorevoli,* despite the presence there of Angelo Ingegneri, one of the very few Italian intellectuals of the time indifferent to the virtues of *Il Pastor Fido.* Angelo Ingegneri, incidentally, was to be punished for his indifference; three years later we find him completely forgotten in Guastalla manufacturing soap. Yet, like all the other poets, he kept a happy memory of la Sanseverina.

Great, mediocre, or unknown poets were always welcome at Barbara's palace. Muzio Manfredi, whose *Semiramide* was then praised as the greatest of all Italian dramas, was one; Porrino, a Petrarchist, "one of the few who don't make one yawn too much"—according to a reader's note in a sixteenth-century edition—was another, as was Giacomo Marmitta, also a Petrarchist, whose specialty was the study of the historic-philo-sophic-astronomic meaning of the horns on cuckolds' heads. There was Federico Asinari, no one of special importance except that he had celebrated la Sanseverina as "the nymph of Baganza," which was sufficient to have made him someone. Occasionally, Bishop Maffeo Veniero, the most gifted in his family of poets, turned up at Colorno. His father, Lorenzo, owed his fame to two bawdy sonnets, and his cousin Luigi had exchanged verses with Veronica Franco, the famous Venetian courtesan. But Maffeo was considered the best vernacular poet of his time. He was a worldly and restless man, compensating through literature and travel for the bitterness of an enforced ecclesiastical life. Sometimes, led by him, Colorno's court crossed the Po to visit Vespasiano Gonzaga, Duke of Sabbioneta, a fanatic on mythology and Augustan poetry, and a ruler absorbed in the humanistic dream of making of his small duchy a model state.

*

But Barbara's closest friend of all was young Vincenzo Gonzaga, the handsomest member of the Mantuan dynasty. His good looks would not have been exceptional had not the Gonzagas been, for generations, all very ugly and often also hunchbacked. Their hereditary deformity clung to them like a curse, and the family's history is the story of girls rejected by their fiancés because of a curved back, of boys forced to enter the ecclesiastical career as the only one in which people would not stare at their shoulders, of parents anguished at seeing their children slowly grow deformed. Vincenzo, on the contrary, was straight and fair, with blue eyes and a winning smile. He was an extrovert, and also a bit debauched—which drove his mother, Leonora of Austria, a stiff Teutonic matron shrouded in virtue, to despair. Both his physique and his character seemed sufficient to make of him a popular ruler, and the people of Mantua already loved him. His pride, a certain gusto he had for scandal and the unusual, and his rather visionary and passionate nature, seemed to promise an era of joy after his parents' austere reign. His generosity, compared to his father's stinginess, automatically became a virtue; and people were amused by the idea that a couple so rigorous as to practice, after the birth of the heir, sexual abstinence, should have conceived a son who liked women very much indeed and who was in turn most enthusiastically regarded by them. One could have foretold Vincenzo's future: Lenten sermons neglected for spicy love stories, scandals, and duels; the inauguration of new churches replaced by the production of pastoral plays; the more intimate *concertini* preferred to organ music; the company of poets and actresses substituted for the oratory of gloomy preachers; Leonora's stuffy ladies in waiting edged out by pretty young girls. No one yet asked if Vincenzo would be a good ruler; it was enough to know that he had taste both plebeian and refined, simple and aristocratic —the most important thing, for the moment.

Vincenzo's father, Guglielmo, an unhappy hunchback, introspective, rational, was nearing the end of a difficult life. His regime had been strict, scrupulous, and positive; under him, Mantua had known peace and prosperity, which helped the citizens to tolerate the strictness of his administration, the ornate gloom of the court, and above all the excesses of an Inquisition which constantly found heretics where none existed. Father and son, naturally, did not understand each other. Guglielmo forgave Vincenzo nothing, not his irrepressible need to enjoy life, his whims, his imagination, his slightly cruel pranks nor, above all, his almost offensively perfect health. To see "that complexion of his, that blond hair," that agile and well-proportioned youth, was to be reminded, painfully, of his own ugliness, of his own squat, ailing body, and of a Silenus-like face.

Obsessed by his father's authority, full of confused, grandiose ideas, Vincenzo inevitably came to admire Barbara di Sanseverino and to cherish her alliance. He was fascinated by her insolent, feminine independence, recognizing in her the regality and the authority of a true mistress of life. He felt he could be himself with her and share with her the conviction that life deserved to be savored to the last.

Leonora of Austria of course was informed about this friendship, and she disapproved. She regarded her son with maternal obtuseness, and when he left Mantua she wrote him pathetic little notes: "I beg you not to indulge in excesses. Don't strain yourself, and don't eat too much, and behave yourself; speak properly, not as they do in Ferrara, because it is unworthy of a prince. So that people may speak only well of you for the sake of your honor and my joy. Dear son, I beg you, keep in mind these few words of your mother who loves you."

Colorno was, together with Ferrara, Vincenzo's favorite spot. The atmosphere in his friend's palace was rich and cordial; it accepted the world in its most optimistic guise. The courtiers were men of easy conscience, pleasantly cynical, with the gaiety of uninhibited, sensual people—in spite of "the French disease," which was literally destroying many of them.

The ladies, too, were conscious and voluptuous sinners. Among them was the first link in a chain of women to which Vincenzo remained, to the end of his days, a voluntary prisoner. Her name was Hippolita Torricella. The poet Muzio Manfredi described her, rather generically, as having "a noble heart, fiery eyes and other great charms." In fact, we would know nothing of her today had Vincenzo's secretary not kept, with a sort of mischievous zeal, copies of the prince's love letters. These letters, sometimes quite passionate and sincere, sometimes adopting the elaborate love rhetoric of the time, outline a story worthy of the sensuality and the intrigues of a Renaissance comedy. Hippolita was not a woman easily conquered: she had a husband, perhaps also children, in Reggio Emilia, and a household from which she could seldom escape. But whenever possible, her carriage hastened to Colorno where, with the complicity of la Sanseverina, she enjoyed a love holiday with Vincenzo. This affair, however, did not prevent Vincenzo from participating in the lengthy negotiations preceding his marriage to Margherita Farnese, the granddaughter of the Duke of Parma.

Unlike Hippolita, Vincenzo was not disturbed by the idea of the imminent marriage. Convinced of its importance for the family succession, he nevertheless believed in the traditional conception of men's rights, keeping from the beginning of his engagement to Margherita a clear distinction between love and marriage, so that also later the presence of a wife would never exclude that of one, or even of several, mistresses.

In the imminence of the wedding, the correspondence between Reggio Emilia, Mantua, and Colorno intensified. To the letters, presents were added: gifts for the beautiful mistress, for la Sanseverina, for her discreet ladies in waiting, and also for the dwarf Isabellina, "a lovely little monster" who was a tireless messenger between the two lovers. But then, passion died, and the affair ended in an indifferent separation. Vincenzo, who loved women with an almost lyrical exultation, was soon attracted elsewhere. Hippolita disappeared, reabsorbed by her family. Nobody knows whether she, too, had forgotten, or whether she carried the scars all her life.

Life at Colorno continued with its usual jolly immorality. The marchioness was forever organizing something; it was said that she labored more at her leisure than any workman at his work—hunting parties, carriage excursions to the Po, tarot tournaments, blindman's bluff, garden parties, dances, and parlor games.

With a typical Renaissance taste for conversation and debate, her guests discussed important matters, such as honor, warfare, nobility, and literature; but more often they talked about love, an important problem for the lords and ladies of the time. These intellectual tournaments first became fashionable in 1570, when Torquato Tasso, in honor of Eleonora d'Este's wedding, had held in Ferrara a three-day-long public seminar about fifty love cases. The participants discussed, for example, "whether love is born by choice of destiny," and "whether it is better to love or be loved." The theme of love was analyzed in all its stages: the first awareness of feelings and sensations, the excitement of the affair, the celebration of anniversaries. They discussed the lover's psychology and the various types of lovers in keeping with the traditional classification of love as spiritual, chaste or lustful, which borrowed its philosophical status from the Platonic theories in the *Phaedrus* and the *Symposium*. Spiritual and chaste love, usually classified together under the name of platonic love, was allowed to married women, for husbands ought not to be jealous of platonic lovers, nor they of husbands. "The love a woman has for her husband," said Tasso, "does not bother us, for it is very possible for a woman to love both her husband and her lover. This happens because they represent two different kinds of love. A woman loves her husband as a mate who produces children, as a companion with whom to share the preoccupations of a household and to whom she is indissolubly bound by holy laws. For the lover she feels something entirely different." It would have been useless to point out that often one lapses from "platonic" into "lustful" love. The Colorno gathering was even more engaged in making love than in talking about it.

Barbara, despite her intelligence, was incurably superstitious. She made use of a crystal ball. She wore earrings in the form of horseshoes and on her neck glittered a tiny harquebus of precious stones. On moonless nights she observed the stars— astrology as well as literature was her hobby—and she remained for hours in the dark with her friends; but then, as she was basically realistic and apt to explain everything in terms of physics rather than of metaphysics (the meaning of which she was not too certain in any case), she left the skies and returned to the earth and to the good things that it offered: the white lies, the sparkling conversations, and the parlor games.

La Sanseverina knew dozens of such games, and she invented new ones constantly. For the more simple ones, all that was needed was a quick wit, but for others a certain literary sophistication, culture, and good memory were necessary. For instance, in the game called The Muses' Archive, the participants were required to enrich this imaginary archive with some verses worthy, in their opinion, to be preserved. And in the game of The Epitaphs, the players pretended to consecrate the ladies to a temple of immortality. It was the gentleman's task to declare, in verse, which virtue each lady should be immortalized for. In the one called Lovers' Hell, the players pretended to be lovers' souls which the games master, impersonating Charon, brought to Minos, to whom they confess the particular love sin that has condemned them to hell.

If the company felt like having fun, they played Lunatic Asylum, where mad lovers were "comfortably detained." To enter this asylum, each player had to explain to the "director," in the funniest way possible, the reasons why he went mad. Or else, pretending to select the courtiers to serve an imaginary prince or princess, they assigned inverted roles: to a tall courtier they gave the part of the dwarf, and to the sad man, provided there was one, that of the jester. When they tired of "talk" games, they proceeded to play "mute" ones—pulling faces at each other, for instance. Or, once more back to words, they played the game of The Gardeners, discussing only flowers and using them as allegories for feelings, one of the many forms of that symbolic language so popular in that time.

There were so many games, both intellectual and simpleminded, spicy and bland, that the party could go on all night. But inevitably la Sanseverina would burst into one of her hearty laughs and declare that they all needed a *desinarino* [a little dinner] which, in spite of the diminutive, was almost always a gastronomic triumph: "Great salads, made of animal figures carved from citrons; castles of turnips; walls of lemons; standing-eagle pies; white peacocks with spread tails." It was the apotheosis of spices, of sugar: roasts, game, fish, soups were sweetened, often perfumed water was added—as well as gold dust, which was supposed to strengthen the heart. Mythological figures, castles, pillars—all made of sugar—were brought to the table. "Three statues: Meleager's boar, one of the three Magi riding a camel, and an elephant carrying a turret full of armed men," reads a famous menu in a gastronomic treatise of the time. (The author, Cristoforo Messisbugo, became so popular that after his death he was accorded the high honor of burial at the right side of the altar in the church of Sant'Antonio in Ferrara.)

La Sanseverina imported a game very fashionable in Ferrara: to serve a dinner of only one dish, prepared in many different ways. The idea originated with Gherardo Bevilacqua, a courtier of Alfonso d'Este, who had succeeded in cooking eggs in fifty-six different ways. Moreover, he had done the same with fish, so that, on Fridays, without an ounce of meat being eaten, pious gluttons could feast more sumptuously than on any other day of the week.

After the *desinarino,* everyone danced. Even the most bloated stomach could not deter anyone. Corso, a theoretician of the art of dancing, wrote: "Attractive women are made to have fun, and fun is made for them. For the ugly ones, there is cooking and reciting the rosary." The musical repertory was quite rich: *mattinate, villanelle, strambotti, disperate, siciliane, napolitane, chiaranzane,* all requiring only "languid eyes, smiling mouths, lively hips, innocent hands, ambitious feet." In spite of these pretentious requisites, however, dancing at Colorno meant little more than a rhythmical back and forth walk with some twirls. Choreography was apparently bolder in country dances, for the ladies wore long underwear so as "not to reveal their shame while whirling." During the pre-Lenten carnival season, new dances were invented whose elaborate costumes required months of preparation. Their fashions reflected all the ferment and the magnificence of the late Renaissance, and the ladies' dresses had all kinds of enormous and grotesque trimmings, the greatest eccentricities being accepted as being the most fashionable styles. And, of course, la Sanseverina, engaged in a constant search for the original, the sophisticated, invented the most exquisite toilettes of all. She was not, and certainly never wished to appear to be, a simple woman, least of all in her dress.

For her wardrobe the marchioness went to Venice, where fashions and jewels were works of art, and where tailors and weavers had famous artists in their service. Cesare Vecellio, Titian's cousin and disciple, for example, designed laces; and Valerio Zuccato—who was supposed to be in the San Marco basilica working on his mosaic of the Apocalypse—lingered in the shop among bonnets and millinery. La Sanseverina was a good customer of one Bartolomeo, who also supplied the seraglio of the Turkish sultan. It is difficult to know if she enjoyed more the trip to Venice, with the anticipation of Bartolomeo's treasures, or the return in the carriage heavy with baskets overflowing with new laces, ruffs, parasols, clasps, furs, embroidered underwear, satin-edged stockings, and frilled and perfumed skirts. (Everything was perfumed, even shoes and rosaries—and of the latter there were some with beads made of a fragrant paste "in the service of eroticism, not of devotion.")
Fashion, too, was a game in the sixteenth century, an exquisitely intellectual game, and clothes reflected more than one's good taste; they had a symbolic value. Through their dresses women presented themselves as riddles, as allegories. A skirt of white brocade implied chastity; black slippers signified simplicity; purple stockings, perseverance; a gold damask purse, generosity. Sleeves, too, had several meanings, and they were perhaps the most important part of a woman's dress. They could be fastened, like huge wings, at the shoulders, with buttons, so that each dress could be worn with many different sleeves. (This is undoubtedly the origin of the popular Italian expression "It is

another pair of sleeves," signifying a shift from one subject to another.)

Trousers were, of course, a preoccupation of the male. Fashion required incredibly padded codpieces, which made one think unequivocably, as Montesquieu observed, "of the shape of the part of the body good manners forbids us to mention." At first, the tendency was to adorn the codpiece with bows and ribbons; but in time this intentionally indecent vogue died out, and trousers ended up with innocent pockets containing oranges and candied fruits to offer to the ladies.

To keep up with the fashion, the amiable ladies and gentlemen of Colorno traveled even farther than Venice. They went as far afield as the famous Besançon fair, where merchants, bankers, and traders converged from all countries. La Sanseverina periodically ventured into that noisy mercantile world. On her way home she might stop in Turin, at the court of Charles Emmanuel of Savoy, whose interest in beautiful women almost equaled his passion for political involvement and for warfare. She most probably stopped also in Milan, at that time already a prosperous and enterprising city, and a hospitable and active one. Of her trips to Rome, only one is mentioned in the annals, and that on the occasion of the election of Pope Gregory XIV. Every conclave attracted to Rome the entire Italian aristocracy and many prominent foreigners, for the election of a pope presented a rare opportunity for political intrigue. There, la Sanseverina enchanted cardinals, ambassadors, humanists, and aristocrats with the inimitable flair with which she had hypnotized the simple people of Parma. But the town she returned to most often, the town which offered the best stage for her improvised performances, was Ferrara— sparkling, lazy Ferrara of the turn of the sixteenth century, in decline from its age-old independence. In Ferrara, society was mad for la Sanseverina and her name was the subject of all gossip. It was noised about that Alfonso II, Duke of Este, was in love with her and that they met secretly, heedless of the complications that might arise between such personages who meet precisely to enjoy such complications. But perhaps it was only gossip. In Ferrara, la Sanseverina, a true daughter of her time, was free to act out her singular role, which, once transposed to the provincial and clerical Farnese world, became fatal to her.

Between Parma and Colorno there was a current of intense hostility. On la Sanseverina Ranuccio concentrated his dangerous animosities, and for years the duke had tried to complicate her life by interfering with her private interests, imposing fines, and arousing her serfs against her. *I miei poverazzi* [my poor devils], she called the latter, with detached pity. But she never understood, nor loved, nor did anything to help the "poor devils," and they, for their part, had little affection for her. With the quick intuition that simple people have for survival, they recognized how seriously the duke could injure their mistress and they mustered up sufficient courage to tell him how badly they were treated, how unjust were their mistress's taxes and her demands for "gifts" during holidays, how she forced them—illegally—to contribute toward the upkeep of the manor, to work the fields like animals, and to do a hundred other things they were not legally required to do.

La Sanseverina reacted irritably to these harassments; difficulties always aroused her belligerence. She sent long letters to the duke: "I appeal to you, my lord, and I kneel to implore you to read patiently these lines I am writing impelled by the pain I feel in my heart, for I cannot remain silent under such abuse." So she wrote to Ranuccio the day he took away from her the command of the Colorno garrison. An arrogant captain had taken over the fort and now trampled about in the village, deaf to the marchioness's ravings. "I cannot see why a stranger should be allowed to give orders on my land, land granted to me by their Serene Highnesses your ancestors, without it having been first shown that you have legally annulled my privileges. Have pity on me! I shall fall at your feet crying so much that finally Your Highness's soul will be moved to say: 'Enjoy, my lady, your land, as your ancestors did and you yourself have done for twenty years.'" In reading these words Ranuccio smiled his ambiguous smile; for all he cared, the marchioness could melt into tears; he would never trust her. A woman capable of choosing a scorpion on her personal emblem could not be sincere.

Rarely have two persons been less sympathetic to one another than Ranuccio and the marchioness. He tolerated only quiet, submissive, insignificant women, and the mistress of Colorno was none of these. Even after the age of fifty her beauty was still intact; she had that soft and voluptuous something that beautiful women have when they are happy to be alive. Ranuccio, who had always felt excluded from life's feasts, had fits of envy and anger at the vitality, the exciting aura of dissipation that surrounded the apparently eternal Sanseverina. The devotion she had inspired in his father and grandfather was the only thing he despised in the life of the two men he tried to imitate in every other way.

The antipathy was mutual. Barbara did not even dream of capturing his admiration, let alone his love. A woman who had charmed two generations of Farneses and attracted the attention of the most notable Italian rulers could afford to be indifferent to such a sinister man. But the truth is that the marchioness had no sense of history, and though convinced of the contrary, had no understanding of politics. So long as she could exploit, by her femininity, the friendship of powerful men, she managed successfully to handle her interests. But when her relationship with Ranuccio soured, instead of showing any real diplomatic talent she failed completely.

Her quarrel with the duke was complicated further by the lack of solidarity in her family. Devoted to a daring, free life, la Sanseverina had never had either the time or the desire to mother her children. The meaning of sacrifice for her children's well-being, the pride of having their friendship and alliance in life's difficulties, were unknown to her. Her children were strangers, almost enemies, ready to reprove and to judge her. The step-daughter Eleonora who, as her contemporary, expected no motherly love but only a friendly camaraderie, died at twenty-two, in childbirth. Barberina had grown into an ordinary and rather dull woman; unhappily married to a nobleman of Burgundy and soon widowed, she had been remarried to one Ferrante Novati, a man of dubious lineage, and had gone to live at Calisco, near Bergamo. La Sanseverina disapproved. How could a respectable person live in Calisco? Partly through spite, partly through distrust of her son-in-law, she ordered the confiscation of the eight thousand scudi of Barberina's dowry. Offended, Barberina never set foot in Parma again. Girolamo, on the other hand, lived with his mother and was destined to die tragically beside her. The only male heir of the Sanvitales, who in Giberto's dreams was to become "a prodigy of sainthood, a joy to the Church, and a glory to the world," was in reality a mediocre fellow living an irrelevant, uninspired life. He married very young, for social convenience, Benedetta Pio di Sassuolo who, from the little we know, was a wise and docile woman. At sixteen, Girolamo came into his title and patrimony, and immediately gave trouble to his mother, first by refusing the restitution of her dowry and then by withholding his sister's, and finally by threatening publicly to deprive la Sanseverina of Colorno on the grounds that she was a bad administrator. In any case, he was not much better at the job than she, for he entrusted his properties in Sala to dishonest servants and farmers.

It was only to spite Girolamo that la Sanseverina decided to remarry at fifty. It seemed a marvelous idea to her, even if remarriage was an admission of weakness, a proof that a woman —even such a woman as she—needed the protection of a man. But she made a good choice: Count Orazio Simonetta, lord of Torricella, *cavallerizzo* at the court of the Farneses, was an excellent man of very good family. He was sensible, cultivated, and a wise administrator. In Parma he was well liked, and even Ranuccio granted him a measured, silent deference, the highest sign of respect of which he was capable. Count Orazio was precisely what the marchioness needed. "What I need," said she, "is a husband who will be content to live in my house, for I do not wish to leave Colorno." Moreover, he was madly in love with her. Once, before he had met her, Orazio had called Barbara a whore; but as soon as he had met her he was attracted by her stunning beauty and also by a desire to become part of her glamorous milieu. By this time la Sanseverina was almost fifty, but her youth seemed miraculously to have endured; she looked at least ten years younger. "My dear Cardinal," she wrote to her friend, Francesco di Santa Fiora, "I see Your Lordship is very interested to know how it all worked out, and I shall tell you most accurately everything that went on. Imagine! My own son, after having notified me that Colorno did not belong to me any more—an injunction which has been since revoked—threatened Agacio, who had gone to talk to him in the name of His Highness, with a dagger, saying he intended to bring him and all those cuckolds at his mother's service to their knees, and that Colorno belonged to him and he wanted it. . . . When I complained to Count Orazio about my son's impudence and told him: 'Count, I should like to marry,' he answered that, if I found him acceptable, he himself was proposing. And I said: 'Ask His Highness for permission.' And so he did, and I did, too; and everything was settled."

It was, all things considered, a happy marriage and a most useful one. The very presence of a man in the palace of Colorno was enough to dispel the clouds. The hostility of the serfs was allayed. Girolamo gave up making trouble. Ranuccio's animosity dampened, waiting for a better occasion. Life was easy and gay again. La Sanseverina returned to her usual round of pleasures. With her ability to forget her problems, she put out of her mind these first symptoms of Ranuccio's hostility. Banquets, trips, masquerades—and also the meetings with Vincenzo Gonzaga—went on as before, as though nothing had happened.

"The prince seems much changed to me," wrote an agent of the Duke of Urbino, describing the Duke of Mantua. "He has put on weight, he has no beard and almost no color in his face. Altogether, he looks Germanic, like his mother." Grown up, fat but still handsome and incorrigible, Vincenzo was very eager to keep la Sanseverina among his intimate friends. Grateful for the solidarity she offered him during the years of his rebellious youth, he still turned to her for reassurance when he doubted himself and his good star. "She is attractive and fresh as never before," he wrote to a friend after a rendezvous in Maderno, near Lake Garda, in one of the many beautiful Gonzaga villas. To accentuate the erotic flair, Barbara had arrived at the assignation with three of the most attractive, coquettish girls in Parma. The love of beautiful women was the only thing in the world to which Vincenzo, unfaithful by temperament, was and always would be faithful. Women, like paintings, poetry, and architecture, heightened his exceptionally sensuous life. La Sanseverina in any case was not the person to fear competition; in fact she still looked for it as a challenge to her seductiveness, which was always triumphant.

In her intimacy with Vincenzo, however, there was also an element of personal gain. It seemed to her the best possible alliance to offset Ranuccio's increasing enmity. Yet, only her political immaturity could have suggested to her such a naïve expedient, for it was precisely this ostentatious familiarity with the Duke of Mantua that fed Ranuccio's deep hostility toward the lady of Colorno. To imagine them together, the hated former brother-in-law and the loathed marchioness, drove Ranuccio into a fury. Together the sinful pair almost certainly were plotting against the court of Parma. . . . Tormented by such visions, Ranuccio's suspicion grew until it became certainty.

It is difficult to establish exactly when Ranuccio decided to ruin la Sanseverina. He may well have thought of it since he was a boy. Through the years his secret desire had strengthened itself and had finally become a cold determination which later, once he had become duke, fitted in perfectly with his over-all plan to destroy the power of the lords.

To humiliate the great lady and seize Colorno, that lovely rich land, has become a definite program. To perfect it, there was Bartolomeo Riva, a shrewd man from Piacenza who never lost self-control or revealed a secret and whom Ranuccio had chosen as his advisor and treasurer. By temperament inclined to carry out his promises, and blindly devoted to the duke and the state, Riva was the gray eminence of Parma. A master of flattery, he managed to become indispensable to Ranuccio, who shared everything with him from the most guarded state secret to his most intimate ailments, "the weakness of his stomach and his thighs." Riva comforted him like a brother, listened to him like a confessor. No one knew better than he how to justify the duke, cheer him up, approve and encourage his most distorted ideas. When Ranuccio, for instance, had the notion that his infirmities were due to witches, Riva gravely assented and approved of the duke's going to the shrine of Loreto and making a vow to the Virgin Mary that, in exchange for his health, he would wipe out all the sorceresses in the duchy. The consequences of this pilgrimage were disastrous for many women, who were banished or jailed, tortured, or slowly killed by privation. But while all this added to the duke's nightmares and guilt, the treasurer remained free from a troubled conscience and he prepared himself for other, more sensational sacrifices. Indeed, it was while listening to Bartolomeo one day that Ranuccio discovered the means eventually to absorb Colorno into the duchy of Parma. Meanwhile, the only way to impair the legality of the marchioness's feudal title was to annul the two investitures granted her by Duke Ottavio in 1577 in exchange, it was said, for more intimate concessions. Promptly, Riva drew up a list of juridical impediments and technical irregularities in the contract, which would furnish the pretext for invalidating the investitures.

When the marchioness was informed of the duke's claim to Colorno, she was at first taken aback and shouted that Ranuccio was a rascal born only to give trouble to respectable people. Then she reacted the way that well-born people usually do; she turned for help to influential friends. Letters and petitions were sent to the Vatican, to the court of Mantua, to the Milan aristocracy, to the various small principalities scattered throughout the Po Valley, begging all and sundry to put pressure in her favor on the old Duke of Fuentes, the Spanish governor of Lombardy, then the most powerful person in Italy.

The governor, partly to please the marchioness, to whose beauty he was not insensitive, partly because he could not abide the Farneses, hastened to send to Parma the general commissary of the state of Milan with a command to stop harassing the marchioness; otherwise, in view of the protection the king of Spain owed to the lady, he, the Duke of Fuentes, would be obliged to come in her defense. For Ranuccio this curt order was a bitter pill. His Excellency need not worry, he sent word to Milan; the lady will not be troubled. And should one day the irregularities of the investiture come up again, he, Ranuccio Farnese, would personally ask the Duke of Fuentes to arbitrate that embarrassing question.

Once again disaster has been avoided, and at Colorno the atmosphere returned to normal. It was the year 1609, a splendid season from the social point of view. The marchioness plunged into her *dolce vita* as if into a sea of honey. She was almost sixty now, but there was hardly a wrinkle around the eyes, her arms were still fresh and solid, and her slender figure emanated an almost desperate vitality. This obstinate gusto for life made her admirers declare that only she had been spared the shame of physical decay. She never thought of death and, instinctively, with a childish impulse, she shunned anxiety and evaded all gloomy thoughts. Only the sense of being one of the few survivors of a happy generation made her unhappy. Once more time repeated its old trick of making the past seem more beautiful than it really was, more heartbreakingly irretrievable. But la Sanseverina did not surrender. Death had thinned the rows of her friends, but she made new ones, young ones, blue-blooded, rich. Theirs was a pleasant and whimsical world, but irremediably doomed; none of those who loved la Sanseverina as a master of life could know that they were rapidly marching with her toward death.

The most important guest at the palace of Colorno was la Sanseverina's grandson, Gianfrancesco Sanvitale, called *il Mar-*

chesino [the little Marquis] to distinguish him from *il Marchese* [the Marquis], Girolamo, his father. He was nineteen, rather handsome, and sure of himself with that special kind of assurance that comes from being rich. La Sanseverina loved this grandson in whom she recognized all her own unrestrained *joie de vivre*. His insatiable curiosity had induced him, as a Faust *ante litteram,* to sell his soul to the devil, signing the pact with blood—or at least this is what was said in Parma. One of the proofs was that on Good Friday he feasted merrily, and his banquets were everything but meatless. Of this reputation Gianfrancesco was very proud; he liked to see the bishop frown and people cross themselves when he passed by. He was, of course, an expert on women; with his handsome, rascally face, he could not have been otherwise. He threw himself into pleasure with reckless determination, and it is likely that he experimented with homosexuality in order to test the limits of his own debauchery. Some people even maintained that he seduced his mother, Benedetta Pio, but this obviously was an exaggeration. He was married but he behaved as though he were not. His wife, Costanza Sulviati, was a patient girl, the resigned witness of the debauchery of a man who did not care even to keep up appearances. The Marchesino did not love her. He loved, or better, he liked Agnese del Carretto, Marchioness of Grana, who was old enough to be his mother. His real mother could find no peace; it seemed impossible to her that her son should be charmed by a woman even older than herself. She continuously had Masses said, complained to her confessor, and confiscated the lovers' letters.

La Sanseverina, on the contrary, had no objections to this sinful relationship. Since the time of Vincenzo Gonzaga and Hippolita Torricella, she had indulged her feminine inclination to protect love affairs, especially the troublesome ones, and the love affair of her grandson was sufficiently unorthodox to please her and give her, at more than sixty, a twinge of pleasure.

Besides, Agnese del Carretto was one of her best friends. Their intimacy went back many years and hid a love secret whose name was Vincenzo Gonzaga. Agnese, an opulent brunette, was a Neapolitan of Spanish origin. It is unknown what induced her to migrate to the north and why she chose, of all the towns of Emilia and Lombardy, tiny Colorno. Perhaps it was because at Colorno people merrily lost the most precious of things: time. Or perhaps she was attracted by the kind of atmosphere found only in circles whose main occupation was to make love; and at Colorno love certainly was the vocation, the rule of court life, the dominant theme. Everyone had at least one affair, which could range from a platonic flirtation to a more or less all-consuming passion. (One of the conventions of the perfect courtier was to languish, or at least to seem to languish, for love.) At Colorno Agnese lived six years in the constant company of la Sanseverina, who kept her as friend, pupil, and lady in waiting, teaching her the refinements of conversation, good manners and, above all, that passionate art of life which distinguished the marchioness from every other woman. Almost certainly Vincenzo Gonzaga met Agnese during one of his visits to Colorno, the court his parents disliked so much. After one knowing glance, he decided to conquer her with the irresistible gallantry for which he had been famous since his adolescence. Agnese could not resist him.

Vincenzo Gonzaga had the unusual habit of finding husbands for his mistresses. He saw to it that the men chosen were willing to tolerate everything, to say and see nothing. Faithful to this practice which he never regretted, he found a husband for Agnese: Prospero del Carretto, a most discreet gentleman and so observant of his role that he even accepted the paternity of a little Gonzaga to whom he was related only by virtue of the child's birth certificate. Prospero knew that his compliance would earn him many substantial advantages; indeed, they arrived punctually, in the form of estates, honors, tax exemptions —all precious things during bad times.

Agnese del Carretto was the most constant and perhaps most important love of this softhearted prince, the only affair which could wrinkle the forehead of Vincenzo's second wife, Eleonora de' Medici, who was usually wise enough to attach no importance to her husband's love life. The Marchioness del Carretto, however, tried her patience: one day she simply moved to Mantua, into the Té, the famous palace reserved for the Gonzaga favorites, where, among the sensuous frescoes by Giulio Romano, she too held court for intellectuals and poets, imitating la Sanseverina who congratulated her from Colorno.

Years passed, emotions cooled, and Agnese's star began to grow faint. Though now the widow of tolerant Prospero del Carretto and demoted to the position of former mistress, Agnese did not leave Mantua. The termination of her relationship with the duke had not diminished her wealth and prestige; in fact, she remained Vincenzo's good friend—that friendship peculiar to lovers who leave one another without quarreling. Vincenzo paid her long visits, prompted no doubt by courtesy but also by a great tenderness. The children she had borne her husband, and the one fathered by the duke, were well cared for, and she entertained Mantua's best society. Poets and men of letters maintained with her an amiable and intellectual correspondence, as was customary at the time. At forty, Agnese led a luxurious, sophisticated life. Occasionally, she went to inspect her rich properties in Viadana, near the Po, from whence she often visited Colorno across the river. To welcome her there was la Sanseverina, still beautiful in spite of her years and still possessing the talent for inventing happiness each new day.

Among Colorno's habitués, as we have said, there was Gianfrancesco Sanvitale, the Marchesino. To seduce his grandmother's friend, to discover at twenty the passion of a woman of forty, appeared to him a reasonably interesting experience and he decided to satisfy his whim. There is no record of how long he had to court Agnese before she yielded, nor is it known whether, before yielding, she suffered the tortures of temptation. In any case, she surrendered, and when she regretted it, it was too late. Her feelings had reached the temperature of passion, the irresistible passion of women who are offered a last encounter with youth. Unable to restrain herself, absorbed in a tragic and exquisite madness, Agnese permitted Gianfrancesco to follow her to Mantua, then to Viadana. Eventually, what was left to her were the painful intervals between rendezvous. La Sanseverina watched sympathetically; she condoned and favored everything her daughter-in-law disapproved of and hampered. Neither of them suspected the tragedy of which this love duet was but a prelude.

VI

The Spoiled Conspiracy

In 1610 the Duke of Fuentes died. His threatening presence
in nearby Milan had been for years the main obstacle to
Ranuccio's reprisals against the Marchioness of Sala and to
his project of seizing Colorno. Yet, in a way, this forced truce
had helped Ranuccio's designs, for it compelled him to perfect
them by meditation and by secret talks with Bartolomeo Riva,
so that his revenge, although delayed, promised a more exquisite
and rewarding pleasure. Once the fearsome Spanish governor
was dead, Ranuccio promptly revived the Colorno issue. His
first move was to send for Girolamo Sanvitale, because he had
the impression it would be easier to intimidate the son than the
mother. Once he was able either to convince or to crush
Girolamo, Colorno's legal owner, it would be simple to break the
resistance of the marchioness, who was only the usufructuary of
the estate.

Ranuccio's reasoning was entirely correct. Girolamo, lacking
his mother's arrogance as well as her courage, was left to
meditate upon the consequences of opposing someone who had
raw power on his side. The best solution seemed "to rely wholly

on His Highness's mercy," and to trust in the natural evolution of the situation. But after the interview with the duke, when he detected disdain in his mother's eyes even before she spoke to him, he realized how unworthy of a Sanvitale his meekness had been. Recovering some courage, he informed the duke that he intended to have their respective claims examined by some lawyers known for their honesty and skill.

Ranuccio was not caught by surprise. To clear himself of any suspicion of usurpation he pretended to be most willing to submit his claims to an impartial investigation. However, while he officially and publicly retained a group of famous jurists, he secretly ordered his shrewdest diplomats in Rome, where la Sanseverina's cause was supported by the cardinals Gonzaga and Montalto, to bribe some of the most important Roman lawyers. Perhaps to get more publicity, he declared that he would not be satisfied with the opinion of individual jurists and that he wanted his case examined by the College of Doctors in Padua. This was a subtle maneuver on Ranuccio's part, for two years before, the College, one of the most prestigious in Italy, had rendered judgment against him in favor of Count Alberto Scotti of Piacenza, whose estate Ranuccio had confiscated. Now, relying on the authority of the Farnese name, on the ability of his ministers, and especially on the corruptibility of the judges, Ranuccio applied to this assembly for the second time with the certainty that the Padua doctors would not dare to move against him again. Also, this time he made sure to bribe almost all of them. Ranuccio ordered Doctor Giovanni Giorgio Rossi, who supervised this matter for him in Padua, to do his best, it being a matter of indifference if victory cost him more than the entire marquisate of Colorno was worth. These exhortations were followed by bags of scudi to be distributed among the still recalcitrant doctors. The scudi succeeded where evidence might have failed, and only a few of the jurists resisted the temptation; but these few, fortunately, carried no weight. On May 5, 1611, they were overwhelmed by the bribed majority, and Ranuccio finally saw his claims validated by a vote of thirty-three for, and seventeen against.

Then, for the first time, the marchioness cried, giving free rein to her chagrin and behaving as though pain were a new and unnatural feeling. In her dismay, the only thing she thought of was hastening to Colorno, her beloved land of mists, waters, and beautiful trees. People said she wandered about the palace, on the verge of fainting at the mere thought of losing it. So gossiped the *poverazzi* of the village, pleased by her misfortunes. For almost a hundred years that palace had been her family's seat. There she had spent her childhood, her youth, and her glorious maturity, all that magnificent life she loved so much and would have lived all over again without changing an iota of it. She had wanted to grow old among those walls; there she had wanted to die—as old as possible, of course. Suddenly, an unexpected burst of energy, quickened by the idea of defeat, encouraged her to write more letters and reports, to consult lawyers, to send messages to influential people. All this cost money, but for Colorno she would have given anything. "Sell all the wheat there is in Chiavenna," she sent word to her stewards; "try to get as much as possible, and quickly, because we need much money for these consultations and trips and presents." Sensing that hard times were coming for all of them, her friends closed ranks around her. Only her son and her grandson, both of whom she would have liked to rely on in that trying moment, failed her: Gianfrancesco, by boasting and ranting childishly, Girolamo by cowardly suggesting they submit—although, somehow, he found the courage to call on Ranuccio to discuss a possible compromise. But the negotiations (of which there exists an interesting draft in the treasurer's handwriting) were interrupted by other events.

✻

In the winter of 1611, a dull, tiresome carnival was in progress at Parma. "It feels more like Lent than carnival," wrote Marchioness Benedetta Pio to her son, who had remained at Sala. Celebrations and parades were slack; the tournament, which had just started, proceeded slowly, with no enthusiasm. There were no masques, no ladies in their carriages on the main street. The duke, who, in deference to tradition, should have presided over the great show of the nobility, did not appear at all. The Sanvitale clan stayed in seclusion, although they remained attentive to town gossip, which reflected the pessimistic picture Ranuccio's circle was painting of their situation. An atmosphere of heavy uncertainty spread over the town and the court.

It is unknown who inspired the first thought of open rebellion among the dissatisfied patricians, or who sct in motion the snowball which, transformed into an avalanche by Ranuccio's suspicions, ended up by crushing so many people. From the records of the trial, the responsibility seems to belong to Gianfrancesco Sanvitale. The idea of destroying the Farneses came suddenly to him, it seems, during the carnival, and it fascinated him as did all ideas which in one way or another might give him notoriety. He expounded the notion one night to a group of friends in his father's house, while they were complaining about the duke as usual. He created a sensation. No one, however vexed by the Farneses, had ever thought of such a violent but simple solution. Encouraged, the Marchesino repeated his incredible plan; he reinforced it with rigorous logic, made it look indispensable, appealed to the universal concept of honor, revenge, and solidarity in redressing a wrong done to a friend. The others, undoubtedly, envied him the audacity they had not shown; they were mortified and felt more than ever

Ranuccio's victims. The idea of plunging their daggers into the oppressor's heart intoxicated them; to throw off the yoke, to recapture the dignity of the heroic times when knights kept God beside their sword, exalted them.

Fortunately for Ranuccio, the noblemen of Parma did not have the character or the cool drive of Don Ferrante Gonzaga, who fifty years before had planned and executed the perfect political assassination. Compared to Gonzaga, these were inexperienced boys playing with things beyond their strength. Inevitably, incapable as they were to carry out such a project, the lords began to consider their conspiracy more as a remote possibility than an immediate action, forgetting that Machiavelli had warned that delays in a conspiracy lead only to disaster.

La Sanseverina, after some hesitation, had been the first to accept a plan which promised to solve so many of her problems. With the help of her grandson, she encouraged in her friends the forbidden pleasure of defying Ranuccio—in talk, of course. According to her, everyone with a minimum of brains and courage should join the conspiracy or, at least, approve of it. Her husband, still madly in love, approved of it just to please her. Gianbattista Masi and Pio Torelli accepted it because of old grudges against the Farneses, and Alfonso Sanvitale did so to emulate his cousin Gianfrancesco. Teodoro Scotti accepted for friendship's sake; Girolamo Sanvitale, through weakness; Alberto da Canossa, Ranuccio's cupbearer, for money; Giulio Cesare da Madrignano, Ferdinando da Liciana, and Gianvincenzo da Montarese (the three Marquises Malaspina), out of common interest. And last, Bartolomeo Roverzani, a captain in Ranuccio's service, also signed up. More meetings followed in the winter of 1611. The conspirators gathered in Girolamo's house or in la Sanseverina's palace and eagerly exercized their imaginations concerning the affair, since, for the moment at least, the plot was still academic and therefore safe. In tune

with the general mood, Barbara posed as a fearless matron and
uttered Plutarchian mottoes—for instance, that she regretted
as a woman not being able to wield a sword instead of a distaff
—unwary words destined one day to be used against her.

Presently the conspirators began to organize the various details, to find money and men "not to instigate bloodshed,"
they reassured one another, "but in case of emergency." The
Marchesino was assigned the task of obtaining the Marchioness
of Grana's recommendation to the Duke of Mantua for money
and protection. To a priest, Battista Giglio, Gianfrancesco's
confidant, alchemist, astrologer, and treasure digger, fell the
task of going to the Malaspinas in the Lunigiana mountains to
ask for strong and willing men who were to be referred to, in
the conspirators' letters, as "cows." Alfonso Sanvitale was to
make a trip to Modena to ask Duke Cesare d'Este for assistance;
and Girolamo da Correggio was dispatched to Mirandola to
confer with Prince Pico. Onofrio Martani of Spoleto, another
of Gianfrancesco's confidants, was in contact with some brigands
of the Papal States, to have them ready to join the conspiracy
at the right moment. Along the flat roads of the Po Valley, up
the stony paths of the Apennines, a procession of messengers
came and went, muffled in monk's robes and dogged by the spies
of Bartolomeo Riva, who took daily notes of every suspicious
word and movement in the duchy. But although the treasurer
interpreted everything negatively, and the spies did their best
to exaggerate the least significant facts, the reports showed no
real evidence of a plot—merely the intention of one. Both Riva
and Ranuccio, however, were too intelligent and experienced
not to understand that at any moment that kind of mood
could generate the dreaded conspiracy. They agreed to fore-
stall it, to get a step ahead of the enemy by creating the moral
atmosphere of the crime, to give suspicion the consistency of
truth, to strike at the foremost conspirators in order to break up
the ranks of the undecided, and to legalize the confiscation of

their estates. The situation which had been ripening for years, they felt, was finally maturing.

Moreover, to convince Ranuccio that a plot was imminent one anonymous letter was enough: "Cruel Tyrant," wrote a stranger whom Ranuccio could easily identify with any of his enemies, "since for the moment I am—in no other way but by writing—allowed to give vent to my feelings, feelings shared by all of your chained dogs (I cannot call them subjects), I want you to know that those who in the past would have done everything to please you and serve you loyally at the cost of their lives, are now so nauseated by you that they can hardly pronounce your cursed name. And this because of your and your ministers' heartless rule. . . . Tell me, wicked man, is there one bishop still in charge of his church allowed to exercise his duties and privileges undisturbed? Evil creature, don't you realize the cruelties you inflict on the poor, feeding on their blood with ever-increasing taxes and tolls? And daily you affront your nobles, endangering their lives and properties. Heartless wolf, think of all the frauds that you perpetrate because you are greedy for the possessions of others. Do you realize that your crimes are as well known outside of the state as they are inside? Everyone knows about your illicit trading in wheat and other things. . . . Here, only malicious and envious people like yourself—spies, traitors, corrupt judges and false witnesses—have good reputations and enjoy your favor. . . . Tell me, for whom are you piling up so much wealth? Perhaps for your bastard, the son of a Parma whore, or for the one your wife is pregnant of, God will it were a serpent? I tell you: should I find twenty-five people who think the way I do, neither you nor anyone of your rotten family will enjoy for more than a month what you now undeservedly own. . . . I swear to God that you are hated by the whole town; and do not forget that your great-grandfather, Pier Luigi, was assassinated, and that even kings may be killed, as you have seen recently."*

Letters like this gave Ranuccio fits of horror which lasted through his feverish, sleepless nights. The nightmare of a conspiracy diminished only with the dawn, when he could find a little peace by convincing himself that the hypothetical conspirators had "neither brains, nor common sense, nor opportunity, nor means to execute such a project." But by night, the raving started over again; at which point, even his brother the cardinal was affected and wrote from Rome to be wary "of poison, sword, and devils, that is, for enchantments. . . ."

In Parma the conspirators, excited by their own absurd machinations, went as far as fixing a date for the assassination. At first the most suitable day seemed that of the baptism of Alessandro, the child to which the duchess had recently given birth. Once they had slaughtered the duke's family gathered in the baptistry, the conspirators planned to separate: some were to invade the citadel, others to occupy the town's other strategic points. But then they decided against that date, partly because the baptism had been postponed, partly in the hope of finding a more suitable occasion, and partly because, though they were determined more than ever to kill Ranuccio, no one was willing to commit himself to being the actual executioner. They decided to wait until the duke visited the Abbey of Fontevivo, where he sometimes went, usually with a small escort, to be exorcised by the Capuchins. More weeks passed in waiting, and once again, fate changed the course of events.

Alfonso Sanvitale was a collector of capital sins, with a predilection for lust and anger. His dissolute life, however, seemed

* An allusion to the assassination of Henry IV of France.

not to interfere with his reputation of being "the bravest and most fearsome of the duke's men." He was obsessed with the idea of honor. His wife, Silvia Visdomini, probably betrayed him. Ranuccio, with his mania for meddling into everything, had hired a man to spy on the unfaithful Silvia. After keeping watch for a while, the spy reported to Ranuccio that Alfonso Sanvitale was indeed a cuckold. Then, to earn some additional money, he repeated the story to Alfonso Sanvitale himself. "I saw Count Teodoro Scotti embracing Donna Silvia," he told him, "and the count had his stockings down."

Alfonso was not a man to forgive an insult to his honor. In 1598, in the name of honor, he had dueled with Count Fortunato Cesi, with the Marquis Pallavicino, and also with Orazio Simonetta for having called him a cuckold. And, in this instance, also in the name of honor, he decided to do away with his wife. One evening he had her and her mother shot in the garden of his villa of San Patrizio, near Reggio Emilia.

The incident caused a sensation, and since in both Reggio Emilia and Parma Alfonso was known as an extremely choleric man, the shooting was immediately attributed to him. Ranuccio, promptly informed, a few days later ordered Bartolomeo Riva to "enforce the law immediately." And so Alfonso, together with his servant-confidant Oliviero Olivieri, was imprisoned in the Rocchetta on a charge of the attempted murder of his wife and the murder of his mother-in-law. Onofrio Martani ended up in prison, too, at the same time, and with him also some soldiers to whom he had promised a large reward should they succeed in "a certain business."

The inquest was led by Filiberto Piozasco, a Piedmont nobleman, honest in the worse sense—that is, ready to commit any cruelty in the name of truth. He had become famous as the judge in Piacenza's witch trials, which had made him a very powerful member of Parma's Council of Justice. Piozasco took his place in the torture chamber and did not come out until

Onofrio Martani, with shattered nerves and dislocated bones, admitted that "the important business" mentioned in some ciphered letters he was carrying at the moment of the arrest referred to "the business of the duke." Piozasco thought these words sufficient for a case of treason. The following day he did not even have to torture Martani again. "I'll say what I know," said the poor devil. "I don't want more torture, because I cannot stand it any longer, because I have a fever and had to evacuate forty times in four days." At the mere sight of the wheel he revealed the plot, singling out Gianfrancesco and Alfonso as the leaders.

With the conspiracy accidentally discovered, through the shots of a jealous husband and the mouthings of a group of scoundrels, the trial for treason was under way. On June 24, 1611, the Marchesino was also thrown into a musty, filthy cell. In Mantua, Agnese, promptly informed of the arrest, moaned that she wanted to die.

VII

The Trial of the Conspirators

"Alas, my dear Marchioness," wrote la Sanseverina to her friend Agnese, "while I was at the Abbey paying my respects to His Highness, they took my Gianfrancesco to prison. The poor boy went unarmed, as was his duty, and yet they searched him. . . . Let us find hope in his innocence and virtue. . . . As for me, I have forgotten all about Colorno and everything else. Oh, my dear girl, I cannot stand it much longer! Count Orazio hasn't been permitted to see His Highness—maybe he will if I give up my property."

Ranuccio refused to see Orazio or anyone else, and the mood of the Sanvitales can well be imagined. A scribe present at the interrogation had spread the rumor that Gianfrancesco had been arrested "for something to do with women," but it was a vague charge and only added to the general confusion. Hoping to be received by the duke, Girolamo declared he would kill his son with his own hands if he found him guilty of some intrigue. But he, too, was kept waiting in the duke's antechambers.

While his family trembled for him, the Marchesino was, at

least at the beginning, not in the least concerned. He knew, or imagined, that influential friends in Rome would work for his release. To be sure, several people in the Vatican were already maneuvering to this end, especially the Salviatis of Florence and Prince Pico della Mirandola to whom Gianfrancesco was related by marriage. The matter had already been brought to the pope's attention. Also, Cardinal Francesco Sforza, a great friend of la Sanseverina, had gone to Rome and was creating a great stir; he had "slapped Cardinal Farnese in the face and would have killed him had they not stopped him." The Marchesino did not know about the slap, but he had figured out the rest and remained calm.

Shortly after Gianfrancesco's arrest, Ranuccio had set up a secret council composed of Papirio Picedi, Bishop of Parma, Fulgenzio Lucii, Auditor of the Chamber, and the treasurer Bartolomeo Riva, the mastermind of the inquest. Day by day this council advised Judge Piozasco concerning the trial. One of the suggestions had been to put the Marchesino in the same cell with Tomaso Menalotti and Camillo Pilotta, two famous *comprigioni,* that is, fake prisoners who, pretending to have been jailed for some imaginary crime, had the task of winning the real prisoners' confidence and of reporting their words to the authorities. In the case of the Marchesino this was not difficult to do: he loved to talk, especially about himself. He began with cynical, elegant humor to tell all about his "ribaldries" (a blasphemer and a wicked pederast" is written in the transcript of the trial), which were reported to Piozasco, who punctually confronted him with them in subsequent interrogations. These persuaded the Marchesino that indeed his immorality was the only reason for his arrest.

While the days passed in the minute enumeration of Gianfrancesco's obscenities, his cousin Alfonso, who up to now had managed not to disclose any dangerous secrets, under torture finally confessed to the attempted murder of his wife and also admitted the existence of a plot. He told how the Marchesino had confided in him about the project, how they had discussed it together and had organized it with their friends. In the end Piozasco found himself in possession of explosive evidence, and he set about cruelly and competently to analyze it, drawing out whatever he needed for his purpose and discarding the rest. So, while continuing to interrogate Alfonso, he began gradually to divert the Marchesino from the subject of obscenities and question him about other topics—for instance about the motives the Sanvitales could have for disliking the Farneses. For quite a while, these interrogations were fruitless. Gianfrancesco controlled his answers and his reactions, admitting only to a slight disagreement between Ranuccio and his own family, a moderate and polite dispute such as is customary among patricians. Fear, however, must have overcome him because, through one of the guards and the barber, he tried to warn his mother and grandmother to do their best to keep Don Battista Giglio, his manservant Turchetto, and the groom Sandrini out of Ranuccio's reach. In a letter he also begged la Sanseverina to send all three to Mirandola, where they could hide until he got out of prison. The one who most worried him was Battista Giglio, who used to carry his love letters to the Marchioness of Grana. Should Giglio refuse to leave, Gianfrancesco suggested a quick remedy: "to induce him with friendly words to come out of the house and, arriving at a convenient location, to stab him or shoot him to death—in short, to get rid of him." They should not fear the consequences. "Since the place is out of Parma's jurisdiction," he wrote, "there is no problem." As for religious scruples, they should not worry either. Absolution could be bought in Rome "for few pennies."

After three months of questioning, the Marchesino was brought into the torture chamber. The ignorance and the cruelty of the time demanded that all prisoners, before being tortured, be washed and shaved all over, for fear that some evil spirit would entangle itself in the beard or hair, giving the prisoner the strength to remain silent or to deny the truth. At the prosaic ceremony of depilation Gianfrancesco's resistance collapsed. On October 3 he declared that, to avoid torture, he was prepared to admit the existence of a plot and not to contest any accusation of the tribunal.

From that moment on, Gianfrancesco, who had been so cautious in his statements, completely changed his tactics. Seized by a sudden fury of desperation, he denounced not only himself but also his parents, his grandmother, friends, servants, Don Battista Giglio, and two more priests. Then, endlessly widening the circle, he included the least suspected persons in Italy: the Duke of Mantua, the Prince of Mirandola, Charles Emmanuel of Savoy, the viceroy of Naples, the Spanish ambassador to Rome, the Duke of Modena, some of the Medicis, a dozen princes of the Church, Cardinals Lanfranco, Barberini, Giustiniani, La Rochefoucault, and even the pope. The *comprigioni* reported to Ranuccio that the Marchesino expected any day to receive the pact the pope and he had signed dividing the territory of the duchy between them.

This talking fit of the young Sanvitale, which seemed inspired by the muse of absurdity, in reality disguised a subtle plan: "to make the trial the dirtiest, most sordid and complex possible . . . to thicken and to inflate the plot with innumerable accomplices, to discredit it by making it hyperbolic and grotesque, doomed to be crushed under the weight of its own paradoxes, or to elicit protests, scandals, and anger, which sooner or later would rebound on the Farneses." His nightmarish scheme implicated so many people—Scotti, Torelli, Canossa, Rangone, Zanardi, Malvicini, Caracciolo, Anguissola, Pallavicino, Oddi, Mancasola, all the foremost families in Parma and Piacenza— that already hundreds, without knowing it, were under constant surveillance. Gianfrancesco's mania of confession did not stop even when he was brought back to his cell. He continued to unburden himself to the *comprigioni* who, of course, reported everything to the duke.

Without imagining that everything that came out of his cell was being scrutinized by Judge Piozasco, the Marchesino also wrote innumerable letters, hoping to undo by writing the damage he had done by talking. He wrote to each person he had denounced, advising him to flee. To his grandmother he suggested retirement to the chapel of the castle of Sala, which was, in his opinion, invulnerable to any attack. To his mother he sent word to have the case studied by lawyers from Rome, Padua, and Bologna, "to show the world how unjust my arrest has been," he wrote. To the Marchioness of Grana, his mistress, he wrote about his behavior during the interrogations: "When a man is about to die, everything is forgiven him; and the man who is made desperate by so many wrongs is allowed to exaggerate; and if I have to die because of it, I will at least have said what I wanted. For they can imprison and kill me but they cannot humiliate me or make me beg for mercy. I would die dishonorably if I asked and received mercy from a man who would take my life and my possessions."

Parallel to the tragedy of the Marchesino, there unfolded that of Oliviero Olivieri, the servant-confidant of Alfonso Sanvitale, who had been arrested with his master after the famous shooting of Alfonso's wife. Confronted with his master's confession, Oliviero desperately denied everything, although Alfonso, stretched naked on the rack, repeated the accusation to his face and exhorted him to confess. "If you do not tell the truth," he said almost affectionately, "this will be the cause of so much torture that you will be crippled, as I have been, and in the end you will have to confess anyway."

"The devil take me if I know anything," swore Oliviero. Then, overcome by horror and pity for his master, he ended up by agreeing to confess all. In the following days, while Alfonso added more details and names, Oliviero volunteered the key to the cipher by means of which his master used to inform Giulio Cesare da Madrignano of the conspiracy's progress. An example of these ciphered letters exists today.

Toward the middle of October, 1611, thanks to the confessions of Gianfrancesco, Alfonso, and Oliviero, the other conspirators were so irremediably compromised that their arrest seemed imminent. But Judge Piozasco was a man of unusual patience, and he decided to wait for the annual tournament of San Martino, which would bring to the city all the lords who usually stayed in the country till late in the fall. He waited. Had he been a politician, the Guicciardini epithet of *cunctabondo* [prudent] would have fitted him perfectly. On November 9, the time was ripe and Piozasco hauled in his net. The following day the majority of the conspirators were arrested. Gianbattista Masi, Orazio Simonetta, and Girolamo da Correggio were arrested in Parma; Teodoro Scotti in Piacenza, while he was visiting the governor. As for Count Pio Torelli, who had remained in his castle at Montechiaruggiolo, Ranuccio had his secretary, Linati, write the following note to him: "Because His Highness has to send a gentleman to Spain with his condolences for the queen's death, he has chosen Your Lordship and has ordered me to write you in his name, as I am doing by special courier, to be here tomorrow night to speak with His Highness about your mission. Then you will return home to get ready, because His Highness wants you to leave as soon as possible." The next day Torelli was quietly arrested in the duke's palace.

The imprisonment of so many prominent gentlemen on a charge of treason frightened the townspeople of Parma, a fear shrewdly inflamed by the clergy, who maintained that political crimes were also sacrilegious. The general dismay was increased by the rumor that the angry duke had finally decided to consent to the wishes of the ambassadors of Piacenza to make that city the capital of the duchy, a rumor which reopened the old rivalry between the two towns.

To counteract Piacenza's demonstrations of loyalty, the town council of Parma went to the duke to offer its help and to confirm solemnly his sovereignty. It ordered parades, processions, public prayers, and religious ceremonies—all of which, of course, were well attended.

About that time the counselor Fulgenzio Lucii left for Rome to inform the pope of the conspiracy. He was a man very well suited for this role. He managed, in fact, to present the explosive news so delicately, eliminating all the details which Ranuccio preferred, for the moment, to keep secret, that Pius V, without pressing for explanations, congratulated Ranuccio on his narrow escape and offered to assist him in every way. Similar expressions of solidarity were obtained from several cardinals. Duke della Rovere declared himself happy to welcome Ranuccio to Urbino if he should wish a change of scenery after the shock of his trying experience.

Meanwhile, in Parma, Judge Pierasco continued to spring his traps. The first person to be caught was Gianbattista Masi, the gentleman of the flower pots who, some years before, intoxicated with pride and notions of honor, had written to his fiancée: "Things that happen among gentlemen must not be brought to the law, because one man of honor would sooner have his arms broken than denounce another." Instead, precisely so as not to have his arms broken, he readily denounced those companions and friends for whom he had once declared he would risk his life.

Count Torelli was more tenacious. He succeeded in keeping silent even when both Alfonso Sanvitale and Gianbattista Masi, hanging from the ropes in agony, denounced him to his face. Realizing that now he too was about to taste the rack, he decided to confess without implicating Orazio Simonetta and

Teodoro Scotti. But by not involving them he eventually earned those tortures he believed to have avoided in denouncing only himself.

When Count Simonetta saw his own and his wife's friends change from accused to accusers, he became an accuser in turn. And he had plenty to talk about. The Marchesino, in his letters from prison, had instructed him about what to say when interrogated: the names of the accomplices, dates and places of the meetings, the things said, everything—in order that each one's confession match all the others' in every detail—for "the smallest discrepancy is met by torture."

Even in prison Gianfrancesco assumed the leadership of that unfortunate band. He spent entire days writing, dispensing counsel and advice, ordering everyone to follow his plan, which was, as has been observed, to "make the matter the most complicated in the world by implicating hundreds of people." He liked the role. "All these gentlemen," he wrote to the Marchioness of Grana, "have lost their heads and don't know where they are or what to say, and they all come to me for help." He was the only one who, after a hundred and fifty hours of interrogation, had the bitter satisfaction of having avoided torture. "I did as much chatting as Mercury did with Argus, and I said so much that to this moment I've saved myself from torture." Which unfortunately he could not say for his friends, who were "so mangled that, unless some miracle occurs, they will be broken forever."

Count Orazio Simonetta was the first to mention Captain Bartolomeo Roverzani; and the others, who had almost forgotten this minor character, immediately accepted this new name to include in the merry-go-round of incriminations. It is difficult to say today if Bartolomeo Roverzani was a simpleton or naïve—or both. Candor and stupidity proved fatal to him, the only one of the group who might have saved himself. Friends in Bologna wisely exhorted him to flee as far as possible and to cover his tracks; he, instead, decided to surrender himself in order to explain his position in the conspiracy and clear his reputation as a soldier. His friends continued to implore him. It was crazy, they said, to return to Parma. The matter was so serious that he "could not be sure to escape the death penalty or life imprisonment." But Bartolomeo, following a fatal impulse, took the road to Parma, "resolved to go there," even if he "should be cut into pieces."

At the Rocchetta, where they immediately put him under lock, they did not bother to torture him, officially because of his hernia, in reality because "Roverzani cannot be trusted," as Ranuccio wrote to his brother the cardinal. Someone capable, as he was, of jumping into that hell voluntarily would not hesitate to be tortured to death without talking.

Instead of talking, Bartolomeo wrote. He wrote to the duke, to the treasurer, to the judge protesting his innocence. "I bring to your attention," he said in his last letter, written a few days before the bloody end, "that I am here not to be thought ungrateful and because I believe in Your Highness's justice. Therefore, I beseechingly entrust to you my honor which men's falsity has deprived me of, for nothing beside my soul is dearer to me. Only Your Highness, my second Lord, can preserve my honor. May God inspire Your Highness to relieve me from the terrible suffering in which I find myself."

✳

On February 2, 1612, an official of the ducal court was shown a cadaver. His report observed: "A rather large man, about thirty-four years old, he is lying on a cot in the lower section of the Rocchetta, at the head of the lower corridor, near the first cell. Examination showed no evidence of suicide. He has been identified as Count Teodoro Scotti."

This sketchy, bureaucratic note officially concluded the case history of yet another character in the trial. They had arrested Count Scotti in Piacenza on November 10. From the very first interrogation it was clear that, unlike the others, he would obstinately deny everything, perhaps expecting in this way either to save himself or to die nobly so that the name of his children —he had five—would not be dishonored. As Machiavelli had said, "A good death honors an entire life."

In the records of the trial are meticulously reported the interrogations, or *costituiti,* as they were then called, of the conspirators. Those of Teodoro Scotti distinguish themselves for their chilling monotony. "Tell the truth, and you won't be tortured," the judge benevolently urged him. "I have said it, I have said it," answered the count while his shoulders were noisily dislocated. "Tell more truth, then, and more fully, because your obstinacy does not neutralize the evidence against you," insisted Piozasco. "I have said it, my sweet God. Oh, Saint Francis of Assisi! I have said it, O Madonna of Loreto!" The records always included the invocations and the screams of the interrogated. While a gigantic sand clock marked the hours, the executioners demonstrated their professional ability. From the spike they passed to the rope, from the rope to the rack, from that to the iron screw, and then all over again. When the torture was increased the count merely sighed: "I am a bit uncomfortable," or "I am thirsty. May I have some vinegar, sir?" After three hours of this, Piozasco would go to eat and be replaced by the notary Moreschi. Suspended on a rope drawn almost to the pulley, the count would say: "If you let me down, you'll do me a favor." The notary would reply: "Do me a favor, too, and tell the truth." And they went on this way for a while. After four days Teodoro Scotti was at the end of his endurance; his lips parted only to whisper prayers. The jailers felt his thighs and said there was "no danger of death," but his legs had become rigid, an icy sweat ran down his body, and he was shaken by convulsions. The onlookers began to fear that he would die without having confessed. Piozasco had him brought back to the cell. On January 30, burning with fever, Teodoro Scotti lost consciousness. The first doctor called, Girolamo Masevi, said he was too sick to come and sent word to give Scotti citron juice. Another ordered "candied sugar to keep in his mouth and a little licorice." A third, Alberto Urbano, prescribed barley water and powdered pearl. Scotti was in his death throes. A priest was called who remained with him to the end. On February 1, Scotti died after having whispered with his last strength this lapidary will: "My soul to God, my body to the earth, my honor to me."

From orders issued the following day, which have been preserved, we know that the court intended to leave Scotti's body unburied until after the execution of all conspirators; but fear that the body would be decomposed by then made the zealous Bishop Papirio Picedi propose to quarter the body and nail it to the gates of Piacenza "for the terror it would inspire and as a warning to others." It was only thanks to the unexpected kindness of Ranuccio the only humane touch in so inhuman a story—that the count was buried, quietly and without being quartered, in the Chiesa de' Servi in Parma, two days after his death.

The news of Scotti's ordeal was kept secret, and those few who knew of it did not speak. This does not mean, however, that the count was not discussed both inside and outside the duchy. There were those who thought he would save himself, and others who maintained that "he has been so tortured that you can see his entrails." No one suspected that he was already dead. Parma's ambassadors to the courts of Europe were given strict orders on that score by Ranuccio: "Should you be asked if Count Scotti is dead, say you don't know." Ranuccio, however, did not dare to hide the truth from the pope. Fulgenzio Lucii, who was again sent to Rome to discuss the legality of the death sentences which the tribunal of Parma was planning to impose, announced that "Count Teodoro Scotti will be exempt from execution because he has died in prison, of fever." He said to the pope: "He was a troublemaker, a malicious, overbearing man, a friend of criminals." The pope accepted the story of the fever, but he did not bother to inform the other Italian princes of it. The truth of Teodoro Scotti's death remained unknown for more than two hundred years until, at the beginning of the nineteenth century, it was possible for the first time to examine the documents of the trial.

Five children survived the count. The four daughters ended up in nunneries. Giacinto, the only son, was placed in the Collegio dei Nobili di Parma by the order of Ranuccio, who liked to make public exhibitions of generosity. A few days later, however, he arranged to have "the students make a petition to remove the boy from the college." And since not even a duke could force the children of his subjects to live with the son of a traitor, Giacinto was expelled and sent to live with a family of peasants near Corniglio.

Toward the middle of February, Judge Piozasco had enough confessions in his hands to proceed also against la Sanseverina, her son Girolamo, and her daughter-in-law, Benedetta Pio. From the ecclesiastical authorities he obtained permission to arrest them in church—for being convinced that flight could no longer save them, they practically lived in the family chapel among prayers, novenas, rosaries, and blessed candles. Girolamo and his wife were taken in the castle of Sala. To capture them were mobilized, besides the constable with his officers and deputies, twenty-five musketeers, twenty-five foot soldiers, two sergeants, ten archers, fifteen horsemen—a small expeditionary force followed by "a horse-drawn petard carriage."

Barbara's arrest was less theatrical; it required only one captain, eighteen soldiers, and two corporals. "Sir," began the great lady when interrogated the first time, "if you allow me to say a few words, I'll say them willingly." Displaying all the aplomb she had acquired by years of practice, she behaved as if they were meeting to clear up some small misunderstanding. Filiberto Piozasco, assuming a conciliatory manner, tried to play along with her ladylike approach: "Say whatever you like, freely." "Sir," the lady continued, "all this time I have been detained, I have been wondering what the charges against me could possibly be, but I cannot imagine any, for I have offended no one. Since people in my position are not treated this way unless there is some serious cause, I suspect some great treachery against me. Consequently, I beg you, when the time comes, to let me defend myself with the help of suitable attorneys who will prove my innocence properly."

She was brave to the end, but she had no chance. She held fast when confronted with her disfigured friends and relatives, unrecognizable from their suffering. She said nothing when they were tortured again. She denied their accusations, calling each one a liar and a coward. Only young Girolamo da Correggio's words managed to shake her: "My dear Marchioness, may I offer Your Ladyship advice as from a son, for I have loved you as a mother. Tell the truth. Obstinacy is of no use; it is nonsense. Stronger men than we have confessed. I have not been the first one, my lady; I too wanted to resist and not tell the truth but in the end I did speak because it was impossible not to. I feel sorry for Your Ladyship—yet there is nothing to do." "Are all of my race traitors?" she sighed. "Very well then, Holy God and Blessed Virgin have pity on me, and the prince be merciful. I admit that what these gentlemen, Count Pio, Count Girolamo, and Count Gianbattista, have said of me is true. It is true that during last carnival I went to dine at the house of my son Girolamo, and after dinner, all these gentlemen—that is, Count Orazio, Count Pio, Count Gianbattista, Count Alberto Canossa, Count Teodoro Scotti, Count Girolamo da Correggio, and also Captain Bartolomeo Roverzani—came and outlined the conspiracy to kill His Highness, the cardinal, and the child, I mean, the young prince, and Don Ottavio. . . . There, I have said it. I am a villain, I am a traitor! And it is true that my husband, my son, and my grandson were present at these discussions. And it is also true that at a later time (exactly when I don't remember, if it was during carnival or Lent—on this I'll trust them) all those mentioned were in my house on the occasion when my daughter-in-law, the Marchioness, came to dine there, and that these gentlemen discussed and reached the same conclusion they had reached in my son's house. I was present there, too. And the Marchioness Benedetta, my daughter-in-law, was present with me in all the places mentioned, and she too, as I did and everyone else, agreed to the plan. The Marchesino said he would find the men and all that we would need, assuring us he had the support of other rulers. It is also true that the Marchesino had the idea first. I warned him, and I think . . ."

At this point Judge Piozasco interrupted the interrogation. There was no need to continue any further.

VIII

The Justice of Parma

Toward the end of March the trial ended. The warrants and the death sentences were presented to the general council of Piacenza for validation, which was easily obtained. A month later the *inquesto*—a summary of all that had been revealed during the trial—was posted at the Palazzo Vecchio della Comunità, at the Porta del Pretorio, and at other important buildings in the city. The executions were to be very special, complete with dragging of the corpses through the streets by horses, decapitations, quarterings, and finally the displaying of the parts "at the usual places." Ranuccio, however, was satisfied to have his enemies destroyed and cut the sentences to their bare essentials, omitting the most spectacular and bloody specifications.

Counselor Fulgenzio Lucii left for Rome to inform the pope of the verdicts. Ranuccio was almost certain that Pius V would present no obstacle to the decision of the tribunal; all the same, to avoid the slightest possible interference, the counselor was ordered to make his trip to Rome last very long "under the pretext of illness and the like." Accordingly, Fulgenzio took his time and traveled only a few hours each day, announcing at a given moment that he had developed a stomach pain, which improved only after a prolonged sojourn at San Quirico and allowed him to reach Rome on May 16. It was too late for the pope to send any counterorder to Parma; the executions had been set for the nineteenth of the month. Pius V, after having made certain that the names of the Italian rulers implicated in the conspiracy were obliterated with sealing wax from the court documents, could do nothing but give his sanction—all the more easily given because Vincenzo Gonzaga—the most seriously implicated of all rulers, according to Ranuccio—had just concluded his "sinful life" with a good death.

At the beginning of May the conspirators were allowed to organize their defense. With the exception of Girolamo da Correggio and Girolamo Sanvitale, who adhered to their confessions, and of Benedetta Pio who had protested her innocence all along, the prisoners retracted their confessions. But when the moment came to choose their lawyers, they preferred—with few exceptions—to throw themselves on the mercy of the duke, forgetting or ignoring the fact that Ranuccio was incapable of mercy. Alfonso Sanvitale, however, went so far as to write a letter to the pope, a letter which naturally never arrived. "Do not think ill of me for having lied," he wrote. "Judge Piozasco had so tortured me that for the rest of my life I will have the use only of my right hand, and even that so poorly that it has taken me two or three days to write this letter. I confessed out of fear, for in Parma there is no reluctance to torture." To the distorted signature he added the postscript: "If Your Holiness wants to be certain of the truth, ask Father Constantio Tordello of the Order de' Servi."

In a letter Oliviero Olivieri wrote to the duke there was a sense of otherworldly threat: "I beg Your Highness to recognize my innocence and to consider well that, if you damage me or my property, it will be a grave injustice. Remember that the blood of the just always cries for vengeance before the Majesty of God." These words probably gave pause to Ranuccio, always impressionable, and struck an old chord of uneasiness in him; but he contained himself, for he never allowed himself remorse or flexibility. He gave orders that those conspirators who had refused legal assistance be given ex officio lawyers, who were asked to serve impartially. But the latter all refused to take a case against their prince.

Benedetta Pio, Orazio Simonetta, and the Marchesino did ask for lawyers, Doctor Rodesi and Doctor Pettorelli. And they would have been defended had not the two lawyers suddenly been called away, allegedly on their clients' orders, but actually on one forged by the treasurer. "Have them stay away a long time," reads a note from the powerful minister. Which meant: until after the execution. Rodesi and Pettorelli were not the only ones who had been sent away on the pretext of urgent missions. The same thing happened to Bernardino Noceto, notary of the Holy Office—i.e., the Inquisition—of Parma, and to some judges of the ecclesiastical tribunal responsible for examining the case of Don Gabrio Campanini and Don Battista Giglio, the two priests involved in the plot. Some of the judges were thought not sufficiently loyal and were immediately transferred, as it appears from the treasurer's interesting draft: "It is convenient for our purposes that Father Ronca be absent from Parma until the twentieth of this month; and when he arrives there (as you will see, the Bishop of Parma wants you to look into the issue of the state border) make sure that he is kept busy and that he does not leave before the given time. Make sure, with your usual caution, that he does not suspect anything. . . ."

The only one not concerned by the absence of a lawyer was, or at least seemed to be, the Marchesino who, a month before the end, still brought himself to say: "I don't think there is enough against me that a hundred scudi couldn't pay off." He would soon be out, he said to the bewildered *comprigioni,* "and then I will really make a plot against the duke, which I'll carry out and not just talk about."

La Sanseverina, on the contrary, was pessimistic for the first time in her life and lived in paralyzed dismay. While her daughter-in-law, impassive and pale, said the rosary day and night, she cried disconsolately or else raised a rumpus. To the jailer, Mazza, one of the few men allowed near her, she spoke uninterruptedly of the years during which she had been powerful, admired, and loved, almost as if the memory of those happy times could give her the strength to bear prison and her imminent execution. When the final sentence was passed, she decided to write to Odoardo Farnese, Ranuccio's brother, who had once been her admirer. And perhaps Odoardo, who was a good fellow, would have tried to obtain mercy for her, if Ranuccio had not quieted him with a consideration to which he had no answer but a gesture of philosophical resignation. "About your proposal concerning Her Ladyship the Marchioness," the duke wrote him, "it would seem to me perfectly acceptable, if the people were not so aroused as they are against her; and truly, when the people have not the satisfaction for which they have been waiting so eagerly, they might put in doubt all that has hitherto been so clear to everyone. . . ."

On April 16 the judge sent to la Sanseverina the two law-yers chosen by the court, whom she rejected with the haughti-ness of a great lady. But by Easter she had grown desperate again and, in desperation, she found the humility necessary to beg Ranuccio for mercy: "Today when all Christians are cele-brating the great day of mercy, I remind Your Highness that our Lord Jesus Christ, nailed hands and feet to the hard wooden cross, turned his divine head to the sky and in that profound silence cried out, 'Eternal Father, peace; forgive those who have offended Thee and have offended me. . . . Discard vengeance and let there be peace and clemency.' I place Your Highness' heart between these passionate words and that divine face so that, wounded by those arrows of love, your heart may burn with divine love, and there be born a flame of charity toward us miserable and unhappy ones which will burn and consume our errors and sins and, phoenix-like, be reborn in a bonfire of incorruptible and immaculate faith, with which we would shed every drop of blood in our veins in the service of Your Highness and your house. . . ."

Girolamo, la Sanseverina's son, also implored the duke's pardon. Along with the young Girolamo da Correggio, as we have said, Girolamo Sanvitale was the only one not to retract his confession. However, he placed moral responsibility for the conspiracy on his mother, on his wife, and especially on "that wretched criminal," his son. Something told him that if last-minute pity were to be born in Ranuccio's heart, he would be its first beneficiary, in consideration of his submissive behavior at the time of the Colorno affair.

On the night of May 18, a group of Jesuits, almost all from outside Parma, received orders to appear in the Rocchetta to inform the prisoners that their death was imminent and to remain with them to the end as their confessors. These priests, who had been chosen from among the most servile and faithful to the Farneses, were all under the orders of Ippolito Cavatorta, the hermit whose letter of congratulations to Ranuccio for discovering the conspiracy has been preserved: "If I were not in the condition in which God put me, then overcome by just passion and righteous anger, I would be there to wash my hands in their blood, hoping to see the name of Judas branded on their hearts."

From a report by Abbot Vittorio Siri, we learn that most of the condemned were tranquil and resigned, savoring their agony drop by drop and praying incessantly. Gianbattista Masi, recalling that he was a poet, wrote his last verses, which are the only ones of his left to us today.

While souls were taken care of in the prison, on the Piazza

Grande other preparations were being made. Against the Palace of Justice was erected a great scaffold, covered with black sheets, that could be seen from every side of the piazza. It reached the height of the palace's first floor, where the windows' parapets were removed to allow the condemned to walk out more easily. On the scaffold were placed the blocks, the axes, the nails, the poles, and all instruments secretly brought from Piacenza to keep Parma in the dark to the last moment. From Piacenza the executioners arrived, along with two squads of horsemen who, added to Ranuccio's regular guard, were placed at the entrances to the piazza. Two hours before dawn the condemned were transported to the Palace of Justice and locked in separate rooms. The record of their exact distribution in the building still exists.

The morning of the nineteenth of May—Saturday, market day—a warm sun was shining on the piazza which was thick with people. All those silent spectators, shivering at the slow tolling of the bell, "rendered," according to a chronicle, "a portrait that was dismal yet awesome." The waiting lasted until noon; then everything happened swiftly. The first to appear on the scaffold was la Sanseverina, dressed all in black, pale, dazed, but still beautiful. At the sight of the block she hesitated, but a monk from San Giovanni who accompanied her whispered something in her ear and she proceeded. The executioner pushed her down. It was a suspenseful and eternal moment, as in a bad dream. She died badly. She had raised her head slightly, and the ax struck her shoulder; the executioner had to use a knife to finish the job. In dying her face was incredulous, like someone unexpectedly wronged. After her came her husband, Orazio Simonetta; then her grandson Gianfrancesco, stripped of all his arrogance, he too incredulous that the end had come for him. Next was Girolamo, who died as badly as his mother, under the blows of the executioner's helper. Then followed Alfonso Sanvitale, Pio Torelli, and Gianbattista

[10]   Margherita Farnese, wife of Vincenzo Gonzaga (later Sister Maura Lucenia). A miniature in the Galleria Nazionale, Parma. PHOTOGRAPH BY VAGHI.

[11] Odoardo I Farnese, fifth Duke of Parma and Piacenza. Artist unknown. Galleria Nazionale, Parma. PHOTOGRAPH BY VAGHI.

[12]   Ranuccio II Farnese, sixth Duke of Parma and Piacenza. Anonymous Tuscan painter of the late 16th century. Ordine Costantiniano di
San Giorgio, Parma. PHOTOGRAPH BY VAGHI.

[13] Francesco Farnese, seventh Duke of Parma and Piacenza. Artist unknown. Ordine Costantiniano di San Giorgio, Parma. PHOTOGRAPH BY TOSI.

Masi. Finally, on a gallows in the middle of the piazza were hanged the priest Giulio da Scurano, Onofrio Martani from Spoleto, Oliviero Olivieri, and Captain Bartolomeo Roverzani. The latter was terribly offended to be excluded from the treatment reserved for the nobility and loudly protested that he wanted to be decapitated, not hanged. They hanged him though, and the crowd witnessed the strange spectacle of a man more concerned with the mode of his death than with death itself.

The show closed with a little incident. Cesare Doli, one of the executioners, on undressing the corpses lifted la Sanseverina's skirt and pinched her bottom with the gesture of a connoisseur. By order of Judge Piozasco, a great moralist, Doli was immediately put in jail for twenty days; he would have stayed longer had not some members of the Congregation of the Charity of Parma interceded for him.

*

The "Great Justice," as it came to be known in Italy, left the people in the duchy terrified and mute, exactly as they had been on that fatal Saturday in May. A contemporary recounted: "Everyone in town is so frightened of displeasing the Prince that no one speaks to anyone, and to feel pity for the executed is almost a crime of *lèse majesté.*"

After the execution, a Jesuit, Father Albrizzi, mounted the blood-splattered scaffold and from that pulpit, decked with heads and contorted faces, he said "a few words, as was customary, to exhort the people to be faithful to their ruler, and to assure them that the crime of those few would in no way diminish His Highness's love for Parma." On the following day, there appeared a proclamation from Ranuccio declaring his wish to practice, in the distribution of the confiscated estates, that generosity which his concern for the public interest had pre-

193

vented him from showing to the criminals, "not wanting even the smallest part to remain in Our hands but to be used for the benefit of everyone." Whereupon the duke ordered that all the creditors of the conspirators be paid, that the widows receive a pension, that one-seventh of the estates go to charity, one-sixth for other uses, and the rest to the state treasury and to the future creation of an order of knights.

A few days after the execution, the town council went before the duke to ask "His Highness to oblige them and destroy the houses of the criminals." At the same time the people of Piacenza decided to erect in the piazza a monument to Ranuccio, for the greater glory of the Farneses and as a token of gratitude for his narrow escape. In order to obtain the duke's consent to the construction of the statue, it became necessary to send more than one ambassador to Parma; but out of modesty Ranuccio continued to decline the honor. Finally, the council of Piacenza thought to assign the task to Doctor Giovan Giorgio Rossi, a man to whom Ranuccio had entrusted the most difficult problems and who had worked so well for him in Padua during the time of the Sanvitale affair. Ranuccio allowed himself to be begged a little longer, and then finally yielded to the advocate's persuasions. To the people of Piacenza he addressed a splendidly hypocritical letter: "We have been informed that you begged Us again, with much insistence, to grant you this favor, which you say would represent for you one of the greatest honors in the world, and that Our refusal would make you desperate and inconsolable. This being so, We could not help but moderate Our firm resolution; for the love We feel for you would not allow Us to inflict upon you any unhappiness or sorrow." So Piacenza got its statue.

Benedetta Pio, la Sanseverina's daughter-in-law, had escaped the massacre of the Sanvitale family, but an impenetrable mystery veils her end. The last record of her is a footnote in the registry of the Rocchetta: "September 17, 1617, Benedetta Pio

Sanvitale will not be sentenced until new orders are issued; another prisoner should be made to keep her company." The fact that she had been excluded from the "Justice" of that memorable Saturday gave rise to the most disparate rumors. Some people said that the queen of France and the Duchess of Parma herself had asked that her life be spared. The more malicious suggested that, because she was rather attractive, Ranuccio wanted her for his bed. Perhaps the real motive was that, as a certain Brother Ippolito da Sassuolo said, "It means something to have a purple hat in Rome, and Marchioness Benedetta was spared because she is the cousin of Cardinal Pio, a man who deserves to be respected and feared."

One other person was not executed: Count Girolamo da Correggio. But in his case documents help to reconstruct the motives for a treatment, different but no less cruel, which Ranuccio reserved for him. The death of Girolamo da Correggio, the only heir of his family, would have opened a delicate problem of succession. One of his castles in the Modena area, the Rocca di Rossena, would have probably passed, by investiture of the emperor, to Cesare d'Este as the legitimate lord of the land on which the castle was situated. To take possession of this fortress halfway between Modena and Parma, strategically important and well constructed, was one of the most secret and pressing desires of Ranuccio, who in the passion for owning things employed that cold light of ingenuity which occasionally illuminated his dark personality. To impound the estate, Ranuccio made certain that Girolamo would neither die nor be released. "It is best not to pardon him, but to keep him in prison; and with time the proper solution will appear," we read in one of the weekly reports the duke sent to his brother. Wishing to live, encouraged by the hope of being spared because of his youth, Girolamo did not hesitate to sign everything the treasurer Riva put under his pen—even an authorization for the duke to administer the fortress of Rossena for all the time he would be absent from it. Cesare d'Este, Duke of Modena, needless to say, was very disappointed, and if he did not turn to force it was only because Ranuccio's maneuver was made legitimate by the owner's signature. Girolamo da Correggio died a natural death in the Rocchetta, but it is difficult to know exactly how much his jailors contributed to the "naturalness" of it. His end was kept secret, so that Ranuccio could continue to collect Rossena's rich revenues and also to conclude the negotiations with the emperor for the definitive possession of the contested castle. Rossena was finally granted to him at the price of sixty thousand florins.

For some time people believed that Girolamo had fled and that Ranuccio had given up pursuing him so as not to worsen the political repercussions of the trial, or perhaps because he feared the reprisals by the powerful Correggio family, which had many important connections. After a while, people stopped talking about Girolamo.

As for the Malaspinas, one, Ferdinando da Liciano, was found mysteriously assassinated in his castle at the beginning of the trial. Another, Gian Vincenzo da Montarese, was tried *in absentia,* and had the incredible courage to surrender on May 13, 1612, confident of being the least guilty among the conspirators. The matter seemed so strange to everyone that to make sense of it many speculated that Montarese had bought mercy by becoming the informer in the conspiracy. He remained in prison until 1618, when he was pardoned on a ransom of fifteen thousand scudi. Widowed and disillusioned with the world, he became a Capuchin monk in Genoa under the name of Father Felice. The third, Giulio Cesare da Madrignano, captain of the guard and an intimate friend of Vincenzo Gonzaga, prudently remained in Mantua, where he limited himself to sending letters to various Italian princes maintaining that the accusation of conspiracy against him was "an outright lie." "I would be ready," he wrote, "to defend myself in Parma if

I were assured of a fair trial." It was a commendable prudence. He never again set foot in Parma, and he died a sad man twenty years later.

The two priests, Don Battista Giglio and Don Gabrio Campanini, were hanged on August 11, 1612, in the piazza, after their clerical privileges had been stripped from them by the bishop in the chapel of the Rocchetta. After two years several servants and grooms who had taken refuge in Mirandola were also apprehended and hanged.

Of the Piacenza aristocrats compromised by the Marchesino's confessions—the Zanardi, the Pozzi, the Caracciolo, the Pavesi, the Anguissola, the Pallavicino, the Oddi, and other families—the omnipotent Bartolomeo Riva succeeded in jailing and executing many, after some time, for crimes extraneous to the conspiracy. It was done in this way because Ranuccio did not wish Piacenza to seem as rebellious as her sister town.

The tragedy left the Sanvitale family with several orphans. Barbara, an illegitimate daughter of Count Simonetta, whom la Sanseverina used to call *la putta del Conte Oratio* [Count Oratio's whore], was seventeen years old when her father was decapitated. In one of the papers referring to the trial we read that "on November 1, 1612, Lady Barbara Simonetta, by order of His Serene Highness, was sent to be boarded in San Girolamo di Piacenza at the cost of two hundred and fifty lire a year." All that is known is that she was still in the convent in 1620.

The only daughter of the Marchesino, Maria, was sent to the convent of Sant'Odorico in Parma, where she later became a nun. Virginia, another of Girolamo Sanvitale's daughters, born in Sala in 1599, was also forced by Ranuccio to enter a nunnery. She chose Santa Chiara in Busseto.

And finally there was Giberto, the third son of Girolamo, the only male left of the Sanvitales. He was a child when the tragedy occurred. Many prominent people, friends of his parents and of his grandparents, would have liked to raise him. In fact he was invited to Florence by the Grand Duke, to Mirandola by Prince Pico, and to Rome by Cardinals Pio and Sforza. To prevent his leaving, Ranuccio decided to keep Giberto in the Rocca di Val di Taro, and to those he assigned to take care of the boy he suggested that, when Giberto come of age, they find him a wife of humble origin. Years later Ranuccio was informed that Giberto was in love with a shepherd's daughter and that there were great expectations he would live a dissipated life. "As Your Highness most prudently suggested to me," wrote Count Anguissola, "to distract him from his studies, I gave him money for gaming." Eager to marry, Giberto asked that the ducal treasury give him an income of four hundred scudi a year, which they were most happy to give him, hoping that he would soon have a family. When, in 1631, he and his two sons died of syphilis, the splendor of the Sanvitales was less than a memory.

In Parma and Piacenza the "Great Justice" was accepted submissively, but outside the duchy it damaged Ranuccio's reputation and provoked violent criticism. Indeed, there was no aspect—public, private, political, legal, administrative, or feudal —under which the trial was not censured. The entire investigation appeared full of absurdities; the supposed plot to divide up the duchy was itself absurd. Allegedly, the land that the Farneses held in the Abruzzi region was to go to the Duke of Modena; Castro and Ronciglione, to a nephew of the pope; Piacenza, to the Duke of Mantua. Parma was to be transformed into an oligarchic republic. Absurd, too, was the supposed plan to ransack the town, to despoil the churches, to violate virgins and nuns, and other crimes worthy of the most barbaric German mercenaries; absurd, because this would have forever alienated the conspirators from the support of the city just conquered. The entire plot was beyond credibility, for no one had ever heard of a plot handled by dozens of people (men and women, aristocrats and commoners, laymen and priests, gentlemen and soldiers—a small army) who, spellbound by a disastrous ambition, organized themselves, sent messages, made and remade plans of action, and inexplicably compromised themselves for almost two years. Some of those close to the duke whispered that Judge Piozasco had confided to a friend that "the conspiracy of Parma had no substance, but that he had to obey orders."

The investigation had implicated several Italian rulers who, seeing their names on the document of accusation, protested energetically. In reparation for their tarnished honor, they demanded that the trial be reviewed by the pope or by some reasonable, objective person who would inform them of the specific charges against each one, to allow them to "defend themselves legally and otherwise." Cesare d'Este, the Prince of Mirandola, and Francesco Gonzaga, son of the late Vincenzo, not only demanded apologies and compensation but spoke of war against Parma. Words were followed by military preparations intended to show the firmness of their intention to fight. Ranuccio, faithful to his policy of compromise, maintained a reserved disdain amid the uproar, punctuating it from time to time with evasive and noncommittal answers. His political instinct told him that, notwithstanding the tension created in Italy by the "Great Justice" and the publicized military preparations, there would not be a war because at that moment everyone had reason to fear it and also because his enemies lacked the passionate determination which alone ensures victory. The controversy, which had engendered widespread anger and tension but also a sense of futility, would resolve itself with time. Italian rulers were no longer intemperate and impulsive men of the Renaissance, ready to put themselves to the test at all times; quite the contrary, though continuously speaking of war, they clearly showed they did not want to run the risk of one.

Exactly as Ranuccio had predicted, time contributed to ease matters. When it became clear that, in case of a conflict, the Farneses would have the help of Spain, while their adversaries would not have that of France, the alliance among Mantua, Modena, and Mirandola went to pieces. Between Modena and Parma the "brawl," as the pope called it, was resolved "without uproar." After an exchange of letters and the intervention of the Duke of Poli, Ranuccio was able to obtain from Cesare d'Este, as a token of reconciliation, the promise that he would ban from Modena Count Alberto da Canossa, one of the conspirators still at large, who was living in Reggio Emilia under Cesare's protection. Anxious, after all, to be in formal if not actually cordial rapport with Ranuccio, Cesare d'Este decided to sacrifice the unsuspecting Canossa to his own desire for peace. On the night of December 9, 1613, the count was summoned before the mayor of Reggio Emilia. Being that "it was such an unusual hour, he was frightened, he was more dead than alive, his voice trembled, and he did not know if he was in this world or the next." They told him he had to leave forever. His angry protests served no purpose. After his departure Ranuccio consented to write to Cesare d'Este a letter of reconciliation in which he also expressed his good will toward the Prince of Mirandola.

In this way the controversy was practically limited to the Farneses and the Gonzagas, who more than the others felt insulted by the trial. Venice, Florence, and Urbino recommended reconciliation, the pope invited them, out of respect for the public good, "to put away their personal animosity." Spain also tried hand and foot to make peace. However, the first act of mediation by the Duke of Savoy failed. A second mediator, the Marquis of Inoyosa, the new governor of Milan, had no better luck. "Either the Duke of Parma gives me the documents of the trial," he said, "or I shall know why." And, in spite of four cases of tapestry woven with gold sent to him from Parma to bribe him, he managed to extract the records of the trial from Ranuccio. These duly arrived in Milan but remained sealed due to the unexpected death of Francesco Gonzaga, who was succeeded by his brother Ferdinando. The thread of the negotiations was not broken, however, and in 1614 the governor of Milan made the following proposition of reconciliation, in his opinion not too humiliating for one and sufficiently agreeable for the other: Ranuccio Farnese would have to declare that, although Duke Vincenzo Gonzaga had been mentioned in the trial, he, Ranuccio, did not consider him an accomplice in the plot.

Ranuccio then made a counterproposal, saying that he was ready to admit that he "was willing" to believe that the Duke of Mantua was not culpable. On this controversial point negotiations once again foundered. The reconciliation was finally brought about by a Capuchin monk, Giacinto, formerly Count Natta di Casal Monferrato, who had given all of himself to the difficult task. It took him years of appeals, trips, patience, and zeal. After many reversals and disillusionments, in 1617 the old dispute at last ended with the exchange of unofficial letters of peace. Ranuccio assured his rival that he was convinced of the innocence of his father and thanked him for having relinquished the protection of Marquis Giulio Cesare Malaspina, in his opinion one of the greatest culprits in the plot (Malaspina's banishment from Mantua had been the first condition for the reconciliation). For his part, Francesco Gonzaga declared himself grateful that the memory of his father had been rehabilitated.

The official peace was made some months later with an exchange of gentlemen from Mantua and Parma, signing the end to the long enmity between the two dynasties.

IX

Odoardo Farnese

Odoardo placed his pudgy little hand over his heart in a solemn gesture, looked gravely at his tutor, Cremona Vicedomini, and said: "I have resolved with all my strength to excel my illustrious ancestors, Duke Ottavio in wisdom, Duke Alessandro in glory, and the duke my father in wealth and peacemaking. . . ." These words expressed exactly Odoardo's sentiments and principles. He repeated them whenever he knew he was being listened to; and each time he was delighted to detect surprise in the eyes of his audience. Such words from the mouth of a boy indeed made an impression. Odoardo was only ten when, at Ranuccio's death, he became the fifth Duke of Parma and Piacenza.

Waiting for Odoardo to come of age, his mother, Margherita Aldobrandini, and his uncle, Cardinal Odoardo Farnese, governed in his place. Almost ten years separated him from his majority, ten years to be filled with knowledge, strength, and wisdom—to measure up to astrological predictions of his exceptional destiny. "From the tail of the Dragon it was discovered that he would make long trips, be victorious abroad, have a large army, many followers, and numerous children. He would be a liberal and splendid prince." Thus fated to glory by the stars, Odoardo believed in his destiny and doggedly worked toward it, barricading himself completely within the ideal as if within a fortress. His every gesture and thought were a preparation for the day when the mantle of glory would descend upon him. Glory was his ineffable torment, a sort of sacred malady. For her he accepted, while still a small child, an extremely rigorous education with an ardor that partly redeemed his haughty, authoritarian, pedantic character. Using the glory to come as a lever, the tutor obtained results in the young duke's education that were praised to the stars by the obsequious courtiers. Odoardo's day was an almost uninterrupted succession of lessons, each, following the Jesuit system, two hours long. When it seemed that the sand clock was running too slowly, and appeals to Odoardo's pride were no longer effective, the tutor had to resort to strange expedients to revive his pupil's interest. "I have persuaded him," he wrote, "not to let the Bad Thing dominate him; and when he asked me what the 'Bad Thing' was, I told him: 'Evil, which is always fighting against Good.'" In Odoardo's case, evil was an ingrown toenail (treated with lemon juice to mitigate the swelling and the rawness) that would make him suffer all of his life, and even on the least painful days it gave him discomfort.

Eager and ready to learn, the young duke gave his teachers much satisfaction. He was barely five when they began to instruct him in "etiquette and deportment." Each time some prominent person visited the city, Odoardo was made to memorize a little speech "of compliments and courtesies," which he studied and repeated until he knew it "well enough not to embarrass the court." To accustom him to speaking in public, they made him practice in the Rocchetta in front of German guards who did not understand the language. At little more than six years of age, Odoardo knew how to read and write and express himself very well indeed. His first letter to Ranuccio reads: "With all my reverent love to Your Highness, to whom I deferentially bow, I offer whatever my ability may produce." The second was a little note of thanks to Count Annibale Diana di Carrara, who had made him the present of a bitch, "ugly but of good character, manageable as a well-trained horse."

Odoardo had little time for recreation, and even that was granted by his uncle only as a reward for good conduct. It only amounted to some walks in the garden, a little hunting outside of the city, some spear-fishing in the streams, some romping with other little aristocrats. They had tournaments, shot toy bows, and had contests of strength. At such times Odoardo forgot his rank and became a child again. But when the court clock struck the end of playtime, he once more became like a serious adult. Waiting for him, books under his arm, was Cremona Vicedomini, the pedagogue, the severe judge of his progress, the inflexible disciplinarian of his negligence. Sometimes, however, Odoardo forgot that he was to be a future hero. "He picked his nose. . . . He was inattentive at Mass. . . . Tonight, in spite of a warning, he left the table right after dinner and sprawled himself over a chair as if food had weakened, not nourished him. . . ." But this happened rarely, and Odoardo was the first to regret his bad behavior—in a flash of realization, he would suddenly stop picking his nose—possessed as he was by that fundamental aspiration to excel in everything. They would say later that he had lived nobly and with constant self-respect. Meanwhile, he was growing up lymphatic, short-legged, large in the seat, prematurely fat. He was more able to give orders than to make himself obeyed, more authoritarian than strong, more arbitrary than flexible. And it was noted that he was free with his hands—which was interpreted as an extraordinary inclination to warfare. He had a sense of his dignity which often degenerated into haughtiness and insolence. One day, when a playmate accidentally brushed by his sister, Odoardo shouted, "Signor Camillo, you are a clod!" and, red with anger, shook his little finger under the culprit's nose, "You have eyes but you don't see what you are doing. If you had knocked down my lady, you would have felt something."

This haughtiness was a thorn in the hearts of his mother and his uncle, who, although adoring him, had a precise, almost depressingly lucid notion of his limitations. Remembering the dark nature of his father, they had hoped he would be very lovable, given to compassion; and to instill in him this virtue they called on a certain Father Leone who tried to teach him, by gentle persuasion, the rules of human behavior and especially the relationship of a lord to his subjects.

On October, 1624, they added to that gentle persuasion the first practical experience: Odoardo was authorized to make his first official visit to Piacenza. The people from Piacenza shouted their hurrahs from their hearts. The young duke comported himself almost exactly as his mother had wished. Dressed in a black suit with flesh-colored stockings and a feathered hat, he dispensed smiles, heard Mass in the cathedral, where Guercino was about to finish the cupola, visited the arsenal, attended a ball, paid homage to the bishop—all with composure and courtesy. It was the dress rehearsal, the test of his princely manner. His subjects always remembered him as he appeared on that day, fat and affected, puffed up with condescension, his lips frozen in a smile without warmth, full of studied dignity. And indeed, his manner that day was to be the model of his future life style.

In Piacenza, which was to become his favorite residence, he especially liked the fortifications whose appearance gave him as much a voluptuous sensation as when he first held a sword in his hands. "I am a soldier now!" he exclaimed, clumsily waving the heavy sword. And, turning to his courtiers, he pronounced what would remain his favorite aphorism: "Princes who die in battle earn a sweet repose, for their tomb is glory. . . ." Expressions and ideas so prematurely bellicose, which would remain with him all his life, disturbed his uncle, a man of good will and common sense who tried to inculcate in his nephew thoughts of peace; for in them only he saw the norms of wisdom and of human equilibrium. Because he knew his nephew to be so rash and impulsive, on his deathbed the cardinal recommended that Odoardo never make decisions without first consulting some prudent advisor. Death spared him from the knowledge that Odoardo never put his recommendations into practice. In fact, when Odoardo grew up, he became more and more convinced that to be born a Farnese was to be born a hero; and more than ever war seemed to him a dutiful adventure to be fronted with that buoyant contempt for life, that sense of honor to which a good soldier responds as a fine horse to the trumpet.

Even before puberty shaded his upper lip, the young duke was given, according to the Spanish custom, private quarters and his own court, with sentinels, halberdiers, a cupbearer, a chaplain, a valet, a surgeon, and two German dwarfs to keep him amused with their Rabelaisian tricks during the few hours of respite from his many intellectual activities. At twelve he excelled in rhetoric and mathematics, wrote little orations in Latin, discussed the military theories of Livy, knew by heart the verses of Ovid and the maxims of Aristotle, and wrote plays on the Nativity. He also studied German and practiced horse riding, the latter "to reduce his fluids and do away with his sluggishness." Andrea Ughi, his dancing master, would have liked him to be a little thinner and more agile; Odoardo acquiesced so as to dance as gracefully as he could—this too, punctiliously, for his attention always was fixed toward the goal he had set for himself: to become a perfect ruler.

*

Odoardo Farnese was one of those aristocratic children raised, for reasons of state, already affianced. Hardly had his umbilical cord been cut when his family began searching for a suitable wife for him. To young Odoardo the thought of that unknown creature who would one day share his life eventually became pleasantly familiar.

Ranuccio had riveted his attention on the family of the Grand Duke of Tuscany, a veritable mine of eligible brides. Four of the eight children of Cosimo II de' Medici and Maria Maddalena of Austria were girls, and one of the Grand Duke's major occupations was to find suitable husbands for them. Ranuccio, who had no preference, wrote to Cosimo: "I wish to offer to Your Highness my son for one of your daughters. I ask not for the first, the second, or the third, but for whomever you choose, and on those terms suitable to you. I beg you to grant my wish, should it be to your taste and interest." To this urbane offer the Grand Duke, equally urbane, replied that he had first to marry off his numerous sisters, but that he did not exclude the possibility of discussing the matter in the future, at the proper time. All these reservations did not mean that Florence had dismissed the Farnese proposal; nor did it mean that Cosimo was any the less concerned for the welfare of his daughters. On the contrary, being the wise ruler that he was, he saw in that marriage the possibility of a profitable reconciliation between the two families hitherto divided by envy, questions of precedence, and various other dissensions.

Cosimo's reluctance to commit himself to the engagement had its origins in the uncertainty and confusion about the lord of Parma himself. The "Great Justice" of 1612 had given Ranuccio a rather sinister reputation; many in Italy maintained that the conspiracy had been nothing more than the fruit of his sick imagination. Besides, his rule was said to be so unbearably brutal, and the atmosphere about him so rigid and heavy that, understandably, before sending a daughter to his house, the Grand Duke felt it was better to think twice. Then, to complicate the situation further, there was the poor deaf-mute Alessandro, Ranuccio's first born, and the other, the restless bastard son, Ottavio. If Odoardo was to get his wife from Florence, the requirement for Parma was—and Ranuccio knew it very well—to declare Alessandro ineligible and substitute Odoardo as the legal heir, to revoke the investiture granted to Ottavio, and above all to make peace with Mantua. And he would have to refine the atmosphere of the court, to *smile*—the only thing, among all the conditions, that Ranuccio was incapable of doing; he nurtured his hypochondria as one does a precious wine.

In 1619 all these difficulties had been resolved, and the marriage negotiations were resumed under different auspices and with renewed hope. After a few months, thanks to the mediation of a monk, an agreement was signed to celebrate the marriage in six years, when Odoardo and Maria Cristina "or any other that might be chosen," would reach the minimum age to consummate the marriage. Ranuccio, it was said, felt the greatest joy of his life at the satisfactory conclusion of this transaction. "If this comes off, it will be a great coup for us," he wrote to the faithful Bartolomeo Riva. He was so eager to see Odoardo married that he imposed no conditions, made no difficulties, and signed the contract without changing a comma. He agreed to the bride's dowry, the composition of the court she would bring to Parma, the invitations to be sent to the various European courts, and the program of public festivities to be celebrated in Florence. To show the Medicis every possible consideration, Ranuccio even consented to Cosimo's request—and God knows what it cost him—to pardon Marquis Giulio Cesare da Madrignano, one of the principal conspirators, according to Ranuccio. Abandoning for the moment his usual parsimony, he even sent to little Maria Cristina precious gifts, among which was an escritoire filled with all kinds of dainty objects.

Ranuccio was not able to enjoy his triumph for very long. Hydropic, suffering from colitis and kidney trouble, he died on the fifth of March, 1622. In the face of death, his ravings, his fears, his obsessions with witches and witchcraft were finally over. What remained to him was the knowledge that he was leaving behind an ordered and peaceful duchy, a full treasury, a government entrusted to a capable regent, and a not-too-bad memory of himself.

Odoardo's wedding took place seven years later, yet Ranuccio's presence was somehow still felt. During those seven years, the young duke lived in his usual manner, his days brightened only by the thoughts of his little Florentine sweetheart. The fact that Maria Cristina had died in childhood and had been promptly replaced by her sister Margherita did not disturb him. Odoardo was too young to make fine distinctions, and the two girls seemed alike to him; and Margherita, made glamorous by distance and expectation, beckoned to him. A special messenger to the court of Tuscany described her minutely in his letters: "I estimate that she is as tall as Your Highness, and she prefers French shoes to flat ones. Her waist is slender and well-formed; she has good features, white skin, and a good complexion. The hair is blondish, and as far as one can see, she has a tendency to plumpness. . . ." The description was followed by a portrait. "I can assure you," wrote the emissary, Bolgarelli, "that the painter has not lied in this portrait; in fact, I am certain that when you compare it to the model you will like the model better, even though I am no great judge of features, complexion, or beauty. . . ."

Despite all these assurances, Margherita was not, as was said of beautiful women, a "sunshine." She had, however, the style of the Medici women, an impeccable education, an amiable disposition, and a goodness which was to win for her the love and devotion of her husband and subjects all of her life. Above all she was gay and carefree, having had the good fortune to come into the world at a time when the Medici family was stable and united as never before. Margherita's parents, her numerous uncles and aunts, brothers and sisters were all extraordinarily amiable and sophisticated. The father, Cosimo II, was an unusually enlightened man; he rehabilitated Galileo Galilei and gave him a villa in Arcetri and the title of Master Mathematician. When paralysis confined him to a chair at only twenty-five, he did not let it crush him, and with a tranquil strength he continued, for the six years he had left to live, to interest himself in art and literature with all the traditional enthusiasm of his clan, and to organize holidays for the people and parties for the nobility at the newly expanded Palazzo Pitti and at his favorite villa, Poggio Imperiale. His most beloved daughter was Margherita, who at eight had started to play the role of the young Farnese's fiancée, daydreaming of her future husband in Parma as he was preparing himself to become a great ruler in order to please her. She trembled with adoration each time the ambassador, showing her Odoardo's portrait, would describe how skillfully he handled the pike in tournaments, or meditated on his Plato or, more childishly, dug holes and built sand fortresses in the garden. To the excitement of this children's idyl was added that of the wedding preparations, for both the Medicis and the Farneses agreed to make a great celebration. While in Florence the servants and courtiers who would accompany the bride were being selected, and the hope chests were being filled, in Parma Ranuccio's widow was ordering for Odoardo "the most beautiful suits, for town and travel, black and colored ones, and formal coats"; she bought drapes and tapestries and bed linen. For herself, although aware of her obesity, she yielded to vanity and ordered gold-spun dresses and sent to Constantinople for pearls and diamonds, which were cheaper there. In the cordial atmosphere that now prevailed between the two cities, the future mothers-in-law carried on a warm exchange of letters, while the little fiancés "shortened the distance by a battery of love letters"—brief notes with real tenderness, despite the epistolary rhetoric already mastered by both.

It was a pity that the serene atmosphere was disturbed by the sudden death of Cardinal Odoardo. He had been the regent for four years and, unlike his brother Ranuccio, he was a man of incomparable good will and humaneness. No one in Parma remembered him ever to have lost his temper—not even when four students were caught masquerading as Jesuits, an order dear to him. Everything was settled by the cardinal's mild admonition that "that habit was unbecoming to them and should be taken off." He liked to be addressed simply as *Cardinal Padrone* [Cardinal Master], dropping all the more magnificent titles which were his due. Ranuccio had kept the people and the courtiers at a distance, but the cardinal drew them to himself. Law under him did not embitter the people but served them. Ranuccio was a maniac on protocol and court etiquette, while the cardinal even dismissed his personal guard of honor. One brother prevented the young aristocrats from traveling outside the duchy, the other urged them to live abroad in order to study and widen their perspectives and to enrich themselves through firsthand experience. The duke interfered everywhere, even in the marital relations of his subjects, and had adulterous wives spied on; the cardinal urged that "women's weakness be understood, so that peace may be kept between married people," as we find in a letter written to Judge Piozasco, whose wife had deserted him and later was returned to him thanks to the diplo-

macy of the cardinal himself. And finally, Ranuccio was dominated by a fear of the supernatural which became overwhelming
at the thought of death; his brother lived fully, never thinking of
death. In sum, the Cardinal Padrone resembled his brother only
in his obesity and in the Farnese passion for owning beautiful
things. Accustomed to his great palace in Rome, to the blue
sky of the Roman countryside, to the ilex groves and the orchards
on the Palatino, the splendid villa of Caprarola, the cardinal
had some difficulty in getting used to the starkness of the Pilotta,
the fogs, the almost metaphysical grayness of the Po Valley.
But he soon became acclimated. He started new art collections,
built and redecorated the palace wherever possible, and, in
particular, he indulged his passion for cultivating flowers. At the
end of a year the ducal gardens had the most beautiful flowers
in the area: red and yellow tulips, Spanish daffodils, asphodels,
anemones, buttercups, and so forth.

It is a matter of dispute whether the cardinal was more
concerned with raising his flowers or cultivating his table. At
any rate, he was the first of the Farneses in whom obesity was
an expression of a *gourmandise* rather than of gluttony. And
what in the cardinal was the measure of his grand style, to the
succeeding generations of Farneses became a matter of greater
gluttony and obesity, leading them to ever-shortening lives. In
his later years the cardinal himself suffered from gout, which
had crippled his right hand, he had the inflamed complexion
of the apoplectic, and his stomach troubled him every few days.
Regardless of all this, he supervised the court kitchen, discussed
the dishes with the cooks, and personally chose the wines and
oils for his well-stocked cellar. Such concern for material pleasures rapidly brought him to its logical end. On February 26,
1636, while watching from a window his nephew at military
drill, he suffered a stroke. He died three days later, leaving
behind the sorrow of those who had enjoyed his brief reign.

*

With the title of Curator and General Administrator, the fat, virtuous widow Margherita became regent. One of her principal concerns was to continue the preparations for Odoardo's wedding which, in view of the enormous expense, among other things required the selling of some land. The following year, after the ceremony of the exchange of the wedding rings, which took place by proxy in Pisa, the preparations multiplied. Parma elected a committee to decorate the town with triumphal arches and selected thirty-six pages to bear the bride's canopy. The master-at-arms, Girolamo Rho, drilled the soldiers for the great parade. At the court, emblems, heralds, and coats of arms were chosen; painters, sculptors, historians, and writers were hired for the occasion. In keeping with the fondness of the time for dramatics, the court organized "pastoral plays, tragedies, comedies and the like, in addition to original ballets and songs in honor of the prince's magnanimity." At last, the huge theater constructed by Ranuccio would have the right material for a proper inauguration.

In the middle of all this excitement, a spark was set off that for a while threatened to destroy the whole project. In Paris, Marie de' Medici, queen mother of France, got the idea that her niece, Margherita de' Medici, should marry her second son, Gaston d'Orléans, who was virtually the heir to the throne of France since his brother Louis XIII was without children. This project had the approval of Richelieu, whose every word was sacrosanct to the queen mother. Thus, certain of Richelieu's approval and most probably guided by him, Marie de' Medici set about, with the ability that only women have in these matters, to engineer the Florentine marriage. Young Margherita then was to marry Gaston. (If necessary, the pope could be influenced to break the contract between Parma and Florence.) As for Odoardo Farnese, since he was still young and did not need heirs immediately, there was nothing wrong if, out of deference to the powerful ruler of France, he relinquished Margherita and contented himself with her younger sister Anna.

This plan, which seemed to Marie de' Medici diplomatically sound, did not take into account one important detail: Odoardo's enormous pride. Odoardo was indeed intolerant of impositions and was now old enough to feel how painfully ridiculous it would be for him if anyone, even one more powerful than himself, should snatch away his bride on the day of the wedding, substituting another girl who was said to have "long and rotten teeth, one shoulder higher than the other, and red-rimmed and drooping eyes." There was also Odoardo's education itself, intended since the cradle to inculcate in him reverence for the Farnese name, which he felt honored to bear and bound to uphold. With these ideals in mind he could not possibly begin his political career with such a clamorous and humiliating renunciation. He decided to ignore the queen's project and, behaving as if nothing had happened, continued the wedding preparations, which were now at their height. He commissioned poetry for the occasion, arranged fairs and banquets, and carefully chose the actors for the comedies and the tragedies, in order to impress the snobbish Florentine guests, who probably thought that in Parma people did not speak as pure an Italian as they. Claudio Achillini, one of the most fashionable poets of the moment, wrote verses in great quantity, which were judged excellent. Only the duchess mother thought them not decent enough, but was put to silence with a dry, "My Lady, we are celebrating a wedding, not a Holy Week." When the time came to decide who should set the poems to music, the prima donna Setimia Ghivizzani petulantly declared she would sing only to the music of Monteverdi. After a proper amount of pleading, Monteverdi agreed to leave Venice just to please the duke and the great singer.

Odoardo savored with complete self-satisfaction each moment of these important days of waiting. To the letters from Florence attempting, because of the pressure of the queen of France, to delay the wedding, he answered in vague terms which ignored the French machinations, but which did so graciously, with impeccable manners and a candor so disarming as to be implacable. Finally, when he felt he had waited long enough, he decided to force the Medicis' hand and wrote to the Grand Duke: "With this messenger I inform Your Highness that I plan to leave here on the twentieth of next month, as we have agreed, and I will be in Florence on the twenty-fourth. I am also informing Cardinals Aldobrandini and Ludovisi of my departure so that they may have sufficient time to be at the wedding and to pay homage, as arranged, at your home, to both Your Highnesses. I cannot wait for the moment when I shall kiss the hands of the Duchess, my bride, and of all Your Highnesses."

With Odoardo about to arrive, the queen of France busy sending messengers, and the pope interfering personally in this delicate matter, the embarrassment in Florence was indescribable. At an emergency meeting of all the Medicis it was decided to send a courier to Parma to stop the duke. The message was delivered to Odoardo at the very moment of his departure, while he was surrounded by his retinue, and his subjects, crowded around the palace, were cheering him farewell. It was a bad moment. Before the eyes of the citizens and his anxious mother, the future hero had a moment of rage, quickly dominated. To those present he seemed merely to stroke his recently grown mustache. "My Serene Lord," blurted out a courtier who was beside him, "if it is necessary, we all have blood to spill in the service of Your Highness!" And he drew his sword, judging the incident as good as a declaration of war.

But Odoardo, though appreciative of the Gongoresque style of his knights, managed to bow in a gesture seemingly humble but in truth most calculated. He continued to behave as if nothing had happened. "Not to make a move," was the order of the day, "to wait and see, and go on as if the contract were still valid." To hold firm, even at the cost of endangering himself, was one of Odoardo's characteristics. "Your Highness's courier found us home," he wrote back to the Grand Duke, "and we shall await further word from you. This postponement has come at the right time, for it enables us better to discuss the arrangements, and gives us more time to prepare ourselves to satisfy Your Highness."

Fortunately the mix-up was resolved without damage to anyone, and the marriage was finally celebrated. What made it possible was Odoardo's almost spiteful vow to resist Paris, the conviction of his rights, the approval of his subjects, the tender, faithful eyes of his beloved ("Margherita won't listen," the Medicis sighed, to the idea that the little hardhead might have become queen of France); but above all it was due to Gaston d'Orléans's aversion to marrying an Italian.

The wedding took place on October 11, 1628, and was the subject of conversation all over Italy for many months. Among fireworks and bell ringing, Odoardo entered a Florence streaming with banners. He met his bride: a romantic, speechless meeting, almost as if they feared, as some of the onlookers later said, "to show themselves too human by expressing their extraordinary happiness." Then came the ceremony in Santa Maria del Fiore, which was decorated in crimson velvet, scintillating with lights, filled with beautiful women and ecclesiastical princes, and an endless throng of noblemen. The crowd pointed out the bride's "long-faced, grave brothers," the knights of Parma and Piacenza: Pallavicino, Anguissola, Sforza, Landi, Soragna, Dal Verme— names important enough to be well known also in Tuscany. The crowd cried with the enthusiasm of simple people intoxicated by the view of the powerful and the privileged. Banquets at the villa of Poggio Imperiale followed, where the Florentine ladies and those from Parma competed with each other in finery and elegance. Then a fight of wild animals was set up in the amphitheater of the Serraglio dei Leoni in the Piazza San Marco. A tournament was produced by Salvatori and designed by Stefanino della Bella, with splendid costumes, superbly drilled horses, and so many lamps as to make the night look like day. Later, forty gentlemen danced in groups led by Lorenzo, Giancarlo, and Mattias de' Medici, the bride's brothers. At last came Margherita's tearful farewell and her departure from Florence, with a retinue of two hundred and a train of carriages, litters, horses, mules, and carts that took two hours to pass through the city.

Under a slow but heavy fall of snow, the wedding party wound its way through the Apennines en route to Parma. According to tradition, wedding parties received the hospitality of the territories through which they traveled. In Bologna, where they were warmly welcomed by the cardinal, they spent two days in making visits, exchanging pleasantries, and admiring fireworks. Whoever was of any importance went to the city walls, with his pages and footmen in new liveries, to salute the bride. In Modena, the old Rinaldo d'Este, after doing the same, caught pneumonia and died four days later. At the border of the Farnese territory, they passed under an arch erected for the occasion. The arch was surmounted by a crowned lily with two stucco branches from which sprung foliage, flowers, wheat, and fruits of every season. It was still snowing when they entered Parma. The night of the arrival, to add to the excitement, there were two earthquake tremors, which were optimistically interpreted as signs of approval from the Farnese earth because the illustrious couple was making love on it for the first time.

On the following day began the second installment of festivities in that atmosphere of intrigue, of amorous license that accompanied the most conservative of weddings. Odoardo strutted about in a suit of embroidered tabby and a flesh-colored hat with white feathers, accompanied by a tired-looking Margherita with dark rings around her eyes. The expectant citizens watched the bride drive from the palace to the cathedral in a carriage which hypnotized their attention: everyone knew it was covered with twenty-five thousand ounces of silver and had taken two years to construct.

The cycle of spectacles, put on in the large wooden theater in one of the palace courtyards, was inaugurated with the *Aminta*, which was not given much attention though, partly because Tasso's work was well known to everyone and partly because the chilled spectators were more occupied in stamping and blowing on their fingers to keep warm than in watching the performance. During the four intermissions a comedy by Claudio Achillini was shown, with music by Monteverdi. This too would have gone unnoticed but for the last scene, in which the combination of mythology and ingenious scenic effects made everyone momentarily forget the temperature. All the theater machinery functioned perfectly; one device made the Sun's chariot sail across the stage, another maneuvered the flight of Fame "directly down to the stage, crossing and circling about —all the time operated by an unseen mechanism." A third, with most impressive effect, opened the abyss of Hell; a fourth cleaved the sky, ushering forward Jove with all the gods; a fifth rocketed the Furies (it was a pity that one could see a piece of the beam which carried them), and the last one parachuted horses and completely armed horsemen who, as soon as they touched the stage, began to play polo. Last in order but first in magnificence was the show of *Mercury and Mars,* which ended in a naumachia for which the Teatro Farnesiano was flooded. "I am not the bravest man in the world," wrote Abbot Folchi, secretary of state under the Grand Duke of

Tuscany. "The whole time I was trembling with fever, as they say, because I was frightened of being in such a huge hall that had to sustain thousands of people in addition to some three feet of water. I had good reason to fear, because yesterday the engineers themselves were worried. . . ."

Fortunately everything went well. Sea monsters, spouting water from their ears and noses and carrying the performers on their backs, sailed across this miniature sea. There followed two floating islands, carrying Galatea with her train of nymphs. At her invitation, Mercury and Mars and all the horsemen stepped onto the islands, which were then joined together to form a platform on which the battle began. Shortly after, the stage-sky opened revealing the gods of Olympus arranged in a semicircle around Jove. At that point the council of the gods advanced to the foot of the stage. When the heavenly choir ceased singing, Jove proceeded to reconcile Mercury and Mars, invoking Peace and casting the Furies into the sea below.

With this, the spectacular ended and so too the festivities. The guests left. The newlyweds retired. Everything had been beautiful and majestic. The reign of the fifth Duke of Parma was beginning.

X

Skirmishes, Obesity, and Glory

In those years, most of Italy had been crushed under the
weight of a dying Spain and had long since ceased to have a
voice in European affairs; even the independent states had a
limited role on the international scene.

Venice, despite tenacious resistance, was in her twilight; yet,
even on the eve of her collapse, her political system was still
an object of admiration. Her eastern empire was crumbling, and
she contented herself with her possessions on the mainland,
maintaining good relations with everyone—including the Turks
—and avoiding political adventurousness.

Genoa, like Venice, had been badly damaged by the shift of
trade from the Mediterranean to the Atlantic and had resigned
herself to her own decline. Of all her possessions, only Corsica
remained—a liability more than an asset because of the primitive
condition of the island and the resistance of the inhabitants.

In Florence ruled Ferdinando II de' Medici, Odoardo
Farnese's brother-in-law. A gentle, well-educated young man,
he was most "diligently watched over," that is to say, dominated,
by his mother Maria Maddalena and his grandmother Maria

Cristina, two bigots, zealous guardians of protocol. Thanks to them, Florence had become more clerical than the Papal States, and the cloister of Santa Croce, which had once seen the frolics of Lorenzo and Giuliano de' Medici, had now become the most fearsome place in town, the headquarters of the Inquisition. Most of the territory of Tuscany was now owned by monastic orders and, as such, was exempt from taxation. Florence crawled with Jesuits who controlled the law courts and all public offices. The censors of the Holy Office had their ears pricked to the slightest irreverence. The general ineptitude of the bureaucracy, the misery, the spreading corruption, the massive ignorance of the clergy, the pompous vacuity of the grand ducal court, all had contributed to the downfall of the Medicis. Still, Ferdinando II had the respect of his subjects, who appreciated his generosity, his gentle manners, and the serenity, the philosophical calm he showed in face of the most difficult problems. His version of Stoicism, which was essentially a fear of damaging his health and shortening his life, provided the rationale for progressively alienating himself from the concerns of government.

Rome breathed a quite different atmosphere. Pope Urban VIII had been reigning for six years. He was young, talented in literature, a master of political intrigue, and concerned with maintaining neutrality and dealing with "the storms of the *raisons d'état*" he felt were liable to blow in the calmest times. Castel Sant'Angelo was fortified with new bastions and stocked with weapons and supplies as though the enemy were already at the gates. The harbor installations in Civitavecchia were completely renovated. A huge arsenal was built in Tivoli; and near Bologna, at the border of the Papal States, the fortress of Castel Franco was constructed. In Rome, the indefatigable pope raised troops, had weapons forged, and acquired horses for the cavalry. Unfortunately, he gave order to melt down some of the most beautiful bronzes of antiquity for his artillery. These

measures, born of pure prudence, had as their goal the maintenance of papal prestige as a secular power, the better to earn
respect for his neutrality. Military violence, ideological crusades,
and repressions were not in the style of Urban VIII. He was
a Florentine skeptic and rationalist who rejected fanaticism in
any guise and shunned coercive measures even in the fight
against the Protestants. The struggles Urban loved most were
the cultural ones, those of architecture, of beauty. He was young
Bellini's enthusiastic patron, and under him Rome was transformed into a fantasy of architecture and statuary. His "secu-
larism" was profoundly disapproved of in many European
countries, where the princes would have much preferred a pope
in the style of Gregory XV or of Paul V, one who would devote
his energy to the Counter Reformation. But Urban was unconcerned with criticism and, faithful to the idea of diplomacy
and the effectiveness of reason, he continued to battle for the
triumph of the Church by means other than warfare.

Warfare, on the other hand, was Charles Emmanuel of
Savoy's very reason for existence. Ambassadors said of him that
"he was so driven to gain more power for his state that he
scarcely administered what he already possessed." The war he
initiated to acquire Saluzzo, Dauphiné, and a part of Provence
had earned him the unflattering nickname of *ladrone savoiardo*
[Savoyard robber]. Yet, Italian rulers were openly envious of
him for being the only one among them to have the nerve to
ignore Spanish power and to exploit all the possibilities of under-
mining the authority of the king of France.

In reality, the expansionistic exploits of Charles Emmanuel
were minor things in comparison with the bloody conflicts that
seemed to have become the norm in the lugubrious, sumptuous
Europe of the early seventeenth century. Born from the split
between Catholics and Protestants, worsened by the conflict between the Hapsburgs and the autonomous German states and
by the rivalry between the Austrian and the French monarchy,

the Thirty Years' War, then at its height, flared up along the Rhine and coasts of the Baltic Sea, in the Alps, in the plains of Denmark, in the Bohemian forests, in the outskirts of Vienna, and in a hundred other places. Its ramifications extended to all the major countries of the continent. It was a war of gallows, of fanaticism, of refugees and victims of the plague, a war which involved civilians as well as professional soldiers. Europe was cut in half like a great ripped cloth, and the rent went through every country, every town, every house. Hordes of worn-out and hungry mercenaries, indifferent to everything but the prospect of salary and loot, wandered through a Germany that had been systematically devastated by Spaniards and Frenchmen, by the troops of Wallenstein and Mansfield and by those of Tilly and Gustavus Adolphus.

Italy, as usual, paid the price of the war. Along her roads, cluttered with carriages and mules, swarmed endless columns of men of every nation. Corsicans, Neapolitans, Dalmatians, Spaniards, Albanians—dirty, with tattered hats, their pants in rags, their boots flopping over the knees—all headed north, where they were destined to become just more cannon fodder.

✳

Odoardo Farnese dreamed of assuming an important role in the disastrous present and the bleak future of this turbulent Europe. But for the moment his attention was distracted by other events. In 1628 the succession to the duchy of Mantua, opened by the death of the last Gonzaga, had provoked bloodshed and rivalry in Italy too. Backed by Richelieu, the most likely heir was Charles from the collateral branch of Nevers. To contest his claims, Spain and the emperor had entered the lists, and so, too, Charles Emmanuel of Savoy who, profiting as usual from the rivalry of others, had this time set his heart on a section of Montferrat.

Odoardo, recently enthroned and perhaps still under the influence of his uncle and mother, both great exponents of neutrality, unwillingly kept himself apart from this conflict that culminated in the tragic sack of Mantua by the imperial lansquenets. An outbreak of the plague also served to dissuade him from thinking of war. To drive away this pestilence, the Bishop of Parma ordered the celebration of 6166 Masses, in honor of the number of lashes suffered by Christ; and he himself, followed by barefooted altar boys, walked through the town dragging his vestments and carrying a large cross. People begged God for mercy and pardon for their sins; they fasted, followed processions, sang litanies, attended High Masses, and built altars on the crossroads. Taverns were closed, markets were shut down, the gates of the city barred. No one could enter the town without proof of his good health. The duke repeatedly ordered that the streets be cleaned and the debris removed. Yet the plague, "swellings in the groin and in the glands, and other maladies that God keep us from," spread rapidly, and at the end of the year had swept away a third of the duchy's population, emptying towns and devastating the countryside. Bodies and carcasses floated in the rivers; the priests had to abandon the churches because of the stench from the heaps of dead bodies.

Odoardo had taken refuge in Cortemaggiore. While waiting for the plague to subside, he occupied himself with thoughts of how he would attain sufficient early glory to distinguish himself from "that bunch of Italian princes," as Charles Emmanuel used to call them deprecatively, being the only prince who *had* distinguished himself. The memory of the past, an awareness of the present, and anxiety for the future, made Odoardo believe that France was the only means by which to vindicate the humiliation inflicted by Spain on his grandfather Alessandro and his father Ranuccio. Such a solution also would allow him at the same time to test his military and political talents and to extend the duchy, an old family dream.

During that time he chose as his personal secretary a nobleman from Provence, Jacopo Gaufrido, his former teacher of French. Once in office, Gaufrido lost no time in encouraging the young lord's new Hispanophobia and in feeding him ideas about the necessity of liberating Italy. The advice of this gray eminence very shortly bore fruit. Odoardo's ambitions took shape and multiplied; already enamored of everything French and burning with dreams of glory, he joined an anti-Spanish league with which Richelieu intended to keep the Spanish forces in Italy occupied. This initiative was Odoardo's debut on the political scene and marked the beginning of fourteen years of futile military show. For almost fifteen years the duke was to act out literally all of Machiavelli's suggestions on how the prince should go about "acquiring territory," yet his efforts led him nowhere.

The plague was scarcely over when Odoardo began to recruit soldiers, clean up the barracks, stock up provisions, restore fortifications. He also found time to entertain Monsieur de Crequi, marshal of France, the most famous *condottiere* of the time, who had come from Paris to make the final agreements with the Italian rulers about the anti-Spanish league. To Odoardo he brought assurance of the unconditional friendship of the king of France and of the esteem in which the king held his valor and his family.

A great psychologist, Richelieu had understood that to manipulate the young Farnese it was enough to tickle his craving for glory; and Crequi knew how to do this so well that Odoardo, now completely possessed by the thought of war and with his fantasy running far ahead of the facts, imagined that he already had the state of Milan in his hands. In a moment of euphoria, he had a coin struck picturing an extended arm—his—holding

a sword, bearing the motto: "I have burned the scabbard."
The hour of emancipation from Spanish tutelage had come.
With his eyes turned to glory as an eagle's to the sun, Odoardo
did not suspect that he was on the verge of ruining the duchy
nor did he realize how much it would cost to maintain an
army. With great casualness he went into debt with merchants
and bankers. The ducal treasury was spent; the accounts of the
time record only recruiting of soldiers, gathering of ammunition
and horses, new taxes, construction of fortifications, maneuvers.

Almost with relief we read of some celebrations for the birth
of Odoardo's son, the first of a long series of children that the
Duchess Margherita would bring into the world every two years.
Another peaceful diversion was the arrival of the king of
Ethiopia's brother, a handsome young Moor, baptized in Rome,
who was touring Europe telling everyone that he had left his
country with forty camels laden with gold; these, without ever
appearing, were enough to ensure him a warm reception everywhere. Naturally, not to lose face, the Farnese court too had
to give him a cordial welcome, with feasts, ceremonies, and
military parades. But once the exotic interlude was over, the
noise of war sounded more loudly than ever. Toward the end
of winter the rivers unexpectedly froze, putting the mills out of
commission. In Piacenza, where the troops were stationed, all
the citizens, including the nuns, were ordered to use up their
stocks of flour to bake bread for the troops, and foreigners were
asked to leave the town so as not to deprive the citizens of
their precious bread. When warm weather returned, it became
necessary to redouble the military preparations, and Odoardo
forced the farmers to leave their fields to work on the fortifications and to guard the bridges.

Finally the anti-Spanish league—comprising France, Piedmont, Mantua, and Parma—was ready to act. Marshal de
Crequi, the military commander, gave the order to proceed and
the word "war" began to have a meaning. One clear summer

morning, Odoardo, his eyes shining with emotion and his head
filled with reckless and glorious projects, ordered the advance.
Among the fluttering of pennons, the laments of the women, and
the blessing of the bishop, there marched through Piacenza the
regiments of foot soldiers—five thousand men wearing green and
yellow coats—the harquebusers, the cavalry made up of aristocrats from the best families, the wagons with ammunitions and
supplies, and lastly the wretched little artillery: four cannons.
The long column left town from Porta Borghetto, marching
under the broiling July sun toward Lomellina, to besiege Valenza,
a hamlet on the Po. Odoardo's first military days were full, easy,
happy. Two of his four cannons were sufficient to have towns
and villages capitulate to him; towns such as Stradella and
Voghera flung open their gates. Near Ponte Curone there was
"a little skirmish" with no loss of life, and in Parma and
Piacenza this was celebrated as a great victory. In August, at
the end of an almost triumphal march through the gentle Lombardian countryside, which lay yellow and green in the ripe-
ness of high summer, the young Farnese joined the French and
Piedmontese troops; "his spirits redoubled," he deployed his
troops by the walls of Valenza. The strategy of the siege had
been studied in every detail, the areas of combat drawn up and
wisely distributed. Yet it was not long before Odoardo tasted the
bitterness of failure and had to admit to himself that he had
been unable to give to his venture that impetus which should
have marked the beginning of his career in glory.

If the siege of Valenza had stabilized itself almost immediately
into a tedious routine, it must be said that the fault was not
entirely Odoardo's. The forces of the besieged city made successful sorties, engaged in skirmishes, and in all were more capable
than the besiegers. In the camp of the allies, on the contrary,
every good occasion was wasted because of discord, jealousy,
and the laziness of the various captains. Marshal de Crequi had
become abusive and lorded it over Odoardo—a manner quite

different from his earlier French *politesse*. And when Odoardo, hypersensitive to bad manners, complained to Cardinal Richelieu, the situation grew even worse because, as a consequence, the terrible Crequi had now begun to hate the young Farnese. For spite he haggled over everything, cut Odoardo's supplies, and vexed him in a thousand ways. Odoardo's hungry and discontented troops deserted him "like quails in August." Only a loyal few remained with him in the end. At the first sign of bad weather, when the first gray mists hung over the river and the fields turned into vast quagmires, when mud invaded the tents and an icy chill penetrated the cuirasses, when the ever-thickening fogs enveloped the stubborn little town, the siege was ingloriously lifted.

In late fall, after a short rest in Montferrat, Odoardo, with what was left of his army, turned homeward. Before Christmas he was back in town fatter than ever, with his outsized scabbard clinking against his thigh. Odoardo was in bad humor but not crushed; his was the attitude of a hero betrayed by circumstance and his bearing was more regal than ever—regal enough to prevent his subjects and ministers from asking about that expensive, futile venture.

Odoardo's failure, though a dramatically powerful lesson, had dimmed neither his faith in Glory nor his self-confidence. Remaining in Piacenza only for the baptism of his second son, he once more prepared himself to act—this time with redoubled efforts on the diplomatic front, to compensate for his forced military inactivity. In the middle of the new year, with a retinue of ten knights, among whom were the loyal Gaufrido and Fabio Scotti, he left for Paris, where he intended to speak personally to Louis XIII about Crequi's haughtiness and to beg him to protect the Farnese state, which, after the unsuccessful military debut of the league, he feared was in danger of Spanish reprisals. The trip, feeding his need to feel constantly in the stream of history, gave Odoardo some great satisfaction; he himself considered it a masterpiece of diplomacy. He was flattered, reverenced, and listened to; for eleven days Paris spoke of him, remarking on his dignity and pride and commenting that, although Italian, he was unusually chaste and unreceptive to the great seductiveness of the French court. Those who had said he would not sleep alone one single night lost face; none of the Parisian ladies who would gladly have welcomed him in their curtained beds could boast of his attentions. The king gave him a cordial reception, presented him with a necklace of precious stones, distributed diamonds to the men of his retinue and even to his dwarf. But above all the king made him great promises. After a week of talks and agreements and assurances, Odoardo started his journey home, unaware of what was waiting for him there.

During his absence, the Spaniards stationed in Milan had again raided the Farnese territory, sometimes venturing close enough to Piacenza for them to be seen from the town's bastions. In the general panic, the townspeople frantically threw up forts, ramparts, and walls. They dug trenches, filled moats with water, prayed in church, and generally behaved as though the town were about to be attacked. To add to the problem, the French garrison left behind by Odoardo behaved with unexpected brutality. They treated the citizens of the duchy more as inferiors than as their allies and were always ready to shout insults, to draw a sword, to provoke riots. Every day there was some new violence.

Meanwhile, there was no news from Odoardo; his return was despaired of. No one imagined that, having left with the ambition of invading other states, he was at the moment finding it difficult to return to his own. In fact he was forced, to avoid the risk of running into enemy patrols and in order to hide his tracks from the Spaniards who were following him, to sail from Nice, disembark at La Spezia, cross the Apennines and return to Parma almost secretly, like a criminal—he who so much loved triumphal entries. It was the first and only time that his subjects felt affection for their duke; some of them perhaps understood that his futile efforts were somehow pre-destined and that his failure made of him a bitter man and, ultimately, one to be pitied. But their sympathy was short-lived. Odoardo himself, understanding that a pitied ruler is a humili-ated ruler, dispelled it with a decisive gesture. With his usual expression of aloofness and haughtiness he continued toward Piacenza, where things were quickly falling apart. The Span-iards were practically at the gates, and Piacenza was anxiously waiting for French reinforcements and for the money promised by Louis XIII. But when they arrived the men were so few and the money so meager that the citizens were on the verge of despair. Food was running out, and the duke's table itself could only afford one calf a week. The bells rang only to announce bad news. More and more soldiers deserted, lured by the Span-ish promise of one scudo and a passport to go wherever one pleased.

Fortunately, just before the catastrophe, through the medi-ation of the pope and the Grand Duke of Tuscany, peace negotiations were begun. The league was inclined to end the senseless war; but Odoardo, incapable of learning his lesson, presented obstacles, sending the mediators aimlessly back and forth between Parma and Milan. He did not yield until he was almost overcome by difficulties, until hunger had people eating "things more fit for animals than humans," until his table no longer had its one calf a week, until his mother and his pregnant wife fell on their knees before him. Only then did Odoardo sign the peace treaty, which was, to tell the truth, very lenient considering the circumstances and the state of the Farneses' affairs. Odoardo had to swear to return to his old allegiance to the king of Spain, to dismiss the French troops, and, in the future, not to enlist in any alliance against the Hapsburgs. His rendezvous with glory had to be postponed for another occasion.

*

In Parma and Piacenza the year 1639 began with religious ceremonies *ad petendam serenitatem* [to beg for peace]. New troubles were at hand, however, and this time the duke did not have to search them out, for circumstances anticipated him with extraordinary rapidity. There was between Odoardo and disaster a constant, almost affectionate rapport.

As has been observed, Pope Urban VIII was intellectual, prudent, and little inclined to violence even for the sake of the Counter Reformation, which for Urban represented mainly an attempt to re-establish Christian unity through the miracle of art. His interest in art has been thought a counterstatement to the austerity of the heretics, their bare churches, their severe and introspective cult. Under Urban, Rome had become theatrical and monumental, populated by statues of marble and travertine, by obelisks and fountains, and by mythological gods. Fascinated by this fabulous show and conquered by the marvelous unity the Church offered to arts and letters, many foreign Protestants returned to the Church's fold. The most illustrious and representative of them was Christina of Sweden.

Urban would have remained faithful to his policy of peace and neutrality had it not been for his three greedy young nephews from the venerable but impoverished Barberini family. For the sake of Antonio, Francesco, and Taddeo Barberini, Urban revived the grand tradition of papal nepotism. He advanced them in all possible ways, made them cardinals, showered them with titles and honors. He never reached the extremes of Pope Paul, who had separated Parma and Piacenza

from the Papal States, but he allowed his nephews to covet the
small duchy of Castro and Ronciglione near Rome under the
pretext of guarding the interests of some creditors of the Duke
of Parma, to whom the duchy had belonged for over a century.
Pope Urban felt favorably inclined to this project because of
the precedent set by Pope Clement VIII who, forty years earlier, had annexed the duchy of Ferrara without firing a shot,
a maneuver for which Machiavelli and Guicciardini would have
given him their praise.

Sensing trouble, Odoardo went to Rome in November, 1639
—"for purely economic reasons," as he explained to his ambassador in that city. The pope, who remembered the duke as
a child-poet, precociously arrogant and well-read, welcomed
him graciously and gave many receptions in his honor; and the
Barberini cardinals too gave splendid banquets. After a few days,
however, the animosity latent beneath the studied formality
burst forth, and a crisis suddenly arose over a question of precedence, a delicate and important matter to the seventeenth-
century aristocracy. Precedence usually had to do with the
priority of salutations, and when there was good will the
problem resolved itself with the agreement to bow simultaneously
or to enter a door together or to meet exactly halfway across
a room. Unfortunately, between the Barberinis and the Farnese
there was absolutely no good will. Don Taddeo Barberini, pre-
fect of Rome, claimed he was entitled to have precedence
over Odoardo, and Odoardo decidedly believed he was not in
that inferior position and insisted that this matter not be pressed,
for it angered him. For the peace of all concerned, the Roman
chancellery suggested that Don Taddeo should stay out of
Rome for the duration of Odoardo's visit. Instead, Don Taddeo
stubbornly remained, and Odoardo retaliated by not going to
pay homage to Taddeo's wife, Donna Anna. This lady, "ravenous for this homage," had invited several Roman noblewomen
for the occasion, and when her social triumph went up in smoke

she almost fainted with chagrin. At this point, Don Taddeo's brother Antonio entered the scene. He visited the Duke of Parma but was extremely cool to him and omitted the usual courtesies. Far from being overwhelmed, Odoardo re-established the equilibrium by promptly returning the visit and turning his back to Antonio at the crucial moment of the departure. This seesaw could have continued indefinitely if Odoardo, "desirous to be spoken about" and exalted by the idea of showing the world that he did not lack the spirit to tweak the Barberinis' noses on their own ground, had not one morning entered the pope's residence accompanied by his armed knights (a scandalous action never done before). Once admitted to the papal presence, he came right to the point, complaining bitterly against the Barberinis. Probably he exaggerated somewhat, for a chronicler tells us that on that day Urban VIII, under the barrage of Odoardo's angry words, could not restrain his tears; his sensibility could not bear to have his beloved nephews badly treated, not even with words.

Odoardo indeed was very proud of having provoked the old man's tears. He made a magnificently stylized bow, the right foot in front and slightly extended, while sweeping the air with his plumed hat. In the midst of the general astonishment, he left for Parma, after first having sent soldiers to Castro, which was most inadequately fortified and practically defenseless. It was beautiful to return home preceded by the rumors of his Roman exploits, to return to Parma saluted by firecrackers and artillery, and to make an entrance as dignified as the last had been pathetic. It was beautiful to come back to his sweet mother, his children, his dear Margherita who was once again pregnant. It was satisfying to show himself in all his majesty and splendor. To celebrate the birth of his seventh son, he organized a tournament that cost a hundred thousand scudi and left the people breathless with admiration. It was delightful to hear people say that Duke Odoardo was so magnificent that he could afford to spend such a sum out of mere caprice.

It was beautiful and satisfying. And it was brief. Hearing that the enraged Barberini nephews were trying to find ways of acquiring the Farnese estates in the Latium region, Odoardo's indomitable instinct for war was reawakened. Thus began that futile war of Castro that cost more money than blood and brought honor to no one. To dissuade Odoardo from making war preparations, the pope showered him with warnings and admonitions, culminating in the threat to excommunicate him. Examples from the past had taught His Holiness that the threat of excommunication was made more potent if backed up by an army. This time, however, Odoardo, who usually was exemplary in matters of religion, disregarded the ecclesiastical censure and the intimidations and continued to raise troops, well convinced that the pope, always a mediator for peace, would never cause a war in Italy the consequences of which were uncertain. This conviction proved unfounded. When he was told that Castro had been occupied by the pope's troops, Odoardo refused at first to believe it; then, stunned with shock, he remained silent for hours, mumbling from time to time, "My Castro, my Castro . . ." with a feeble whining voice. At first his family and the court were concerned for him, but then, when the usual euphoria at the smell of war—as yet undeclared but imminent—came over him, they knew the crisis was over.

To support Odoardo's conviction that the moment had come to give vent to his resentment against the pope's family was the fact that among the Italian rulers there was a mounting anger and protest against the ambitions and provocations of the Barberinis. Fearful that one day the Barberinis' aggressiveness might threaten territories other than the Farneses', Venice, Modena, Florence, and the ministers of the king of France took Odoardo's side. In 1642, after many unsuccessful attempts to solve the matter diplomatically to the satisfaction of both the Farnese and the Holy See, they decided to form a league.

The interlude of peace had ended, and it was again time to think of war. Piacenza once more found itself at the center of ferment. The citizens unquestioningly consented to contribute both blood and money and once again resigned themselves. They told themselves that no sooner had one trouble ended than a worse one would develop. Artisans, laborers, peasants were put to polishing muskets and culverins, to building and repairing quarters for the cavalry and the soldiers. The indefatigable duke sped from one point of the city to another, hardly slowed down by his obesity. He reviewed troops, chose officers, inspected forts. He organized the buying up of hay, beans, and wood, the gathering of fodder and straw for the cavalry, and had the walls and towers reinforced, roads built, trenches dug. To raise money he went so far as to pawn the family jewels. Meanwhile he talked and talked to his court, his natural eloquence inspired by his passion for war, explaining that this campaign had been predestined by fate. He was so happy in fact that one may suspect he was almost grateful to the Barberinis, who after all had given him a chance to become involved in a new adventure.

The papal excommunication, proclaimed with awesome solemnity at the beginning of 1642, scarcely dampened this enthusiasm. That is not to say that the anathema made Odoardo happy; had he died then, he would be buried in unhallowed soil and gone, as he believed, straight to hell. Besides, he knew that in all probability an interdict would soon follow, which would disturb the peace of mind of many of his subjects. To soften the blow, he ordered all the nonresident clergy to leave the duchy immediately. He had to suffer the humiliation of seeing his orders carried out not only by the foreign clergy but by many local priests as well. Fortunately he obtained the promise from the remaining clergy that, if the interdict was indeed proclaimed, they would continue to officiate.

The formation of the league began to have good results. The Barberinis, informed by their spies of the disposition and strength of their adversaries, grew better disposed to negotiate, and the league, understanding this, halted any direct action for the moment, intending to use time as the most effective weapon in their arsenal. Only Odoardo protested, because his military spirit could not bear inactivity and also because of the problem of maintaining a large army on the Farnese territory, or that, on the other hand, of dismissing them without losing face. Therefore, toward the end of the summer, he decided, amid the protests of his confederates, to take his own lead. On September 10, 1642, he left Parma at the head of three thousand men. Perfectly happy, Odoardo embraced his wife, mother, and children, mounted his horse, and rode off.

The start of this new war was such as to justify Odoardo's optimism. With a march that had all of Europe watching in suspense, Odoardo's army passed beyond Bologna; at the border of Romagna the very sight of the ducal forces put the pope's soldiers to flight. He passed through Imola and Faenza, entered Forlì without meeting resistance, reached the Apennines, and set up camp by Lake Trasimeno. In October, he arrived in Acquapendente almost unmolested.

In Rome the atmosphere was reminiscent of the sack of 1527. As Clement VII had done, Urban VIII took refuge in Castel Sant'Angelo. The Romans were near panic, and "couldn't understand where their troops had disappeared to, and the troops didn't know where Don Taddeo went, and Don Taddeo didn't know where his courage had gone." At any moment they expected the Farnese troops to break into the city and loot it, as Charles V's mercenaries had done a century before.

It did not happen, though Rome had never before been so easy and certain a prey. Odoardo did not take Rome because, at the crucial moment, he lacked the insight, that combination of wit and intuition, which makes the great general. He was frightened, and perhaps he preferred to procrastinate; perhaps the great city, seen from afar secure within its walls, put him in awe. The fact is that he let valuable time pass, enough time to allow the Barberinis to catch their breath and find their courage. By the end of October the brief enchantment that had made Odoardo appear for a moment to be a new Alessandro Farnese, was irrevocably dispelled. He was left with an army weakened by desertion and assumed the melancholic aspect of a man who had lost his chance. In November, the fodder for the horses was depleted, and Odoardo rushed back to Parma in order to benefit from the triumph his subjects were preparing for him while it still meant something.

The winter was long, cold, and uneventful. Before it was over, Odoardo had put into operation a highly extravagant plan: to send five hundred foot soldiers across Lunigiana to the Tyrrhenian coasts, where they would sail from Sestri on rented French tartans, disembark farther south on the coasts of Latium, march to the interior, and take Castro by surprise. Confident in the success of "such a beautiful maneuver," Odoardo waited, trembling at the arrival of every messenger. At the end of February one arrived with the news that the little flotilla had been shipwrecked after a fierce storm; the few survivors had repaired to Portofino and disbanded, carefully avoiding Farnese territory. It was surprise enough that Marquis Labeuf (Lubuffo, as he was called in Italy), who had commanded the expedition together with Odoardo Scotti, had returned to Piacenza. Once more the duke gave way to despondency, his inflated enthusiasm collapsed like a sail when the wind falls off.

Taking account of the events of that year Odoardo found that it added up to lost hopes and aspirations and bitter blows to his pride. Everything had been taken from him but the conviction, still deep, that he was destined to do something great. Because of this he felt that, instead of resigning himself to that year of humiliation, he again should take action—especially since the Barberinis, heartened by his failure, had raised a new army and renewed the idea of punishing the haughtiness of the fat provincial who had thought he could humiliate them in Rome, in their own house, in the shadow of the papal throne.

"I am resolved to move because, by God, I do not know if I can remain in my territory any longer and, confidentially, I do not know how I have been able to manage this long. I have neither supplies nor money. I am like the wolf who must leave the forest because of hunger." With these words Odoardo informed the Duke of Modena that he had made a desperate but successful attack on Bondeno, a rich estate in Ferrara territory guarded by papal troops. "We marched the whole day yesterday and arrived at Bondeno at four o'clock. We made a sudden attack, which was so well and energetically done by my men that we overran the enemy fortifications, put them to flight, and I was left master of the place." Everything went well. War once more was a beautiful thing; Odoardo felt at home in it, like an oyster in its shell. "Long live the Duke of Parma," shouted his soldiers happily. "It's a land of Cockaigne here. May God let it always be this way, with great slaughter of hens and geese, without ever firing a single shot!"

That victory paid back Odoardo for his most bitter moments and exhilarated the soldiers. The news reached Parma and Piacenza giving his exhausted and troubled subjects the thrill of patriotism and the pride of having remained faithful to the Farnese family. The two Margheritas fell on their knees and thanked heaven, and ordered that in all the convents of the duchy the nuns exhaust themselves in prayer, seven days a week, in the hope of obtaining from the Almighty still greater favors.

This time, however, divine favor was difficult to obtain, and events were again taking a bad turn. The allies were tired, sluggish, bored. Odoardo's eagerness and new provocations by the Barberinis, whose troops were spread out ready for battle in the heart of Italy, were required to rouse the league to action. Even Venice, usually so accommodating and peace-loving, began to be suspicious of certain fortifications being constructed by the papal troops near her borders. The Vene-tian senate, famous for its moderation, decided that the pope's nephews had gone too far in trying everyone's patience and needed to be stopped before they made new and serious trouble. Throughout the spring, the various members of the league spoke of nothing but the Barberinis. At last, the complaints reached such a pitch that on May 26 the league, which had been organizing for purposes of defense, took the offensive.

It was all talk. In fact the war, the real one, commenced in early summer, presently stabilized itself into a monotonous see-saw of victories and defeats, all of them indecisive. With a tiny army, as ineffective as it was picturesque, the Duke of Modena fought tiredly in Polesine, sometimes crossing the border in the district of Bologna, while the Grand Duke of Tuscany held the enemy at bay near Perugia and Castiglione del Lago. The battle reports were often contradictory and confused.

As for Odoardo, he remained in Bondeno, proud and happy not to have to worry about supplies, for his soldiers finally could stuff themselves in that rich corner of the earth. Bondeno was a cozy little place in which to put down roots—at least until it was possible to trade it for Castro, the ancient cradle of the Farnese family. It was a pity, and incongruous with the image of a great *condottiere* that, after having made such a brilliant entrance, Odoardo had to leave Bondeno some months later because of a catarrh. He would have given anything to return to Piacenza immobilized by a gunshot wound instead of being wrapped up in woolen shawls. This time, by his request, there was to be no triumphal welcome. But while he was at home the pope and the allies began peace negotiations. Naturally Odoardo opposed them, closing his ears to any talk of mediation and insisting that the war go on.

The general ennui won out. The last month of the year saw the end of the Castro war, and everybody was so pleased that it was forgotten how high a price had been paid for a war which won nothing but a forced peace. The excommunication rescinded and Castro restored to him, Odoardo was made to demolish the fortifications, abandon Bondeno, return the captured artillery, and dismiss his troops.

The new year began in an atmosphere of lightness and gaiety. Rarely had the duchy been so much in need of peace. Parma and Piacenza, with a well-justified sense of relief, gave themselves up to the pleasures of the carnival with no thoughts of impending doom. Even Odoardo was in a good humor and he wanted the court to share his contentment. He organized a series of balls, masquerades, and festivals, on which, as usual, he wasted a great deal of money; this time it was to demonstrate how little affected he had been by the war, thanks to his reserves of strength, ingenuity, and courage. Nothing was more important to him, even in the most disastrous situations, than to maintain aplomb, style, and splendor of surroundings. There was a Farnese tradition of luxury that was respected above everything else. In the two following years, the last of his life, he brought that luxury to heights never before reached, seriously using his talents for the magnificent and the grandiose. In Piacenza the court became the center of sumptuous parties, of theater shows filled with technical marvels in the tradition set by Marino. For whoever came for a visit—the Duke of Modena, for example, or the Spanish governor of Milan, or even some

minor figure—Odoardo organized feasts displaying typical Farnese social brilliance. The guests would depart filled with admiration, and Odoardo would look satisfied with himself. When
his eyes rested on his family, he couldn't help saying to himself
that the *fortunazza paolina* had treated him well. His mother,
the Aldobrandina, was becoming even more noble and charitable in her advancing years; Margherita, his wife, was a woman
dedicated to house and family, exactly as Odoardo wished,
grateful to Providence for having given her a husband so unusual, if in nothing else, his faithfulness. Odoardo considered
it beneath the dignity of a great man like himself to think of
other women. And there were his brother and his sisters, all
contributing to his importance and authority: Francesco was
making progress in the ecclesiastical career; Maria was the
happy wife of the Duke of Modena; Vittoria, a sweet virtuous
girl, obediently waited for Odoardo to marry her off to some
worthy man. And finally, there was the train of children. Eight
had been born in fourteen years; five had survived, four boys and
one girl, all healthy if a bit fat. Odoardo had ambitious plans for
them—a secret pleasure which he shared only with his wife
Margherita.

In July, 1644, Urban VIII died. Odoardo, who for years had
enjoyed himself imagining being at the pope's deathbed, was
very happy but had the good taste not to show it. "Now that
he has restored my possessions," he gloated, "he can sing the
nunc dimittis servum tuum Domine. . . ." He sighed with relief
when he heard that the new pope was Innocent X, from the
Pamphili family, who was well disposed toward the Farnese.
Indeed the pope reconfirmed to the duke the previous grants
and the title of *Gonfaloniere della Chiesa*, generously adding a
cardinal's hat for Odoardo's brother, Francesco Maria.

So the months passed, bringing to Odoardo—or at least so
he thought—the rewards of his difficult years and a whole new
set of sweet illusions. Sometimes he felt himself so anxiously and

confusedly happy that he would have liked to open himself to
Margherita; but sensing the disparity between words and feelings, he would simply hug her affectionately. The future seemed
uncertain but bright. He felt he could go far with his ability to
intrigue and persuade, his military skill, the destiny which had
been predicted to him when he was a child. No, he would never
doubt the stars; he felt his fate was beautifully mapped out.

Instead, in one blow everything collapsed. In June, 1646,
Odoardo's sister, the Duchess of Modena, died in childbirth.
Two months later his mother followed, the victim of an acute
form of tertian fever. And in September, while they were still
celebrating Masses in memory of the Aldobrandina, at only
thirty-four Odoardo died of apoplexy. It happened too suddenly
for him to have time to glance backward, to review his own life
in perspective. But if he could have done so, his immense pre-
sumption would have suggested to him the words of a flattering
biographer: "Captains followed him in glory, soldiers obeyed
him out of love, enemies payed him homage out of fear, his
subjects bowed in gratitude."

It was not true, of course. But Odoardo's death was enviable because it had generously spared him the realization of
his failure, leaving him ignorant that he had been one of the
most dilettantish, scatterbrained, unpolitical rulers of his time,
under whom the house of Farnese had begun its decline. The
legacy of the fifth lord of Parma and Piacenza was a liability.

XI

A Farnese without History

Though embalmed and buried in the beautiful Capuchin church in Parma, Odoardo found no rest. If the souls of fathers are allowed to watch over the doings of their children, certainly he must have turned over in his grave watching the fifty-year reign of his first son, the most bland and static, the most consistently mediocre of all the Farneses. The half a century of the reign of Ranuccio II was, in effect, a long blank page which Odoardo would have filled with dubious political and military achievements; his son, however, merely penned in the history of a torpid, uneventful reign. During Ranuccio's adolescence Odoardo's soul could be at peace in the conviction that his son was like an early bottled wine which, once matured, improves so much as to be hardly recognizable. Instead, Ranuccio, as it turned out, excelled in nothing—not in warfare, nor in politics, nor in cleverness; not even in vice. Unlike his father, who had led a life of constant and eager expectation, Ranuccio never felt the need to vary his daily routine. He did not like to travel. The house is a great invention, he used to say, not being much given to rhetoric. He lived in the style of a country squire, to the detriment of the heroic and the sublime but certainly to the satisfaction of Parma and Piacenza, which had both lived and suffered through too much history to want anything more to do with it. Politically also, Ranuccio, with his rather sluggish philosophy, was an upholder of the quiet life; he abhorred military adventuresomeness, in which he differed from all of the other Italian rulers, who were inevitably caught in the net of Cardinal Mazarin, as zealous a contriver as Richelieu had been of anti-Spanish leagues.

Only once did the duchy have to suffer the anguish of war. It occurred when, in one of those upheavals not rare in politics, Pope Innocent X, favorably inclined to the Farnese family at first, had his troops invade Castro. The pope had paid heed, as did Urban before him, to Ranuccio's insistent creditors who until then had been held at bay by promises and deferments. Unluckily, this trouble coincided with an event destined to remain a black spot in Ranuccio's reign.

To fill a vacancy in the bishopric of Castro, the pope had chosen Don Cristoforo Giarda, a mild Barnabite monk from Novara whose election, for mysterious reasons, displeased the Farnese court. All the attempts to have the Vatican replace him by a bishop more pleasing to Ranuccio had failed, perhaps because of the resistance of the powerful and eccentric Donna Olimpia Maidalchini, the pope's sister-in-law. Don Cristoforo understood only too well that he was not welcome in Farnese territory; from Parma they kept telling him that the humidity of Castro was unhealthy for him. Besides, the good monk wanted nothing more than to remain in the peace and shelter of his cloister. But Innocent X would not listen to reason and, consecrating him bishop, sent him on his way with his blessing. Don Cristoforo left with tears in his eyes; he had had many bad presentiments, all of which proved true during the trip to his see. Near the pond of Monterosi, on the Acquapendente road, he was ambushed and left to die.

The scandal was enormous. The assassins were never caught, but Innocent did not find it difficult to believe rumors that the murder had been ordered by Ranuccio's minister, Jacopo Gaufrido. He immediately interdicted the churches of the duchy, and on June 19, 1649, declared war against Ranuccio, after having made certain that France would not intervene this time. Besieged, Castro surrendered on honorable terms after two months, and the soldiers of the pope entered with drums beating and pennants flying. Yet, victory had never been the occasion for greater inhumanity and barbarism. Without taking into account the terms of the capitulation, the pope's army demolished the town to its foundations, destroyed churches and monuments, forced the citizens to level their own homes and then sent them out naked into the world. The episcopal seat was moved to Acquapendente. Innocent X ordered the erection, among the ruins, of a column which bore the inscription: "Here once was Castro." This column does not exist today, a forest now extends over the ground where the city, the pride of six generations of Farneses, once stood.

All of Italy recoiled at the violence of the pope's revenge. That their injury had to be avenged, Ranuccio understood well. Although he did not have his father's mania for warfare, he put together a troop of three hundred cavalrymen; they were, however, mostly infantrymen mounted on broken-down work horses. Out of a sense of duty he would have led them personally had not his mother dissuaded him. Command of the troops was given to Francesco Serafini, Ranuccio's field marshal, but he refused it. Being a shrewd man, he understood how problematic would be the outcome. It was now absolutely necessary to find someone to take the duke's place. The obvious choice was the minister, Gaufrido, who, exalted by this new responsibility, deluded himself into thinking that he could lead the troops to victory. But Gaufrido had had no experience in war, as became soon evident when his troops met the pontiff's in a ridiculous battle in the Bologna district. The beginning was rather auspicious; the Farnese dragoons turned the enemy cavalry to flight. But soon the pope's soldiers caught their breath and reorganized themselves on a little hill; they then began to fire their artillery —and panic immediately overcame everyone, the attacked as well as the attackers. Presently, the two armies were both fleeing in such hurry that they forgot even to loot the few dead bodies scattered about. Paralyzed by fear, Gaufrido had prudently remained in the background the whole time; and once the incredible battle was over, dreading the duke's anger, he retired to Finale di Modena to brood over his disgraceful performance. Then he sent his brother-in-law to Parma to discover how the court had received the news of the disaster. Gaufrido returned home only after being assured that the duke was not angry, and that "if Gaufrido was safe, nothing else mattered."

As had Odoardo before him, Ranuccio held Gaufrido in great esteem and had almost a filial attachment to him. It is difficult to understand, therefore, how Ranuccio could have abandoned him to the chorus of protests of those who, because of the unfortunate war, felt no compunction about criticizing the court favorite. Chief among those who cried for Gaufrido's blood were Count Serafini, leader of the court's Hispanophile faction, and the duchess mother herself, who was "nauseated by the prime minister's love for France."

Gaufrido's fall was as rapid as his rise had been slow. Because Ranuccio was young, easily influenced, and inexperienced, because political harmony was needed, and because he hated complications and wanted to return to the *status quo* as quickly as possible, Ranuccio finally agreed to condemn Gaufrido to death. In the last days of his life Jacopo Gaufrido showed all the spirit that he had lacked as a general. He prepared himself to die with such resolution and calm that, said a chronicle, "he himself seemed worried that he should appear, by chance, vain and affected."

For the citizens of Piacenza, Gaufrido's execution was an edifying show of courage. Arriving in front of the gallows, he gave away his crimson velvet cloak to the guards, kissed the priest, discussed with the executioner the best way to place his head on the block, and placidly waited for the ax. He died in the manner of a gentleman, perhaps not to seem less so than Charles I, whose exquisitely courteous deportment before the executioner only a few years earlier had made a lasting impression everywhere. "I ask God," said Gaufrido before dying, "that my death may solve the duke's problems!" Ranuccio solved them, but only partially. The territory of Castro and Ronciglione were confiscated by the pope, who granted Ranuccio the right to buy them back within ten years, for 1,000,700 scudi, and the charges against the Farneses for their invasion of the Papal States and the assassination of the bishop were dropped.

After the execution of the prime minister in January, 1650, Parma and Piacenza enjoyed several years of peaceful prosperity. At about that time Cardinal Mazarin proposed that the young duke marry one of his beautiful nieces, with a dowry of six hundred ducats—almost half the amount necessary to ransom the confiscated estates in Latium. The proposition was received with scorn. The Farneses still yearned for Castro, but the haughty cardinal should have known that a Farnese would never lower himself to marry for money. Ranuccio's mother stubbornly declared that such a marriage would be an outrage to the dignity of the family. Her rigidity proved unwise, for later the beautiful Mazarin girls were all married to prominent men, two of them to ruling princes.

For Ranuccio they chose Margherita Violante, daughter of

Victor Amadeus I of Savoy, a sickly, thin girl, with a certain neurotic charm, who had missed becoming queen of France only because at the last moment Louis XIV had chosen, for political reasons, a Spanish infanta. Margherita Violante died the following year in childbirth, and was shortly afterward replaced by a not-too-young, not-too-alluring cousin from Modena, Isabella d'Este. After having brought into the world two girls, "for whom there was neither celebration nor rejoicing," Isabella died in giving birth to a boy, named Odoardo in memory of his grandfather. Ranuccio mourned her only moderately, then married Maria, Isabella's younger sister. Maria was received in Parma with pity for having married a man with the stigma of having buried two wives already. She, however, held on for sixteen years, then died too, without regrets, perhaps because of a kidney disease which had made her life a continuous agony and which toward the end left her "only skin and bones." After her, Ranuccio wanted no more wives. He was no longer interested in sex; and besides, his lineage had been assured. Counting the living and the dead, he had brought a dozen children into the world. He had become fat and lethargic from overindulgence, with a double chin worthy of a Roman emperor of the fifth century. His subjects had grown to feel affection for this duke who was such a curious mixture of austerity and wit, profundity and gaiety, provinciality and urbanity. His moderate nature, extremely peace-loving and adverse to tragedy, recoiled at the dangerous game of politics and was amused only by its possibilities for arranging marriages. He considered matchmaking an important aspect of diplomacy and he certainly would have used his many sisters and daughters for this purpose had not most of them died prematurely. People said he was a good man, a lord like those in the old days; that he was unaffected and was treated with respectful familiarity by everyone. And they concluded that life founded on such simple values was a paradise compared to the "epic" times of Odoardo. Grateful for being spared the horrors of war, they willingly forgave the duke his many taxes (his father had invented the chimney tax and had devised the window and the notary-seal tax) and the moralistic tendencies that made him, in moments of bad humor, forbid masqueradings at carnival.

Ranuccio's home administration, unlike that of the other Ranuccio fifty years earlier, was rather stagnant. But he had an advantage over his grandfather: in the half century of his rule, Ranuccio II made very few laws and statutes, and those few were promulgated in a spirit of acceptable paternalism. Some initiatives in favor of trade, the introduction of corn, two new spinning mills, and a plan for draining the swamps had assured him the reputation of being actively interested in public welfare. His moonface froze into a hard expression only when he was administering justice, which, for the love of order, he meted out rigorously. Thieves, vagabonds, and brigands did not thrive during his reign.

Under Ranuccio the clergy were abundantly—even too abundantly—privileged. Toward the end of the century, Parma had two thousand monks and nuns out of a population of twenty-nine thousand. There were about seventy churches, not including private chapels. Ranuccio personally supervised his courtiers' religious activities, almost transforming the court into a large "home for churchgoers." In this his mother worked with him hand in hand. As she grew older, she became a living code of prudery, so much so that, in a time when matters like this were hardly recorded, we find mention that in 1678 she had given orders for the construction in the Piacenza cathedral of a partition dividing the men from the women. Following her example, the noble ladies were active in works of charity, founded religious clubs, took part in the veiling of new nuns, sponsored organizations for "wayward girls," and competed in founding Carmelite, Benedictine, and Capuchin convents.

Gray and clerical, Parma and Piacenza could boast of no exceptional artists. The cultural ambience was suffocating, literature was futile and pedantic, mediocrity often was confused with talent. The academies, still prospering, now composed epigrams, published chronicles, satirized each other in a meaningless bustle of literary activity. Most prominent on the cultural scene was a small group of clergymen, Jesuits, and monks who spent their lives in the various abbeys of the duchy, researching archives, organizing libraries, and teaching philosophy and theology in the ecclesiastical schools. A little more lively were the university and the Collegio dei Nobili, the two most important schools in the country where, in keeping with the century's interest in alchemy and research, experiments in the natural sciences and mathematical speculation had reached a rather high level. Piacenza more than Parma distinguished herself in having some lords who cultivated a taste for scholarship; they were typical intellectual gentlemen of the seventeenth century, in love with antiquity and at the same time open to the attractions of contemporary thought and life.

For the rest of the population the years passed by slowly, almost all alike, distinguishable only by the famines and the condition of the Po, which sometimes flooded the countryside and sometimes dried up so much that "one could cross it on horseback."

The year 1656 remained in everyone's memory for the battle of the Dardanelles, when the Turks lost five thousand slaves, about twenty ships, and left the sea red with their blood and filled with their corpses. A little of the glory of the great Christian victory shone on the Farneses because Orazio, one of Ranuccio's brothers, had brought home, besides his share of booty, an attractive young Turkish girl, later solemnly baptized in Piacenza under the name of Anna Maria.

In 1663 there was much talk that Maria Caterina, a sister of the duke, would take the veil. The ladies of the Farnese family had always been reticent, domestic, and femininely ignorant. But Maria Caterina was different. Intellectual and dreamy, of a peculiar beauty, full of contradictions, her replies were sharp and easily sarcastic, her conversation brilliant in the best Farnese tradition. She was a strange mixture of the ascetic and the eccentric. She read novels as well as the lives of saints; she exhausted herself with equal enthusiasm in visiting shrines and in hunting. She spent hours in the confessional only to say later that she had no confidence in her confessor. These two personalities, each of equal weight, coexisted without ever amalgamating. Her mother, the sweet, extremely patient Margherita de' Medici, sometimes lost her temper with her. At home they said that Maria Caterina resembled Vittoria Farnese, her distant ancestor, and like her, she promised to become a hopeless spinster. She refused all suitors; one day she was offered no one less than the king of England, and she commented stiffly: "If he proposes, I'll reject him, for a Farnese cannot give herself to an enemy of God." If it was suggested that she take the veil, she interrupted dryly: "My soul goes to whomever gives me most pleasure," and that ended the matter. In 1663, while still very young, she decided to become a Carmelite, out of pique: "I'll go barefooted because I say so, and for no other reason!" And once more she enjoyed shocking those who had said she would be a bad nun by offering them the spectacle of an exemplary life, divided between ecstasies and penances which often transported her to a state of religious delirium.

The year 1667 was a memorable one because of the comet which, they say, dived noisily into the Po. On the following year, Paolo Segneri, a vibrant orator in the severe style of Savonarola, came to preach. All those who heard him felt repentant, worthy of God's divine grace, and were overcome with a great desire to be good.

One time Christina of Sweden visited the duchy, and the

event was talked about for months afterward; it was not every day that one could see up close a queen so eccentric, so histrionic, so capricious, so completely fascinating, who fused a touch of northern madness with Latin skepticism. Christina had come to Italy to escape boredom—and to be converted. Her Catholicism was of so imperial a kind that any sort of religious eccentricity was tolerated in her.

Occasionally, Ranuccio's brother Alessandro came to Parma for a short stay. A former captain of the Venetian cavalry, he had toured the world and now, back home, he enchanted the court with gossip and stories typical of the international traveler of the time. In Parma he was recognized as a man who knew how to enjoy life. A dark, handsome youth who always seemed to be in love, he had a certain romantic air that attracted women's interest. His only grief, besides debts— which he incurred continuously and which Ranuccio regularly had to pay—was his corpulence. To fight it, he periodically decided to diet, but he never succeeded and he continued to weigh more than two hundred pounds. These Farneses, said the Parma people, are good-looking in the crib but they spoil in growing. For some of them, at only twenty, their florid cheeks were the signs of their doom in the same way that hollow eyes and paleness are those of the consumptive.

Another brother of the duke, Pietro, had died because of obesity. Odoardo, Ranuccio's first-born, also was fat, sluggish, and lacked the necessary will for abstinence at table. This Odoardo, who was to succeed his father, was well loved in the duchy for his affable manner and mild nature, which were interpreted as good omens for the future. At the beginning of 1690, he married Dorotea Sofia of Neuburg, daughter of the Elector of the Palatine and distantly related to the Austrian Hapsburgs. Odoardo's subjects greeted the lady with some disappointment; they had expected her to be beautiful but found her only passable. She was typically Germanic, large, blonde, with blue eyes which occasionally had a hard glint. Persevering, neat, without a sense of humor, and moreover afflicted by Teutonic pedantry, she brought to Italy some bizarre rules of health. Her first son, Alessandro Ignazio, died because during a sickness she insisted on treating him solely with brandy.

The festivities for the wedding of Odoardo and Dorotea Sofia were the most luxurious that had ever taken place in the duchy; it seemed by now as though the Farnese weddings were becoming more magnificent with each generation. Accustomed to the small, modest courts of Germany's innumerable princelings where diversions were few and economical, the gentlemen of Dorotea's train were stiff and ceremonious but stricken with admiration over everything. To begin with, there were the curtsies, imported from France, so many and so complicated, as one courtier complained, that "one had to have a dancing master to learn all those capers, for one had to dance a whole ballet before one could begin to speak." The court of Parma was abreast of all the latest vogues; there was hardly anyone who could not turn a compliment in French. At dinner the court used a great deal of silver and sipped coffee imported from the lands of Mohammed. Unlike the Englishmen who smoked tobacco, they chewed it—another novelty—and even wrote poems about it. Chocolate, the latest American innovation, was served mixed with essence of lime and lemon. And everyone was mad for the "amber-colored sherbets" so dear to Lorenzo Megalotti.

To keep up with the ducal household, the nobility went deeply into debt with the bankers of Genoa. They borrowed against rents yet uncollected; they pawned family jewels at the mint of Milan and their silverware at the pawnshops of Bologna. The most illustrious families competed with each other in a ruinous display of luxury. Once in a while, Ranuccio, deluding himself that he could stop the wasteful expenditures of the courtiers, imposed various restrictions; but at the slightest provocation he himself—and even worse his women—very casually forgot them. Elegance of dress found its counterpart in that of palaces, furniture, and carriages. For Odoardo and Dorotea Sofia's wedding, money was spent with incredible liberality, so much so that a deficit was created from which the ducal treasury was never to recover. Indeed, to survive these expenditures, the treasury would have needed the most vigilant and careful husbandry, a task for which Odoardo was totally inadequate. Besides, he felt himself much too much a Farnese to give up the pleasure of astounding his guests or receiving the satisfaction of knowing that they were speaking of his munificence. His ostentation would have been vulgar had it not been tempered by a certain natural charm; but even so, the German and foreign guests, for all their exclamations of pleasure, criticized the excesses of his hospitality.

The wedding celebrations lasted ten days, with banquets, games, dances, horse races, and finally a series of shows whose splendid scenery, music, and ingenious stage machinery expressed Ranuccio's sincere passion for theater and music, the only two institutions which he supported lavishly.

In a certain sense, Odoardo's wedding marked the end of Ranuccio II's long reign. The remaining four years of the duke's life were overcast by the long shadow of a new war. At the turn of the century, the adherence of the Duke of Savoy to the League of Augusta (formed by the major European nations, England, the Hapsburg Empire, Spain, Holland, and Sweden, to halt the growing power of France) had once more brought war to Italy. In a few months the northern part of the country had been invaded by German troops, and all the Italian states which were imperial vassals—such as Modena, Mantua, Tuscany, Lucca, and Genoa—had to contribute heavily to the maintenance of the troops. Ranuccio, an imperial vassal for the towns of Bardi and Compiano, asked the emperor that his duchy be spared the obligation of quartering foreign troops, but Leopold I politely replied that he was forced, against his will, to ask Ranuccio to help subsidize his army in Italy, and that after the war he, Ranuccio, would be reimbursed. And so, for three years German soldiers remained in the duchy, and their barbaric appetite spared nothing. Ranuccio wrote to Leopold, to the pope, and to the king of Spain, denouncing the soldiers' depredations and complaining about the poor harvests, the bad weather, his debts, and asking for help. In answer, he received only words of commiseration and appeals to his patience. Not even Venice, in whose service his brother Orazio had risked his life, offered anything more than vague sympathy.

In 1694 the situation had worsened to the point that in order to maintain the Germans a tax of four lire was imposed on every *biolca* [about three-quarters of an acre] of land. At the same time the imperial commissioner requested forty-five thousand *dobles* to pay the soldiers. The weight of all these taxes rested solely on the people. The clergy, secure in its privileges, contributed nothing. Ranuccio untiringly wrote letters to everyone, begging them not to let "a poor sixty-year-old prince die of grief" by seeing his country reduced to such an extremity. He sent to Vienna the Marquis Pier Luigi dalla Rosa Prati, a skillful courtier, to try to soften the emperor's heart and perhaps to put pressure on the empress through her confessor Father Maget. Nothing was accomplished. Leopold apologized, giving blame to the times and asking for yet more supplies and quarters for his soldiers. Toward the middle of 1694 the impoverishment of the duchy became intolerable. Ranuccio wrote to his ambassador in Vienna: "We have to leave to future centuries the judgment of this situation and the compassion for those who have suffered these years during which sorrow and ruin have been inflicted upon innocent rulers, guilty only of draining the blood of their subjects in order to pay their due to Caesar." After the thousandth contribution of horses and provisions, Ranuccio again wrote: "We have to shout everywhere, we must make ourselves heard by those who have given us only words and have deluded us into hoping for better times, so that they will at least know how badly they have behaved on both the political and the human levels. We have seen the vipers among these flowery promises." The "vipers," in addition to gout and obesity, brought a quick end to his life. He died on the sixth of September, a patriarch surrounded by his children. And although one of his advisors had shortly before written that should the duke die there would be hardly enough money for a proper burial, Ranuccio had a splendid funeral, made more solemn by the genuine tears of his subjects than by the many official eulogies.

Because the heir to the throne, Odoardo, had died a few years before, leaving only one daughter, Ranuccio's second son, Francesco, ascended the throne of Parma and Piacenza. From his father Francesco had inherited intelligence, a tendency to obesity, and a disposition to paternalism. On his own, he added a commendable, providential spirit of economy. His first act as a ruler was to do away with the luxurious trappings of the court; he dismissed the dwarfs, musicians, and clowns; he abolished many unnecessary offices and invested each courtier with several functions. Among other taxes, he invented a steep one on wigs —which were two feet high in that period, and adorned with ribbons, lace, jewels, and artificial flowers. Like his predecessors, Francesco was most skillful in raising new taxes, but he was also capable of saying such things as: "Although we have inherited, as everyone knows, an empty treasury, we shall find a way to feed the poor, even if it means melting into coin the silver from our table. . . ." The interesting thing is that he actually did what he said, more than once providing, at his own expense, grain for the starving population. At seventeen, when only just crowned, he had to find thirty thousand *dobles* in order to pay for the withdrawal of the imperial army, following which the hostilities in Italy were terminated. Soon after, he made another decision which reflected his precocious wisdom and maturity: he married his sister-in-law, the widow Dorotea Sofia, to avoid the painful restitution of her dowry should she marry someone else. This marriage turned out to be important for Francesco. Dorotea Sofia was not particularly beautiful, fertile, or in love—in fact, as the years went by, her natural somberness had ripened into pure meanness. But she had brought into the household a daughter from her previous marriage, Elisabetta, a bony, unattractive, pox-faced girl whose pale eyes reflected an indomitable will power. This Elisabetta was destined to become queen of a great country, and the glitter of her crown was to light the house of Farnese in its declining years.

XII

Elisabetta:

A Farnese for Spain

Giulio Alberoni was a man of humble origins. He was born in Piacenza in the home of a farmer and a flax spinner. The Barnabite fathers of the Church of Santa Brigida, where he was an altar boy, taught him to read and write; and, because he was quick and intelligent, they taught him some Latin, thinking that one day it would help him to enter the lower ranks of the clergy. It was said later that Fortune had blessed Giulio Alberoni; but it would have been more accurate to say that he alone, of all the altar boys who vegetated in the Piacenza parishes, knew how to pursue Fortune, to hold her, to exploit her with the tenacity of a peasant. His very character—his earthy nature and inexhaustible good humor—was destined to earn him the friendship of kings, great lords, generals, bishops, and of all whom he was to encounter in his long, eventful career.

After he left the care of the Barnabites, the Jesuits, who usually did not accept students from the lower classes because of the length and high cost of their system of education, made an exception for Giulio. The exclusive school of San Pietro, with its venerable humanistic traditions, became a springboard for the farmer's son. There he studied, ate good food, learned manners, refined his intellectual capacities, and made useful friends. He lived in an intellectual hothouse where, instead of getting trapped into a genteel life, he nurtured the idea of rising above the insular, obscure world of the Piacenza churches; and this idea was as strong as a vocation. The stages of his ascent followed one another in rapid succession. First, he was secretary to the criminal-court judge of Piacenza; then, steward to the bishop; then, pastor and prebendary of the Church of San Martino; and finally, tutor to the nephew of a prominent monsignor, with whom he went to Rome to be trained in court diplomacy. He used this opportunity to make more friends and to make contacts in high places, and, returning home, he was admitted into the political circle of the duchy of Parma.

Giulio Alberoni reached maturity at the beginning of the new century, when Europe flared up once more in the fight for the Spanish succession. In Italy the first hint of war found young Francesco Farnese, like many other rulers, uncertain and wondering how to emerge from the turbulence of European affairs with the least amount of damage. His perplexity only increased in attempting to guess which of the two factions would win: France and Spain on one side, or Austria and Savoy on the other. So, for the moment, there was nothing for him to do but to maneuver among the powers in the wisest, most careful way possible. Nonetheless, Austrian mercenaries led by Eugene of Savoy occupied several Farnese territories, distinguishing themselves as usual by their brutality. To Francesco's rightful protests Leopold of Austria answered, as usual, that after the war he would be indemnified. Which meant, in other words, for Francesco to be patient and quiet. Francesco obeyed, for common sense showed him no other solution.

After two important victories by the Austrians, one at Carpi and the other near Brescia, the scale seemed to tip in favor of the Hapsburgs. Then the French position improved when the Duke de Vendôme, a general of legendary fame, arrived in Italy with large reinforcements. As soon as Vandomo (as Italians pronounced his name) settled himself and his army in Cremona, Francesco Farnese made a timid diplomatic move. He sent to Vendôme the Bishop of Borgo San Donnino, Alessandro Roncovieri, a cultured man well known in France, with the task of convincing the general to keep the war away from the duchy. The old and gouty Monsignor Roncovieri took a secretary with him, Giulio Alberoni, who spoke French fluently and already had shown a knack for diplomatic missions. So for the farmer's son began a great adventure. He was forty-three years old and the picture of strength and energy. He had a short neck and the ruddy face of certain peasants who can still be seen today sitting at inns in the Piacenza countryside. He had a large nose, good-natured, shrewd eyes, and a potbelly —the beginning of a heaviness that somehow did not diminish his athletic appearance.

Vendôme's headquarters was not the most congenial atmosphere for a priest. His officers, bawdy and rough men, gambled heavily, drank, and debauched themselves; in short, they lived a life in which war was only a marginal activity. In his dedication to the profession of war and to his vices, Vandomo surpassed his men. Without being guilty of the excesses of which he was accused by Saint-Simon, who hated him and left of him a portrait too perfidious to be accepted, he was nevertheless the most dissolute of all—proud, haughty, and always ready to whitewash himself with a coat of religion when he felt he had truly gone beyond the bounds of decency.

Giulio Alberoni acclimated himself to this extraordinary headquarters with a jolly optimism which won for him everybody's affection. The officers immediately appreciated his quick wit and just-as-ready appetite; Vendôme invited him to his table and on his tours of inspection. To make himself useful to those he was to live with, Alberoni indulged some of their weaknesses; he procured many good things for them, but mainly good food. He had organized a messenger service between Piacenza and Cremona to supply him with Parmesan cheese, hard salami, beans of Castel San Giovanni, fresh sausages, and other specialties of the duchy. "To win a Frenchman's good will and preserve his friendship," he used to say, "there is nothing better than these little gifts for the table." And when the Farnese minister of finance seemed reluctant to dip into the moneybag, Alberoni would say: "You know that these trifles are very important and that little things given at the right moment never fail to bring results. These bagatelles sometimes open doors that are kept locked to the largest sums. . . . My dear count, the world is run quite differently from what people believe!" Thus, in a few months, by dint of sausages and bons mots, Alberoni had become Vendôme's closest and most esteemed friend, obtaining from him the latest news about the war and the political maneuverings in Europe. "One joke from Alberoni has more effect," they said in Cremona, "than all the heavy hints of the Bishop of San Donnino"—a good reason to have the old, infirm Monsignor Roncovieri replaced by his assistant. Francesco Farnese immediately made the replacement, confident that in his loyalty to the Farneses, Alberoni would put to service both his mind and his heart.

With the passing months Alberoni and Vendôme became more and more friendly. When one day the fighting shifted toward Piedmont, Alberoni followed the duke, submitting himself voluntarily to all the discomforts of a long military campaign. To Francesco Farnese he continued to send letters, dispatches, and memoranda which, in their sharp and unprejudiced analysis, are excellent examples of diplomatic prose. "The duke should not worry," he kept saying, "for this is a gentleman to cultivate, and we, thank God, know the best way to do it." For his part, Vendôme, won over by such dedication to the cause, wrote to Louis XIV that there was no more zealous Frenchman than the Abbé Alberoni. They remained together for the duration of the war, which, kept at a reasonable distance from the Farnese borders, ended with the first French victory, owing, according to Vendôme, almost entirely to his *cher abbé*. Louis XIV recognized Alberoni's services with a substantial pension that finally allowed the poor emissary to resolve his financial problems and to establish some order in his private affairs.

For all the time that Vendôme remained in Italy, the house of Farnese had found in him, thanks to Alberoni, a sincere and effective protector. But when war broke out again in Flanders and Spain, the French army was forced to leave Italy and abandon it to Austrian occupation. The little duchy once again fell upon bad times, being compelled to quarter and feed Prince Eugene's German soldiers. It was a hard blow for Alberoni, who by now had become passionately Francophile and bitterly anti-German.

After years of rheumatism and dysentery, of battles and sieges always at Vendôme's side, Alberoni temporarily settled himself at the court of Versailles, where he slowly gained influence and prestige. The king, the aristocracy, the ministers all liked him. He was finally sure of himself, and his humble origins and the memory of his childhood no longer weighed on him. "I laugh at and despise," he wrote to a friend, "all those who are ahead of me by virtue of birth rather than of personal value. I tell you that I owe nothing to luck, and nature, for its part, has been unkind to me; nonetheless, I have distinguished myself in the world and I can say without conceit that I have made and am making a better showing than those you have spoken to me about." He was referring to the backbiters of the Farnese court, to whom Francesco wisely paid no attention, having faith in that strange *abbé* who made politics by means of cheese and salami. Nor did he recall him to Parma, being convinced that Alberoni's presence at Versailles in some way could advance the Farnese interests in the event of peace negotiations.

For the moment, though, peace was not being discussed. In 1710 Vendôme was given command of the French army operating beyond the Pyrenees, and for his *cher abbé* there began the long Spanish adventure, the most important event of his life.

*

The Spanish situation was at that time very confused and reflected the ineluctable decline of the peninsula. Charles II, the last sprig of the Spanish branch of the Hapsburgs, had died without heirs; the throne was contested by a grandson of the king of France and by the son of the Austrian emperor, both of whom were related to the dead king. As a result, Spain for some years found herself with two monarchs, each fighting the other.

The Archduke Charles of Austria lived in Barcelona, capital of Catalonia, which had recognized him as king. He was a cold, stiff man, vaguely imperial in a Roman manner, surrounded by a court in which Spanish pomp was mixed with Teutonic austerity. Charles himself, with his hunchback dwarf on one side and his confessor on the other, was too coarse a German to be acceptable as a king of Spain.

Not more suited to the throne was his French rival, Philip V, installed in Madrid where he reigned over the central-southern part of the country. The ambassadors described him as "bland and lethargic," without a hint of imagination, homesick for Versailles, for the plains of Saint-Denis and the forests of Fontainebleau, the thought of which made him cry like a baby. Taciturn, dreamy, he was not well liked and lived a solitary life by choice and habit. A half-ecstatic, half-distracted smile was always on his lips; he seemed constantly to be meditating but mostly he was brooding. He had a gentle, slightly sly manner which discouraged confidence. Though gifted with honesty and a proper sense of values, he was interested in little else but hunting. He suffered neurotic fits and was tormented by a sensuality which could place him at the mercy of any woman who attracted him.

More important than the king at the court of Madrid was Princess Orsini, an old, egocentric intriguer of immense power. This French lady, widow of the Italian Duke of Bracciano, was an emancipated woman of the eighteenth century, intelligent and ambitious, one of the many the century produced. She used her physical and intellectual gifts seductively. In her youth she had lived in Rome where she had made her palace an exclusive salon; later she had become an important figure in Versailles, where her influence on Louis XIV and his morganatic wife, Madame de Maintenon, had made her a kind of court divinity and the object of the most incredible adulation. When the young Duke Philip left to rule in Spain, his grandfather Louis XIV sent her to watch over him and to make certain that the interests of the new Spanish kingdom coincided with those of France. And she knew very well how to manipulate the weak man and to keep him isolated and inaccessible to the court, so that he could literally count on the loyalty of only three or four Frenchmen. Princess Orsini created ministers and generals, she ran the government, and she reigned absolutely. When Philip married Maria Luisa Gabriela of Savoy, she was made *camarera major* [chief chambermaid] to the queen, and became so close to her that the queen saw the world through her eyes.

Giulio Alberoni was too realistic to have illusions about the possibility of winning the old woman's friendship. "Today, on top of the mountain; tomorrow, a hundred feet under the earth," he commented thoughtfully on the precarious life of the courtier.

But while speaking thus, he already was thinking of how to handle the powerful *camarera major*. Once again on the scene there appeared cheeses, sausages, wine, and other delicacies. To finance these "useful trifles," Alberoni often had to meet expenses out of his own pocket, for from Parma there came hardly enough money to maintain his own appearance. He complained to Parma that he was not asking for the moon, but that he did not want to seem miserly and lose face before the diplomatic corps of Madrid. He never tired of insisting on this point; nothing irritated him more than the attitude of Parma, where they were so extravagant, for not understanding that "the world runs more on appearances than on substance."

He had cultivated appearances so well that, when Maria Luisa died of tuberculosis in 1713, thus depriving him of a powerful supporter, his position did not change an iota, and was indeed as solid as ever. After the Treaty of Utrecht, which ended the war and forced the Germans to leave Spain, Francesco Farnese decided to give Alberoni an official position at Madrid. That decision provoked a great deal of uproar, because never before in the diplomatic history of Europe had there been an ambassador who lacked either money or title. And yet, Alberoni managed much better than his colleagues who came equipped with frills and illustrious names. He was, for example, one of the few admitted by Princess Orsini to the presence of the widower Philip V, who was nursing his inconsolable loss in solitude. But the king was only thirty-two years old, sensual and languid; it was clear that abstinence was not for him and that sooner or later the court would have to find a new wife to satisfy him. "A woman and a kneeling-stool, that's what the king of Spain needs!" Maria Luisa Gabriela of Savoy had just been buried and already the court behaved as if she had never lived. The idea of a new queen possessed everyone's imagination and created a flurry of excitement among the various ambassadors.

Princess Orsini was seventy-two years old, too old to replace the dead queen but more than powerful enough to decide who should take her place. The list of available princesses was quite long: the ambassadors from Savoy recommended one of the two daughters of Duke Amadeus; the Bavarian ambassador advanced Maria Carlotta, his master's eldest daughter. A third candidate was the daughter of the widowed queen of Poland. And then there was the daughter of the king of Portugal.

Among these names Giulio Alberoni inserted with studied casualness that of Elisabetta, niece and stepdaughter of Francesco Farnese. At first her name went unnoticed; and not to call attention to it was part of the plan Alberoni had conceived at the moment when Maria Luisa's insistent cough had foretold to him, before everyone else, that Spain would soon be without a queen. While his colleagues were busy lobbying, he behaved with careful indifference—but was always attentive to what they were doing and saying. Each time the old Orsini, a bit distracted by the matrimonial whirl, critically enumerated to him the princesses who, by birth, age, and dowry, were eligible to become queen of Spain, Alberoni made sure that he spoke in generalities, never contradicting her. Counting on his knowledge of human nature (so sharp at times as to border on the perverse), he would say that, in the interest of the king and for the welfare of all concerned, what was needed was a quite, submissive girl, incapable of defying the authority with which she, Princess Orsini, ruled the country. To this reasoning the old *camarera* gravely assented; the *abbé* was right, it was essential that the bride be quiet and submissive. Slowly to lead the princess to drop all the names on the list so that only that of Elisabetta Farnese remained, to convince her, without ever exciting her suspicion nor giving her the feeling that he was forcing his opinion on her, that the stepdaughter of Francesco was the only suitable bride for the king of Spain, and finally to have the *camarera* anxious to conclude the marriage, this was Giulio Alberoni's master stroke. "What kind of a girl is Elisabetta?" asked the princess. "A good girl, made of butter and cheese," answered Alberoni casually, pretending to dislike the role of intermediary. "And how does she spend her days?" pressed the other. He answered, elusively, that she embroidered, sewed, spun. But the *camarera* wanted to know more, about her age, education, intelligence. And he described her as very homey, without malice, manageable, lazy, uneducated, not very intelligent and, to be honest, with that pox face, not even attractive.

Such carefully selected details were more than enough to make the old princess choose Elisabetta. She felt that, on the strength of the girl's gratitude for having been made queen of Spain, and without having to concede anything of her own interests and plans, she would soon limit the young woman to one function: that of mother of princes, and nothing more.

In May, 1714, only six months after Maria Luisa's death, the matter had progressed, and Alberoni could write to his master that he had the impression that "everything will be resolved quickly." Philip V had already assented, for he was bored with sleeping alone. Besides, a new Italian wife would be a tribute to the memory of his first wife—not to mention that Elisabetta was probably the sole heir to the entire Farnese duchy, since her stepfather and uncle had no other children.

Meanwhile, in Parma, "the good girl, all heart and no malice," studied the portrait of her future husband. It was a face of honest mediocrity, a bland face emerging from the curls of an oversized wig and the frills of his shirt front. As the same time, she carefully memorized Alberoni's detailed letters describing the king, the customs of the court, the character of the Spaniards. He spoke of Princess Orsini epigrammatically: "Time and patience are needed to chop down great oak trees." Or: "One must first scout the country to avoid ambush." And: "Before you show your cards, make sure with whom you are playing." But the essence of all his suggestions was that, to the Spanish ambassador who was coming to Parma to observe the future queen's character, Elisabetta show herself not too different from Alberoni's description. And Elisabetta managed to present such a colorless version of herself that Princess Orsini once more gave a sigh of satisfaction and applauded her own choice. What was needed—Alberoni's letters continued—was great caution and shrewdness, to play one's cards right; and he added that, if Elisabetta followed his advice, one day Parma would rule in Madrid, but that if she disobeyed him, the Farneses could be reduced to not having enough power in Spain to create a corporal.

On the sixteenth of September the wedding was celebrated by proxy in Parma. Duke Francesco, choking with emotion over the honor done to his family, stood for the groom before the altar. Elisabetta still wore her bland and bewildered expression, which, it was agreed, would remain with her until Giulio Alberoni gave her the signal. No one noticed the glances of complicity between the bride and the diplomat—or better the count, for Duke Francesco had named him a count as a reward for his superlative matchmaking.

The understanding between Alberoni and Elisabetta grew stronger during the trip, that famous trip in which the young woman planned her first gesture of autonomy, the first almost brutal assertion of herself as the queen. She began by changing the itinerary, disarranging the detailed plans of the Spanish minister of the interior and of Princess Orsini. To prepare for her arrival they had constructed new roads, enlarged and repaired the old ones, decorated and furnished all the palaces in which she was to stop. But Elisabetta in the meantime was taking quite a different course, traveling slowly, leisurely, and oblivious to protocol. On December 23, 1714, she arrived at Jadraque, where her first meeting with Princess Orsini had been arranged. The *camarera* did not leave the palace to meet her, she merely came down a few steps from the staircase, as if to indicate, with that infraction of protocol, her future position with regard to the new queen.

What was said between the two women at that encounter no one ever knew exactly. But everyone remembered for a long time the incredible moment when Elisabetta opened the door and ordered the lieutenant of her guards to arrest the princess and conduct her and only one servant to the border. The most abject humiliation Elisabetta could have devised would not have produced a greater impression. Alberoni was astonished, not so much at the episode itself as at the suddenness with which his most fervent aspiration had been achieved. "You will be surprised," he wrote the following day to his friend Count Rocca of Parma, "and soon the whole world will be surprised. Our great queen conducted herself like a Judith. Her coup was worthy of Jiménez, Richelieu, and Mazarin in one. My dear count, I believe that this remedy alone will cure many troubles now considered incurable."

Then came the encounter with the king, in Guadalajara. The wedding night lasted nineteen hours. From that moment, Elisabetta's life ceased to belong to Farnese history and entered that of Spain. Tired, slavishly devoted to Madame de Maintenon, and too old to bear new complications, Louis XIV, who had been Princess Orsini's great protector, did not defend her; he let her finish her days in Rome. Philip V, temperamentally adverse to problems, did not protest too much at the princess's shocking dismissal. Besides, helplessly in love and exhilarated by the presence of his young wife, he could not bear her a grudge for very long. Elisabetta's first gesture of independence set the pattern for her existence on the Spanish scene for almost a half century.

The placid milk-and-honey girl from Piacenza soon turned into a vigorous, authoritarian, aggressive, and materialistic woman. She showed an incredible aversion for cloisters; she liked to enjoy herself, to make fun of Spanish pomposity, and to eat with an appetite that surprised even Alberoni. "She eats for two," he wrote in his reports to Parma, "and one meal of hers would make two of mine." Although in these first years of marriage Elisabetta essentially dedicated herself to music, hunting, and the theater, one could already discern in her an ability to make the most of any circumstance and an acute sense of self-interest that made Alberoni exclaim in admiration: "I assure you, she is as shrewd as a gypsy, and I cannot imagine where she learned what she says and does, considering she is only twenty-two years old, raised among four walls, without seeing or dealing with anyone, having come to Spain with no experience of the world." Elisabetta conquered and dominated her husband with the most elemental and yet most transcendental of means—sexual love, with which she kept him bound to her, especially in the later years when Philip, more hypochondriac and eccentric than ever, grew less capable of ruling and more than once relinquished his prerogatives to her. Elisabetta, consequently, ruled more than he did, dedicated herself to him and their children, always with a clear and exact consciousness of the complexities of the problems in Spain at that time.

Alberoni remained with her many years as a kind of tutor and inseparable companion; and in his weekly letters to Parma he continued to ask for salami, cheeses, sausages, truffles, and spring mushrooms. To maintain his influence over her, he remained faithful to his old system: "I have rabbit *alla piacentina* prepared for her," he wrote, "noodles in broth and *tortellini* on Friday. To eat these things, she says, is like being back in the old country." From Parma to Madrid traveled caravans of food, watched over like imperial convoys. To Elisabetta, Alberoni was "nurse, confidant, secretary, cook, and father."

That was Alberoni's best period. He was created cardinal, a grandee of Spain, and prime minister; he became arbiter of

Spain and was a proponent of an enlightened despotism which gave the country a brief period of prosperity which partially revived her glorious past. Inevitably, his reforms made many enemies for Alberoni, but this hardly disturbed him. "I may be more hated than a devil," he said, "but if the queen allows me to do what I wish, the rascals will be ruined and the good people made happy."

The remainder of Alberoni's life belongs to another story. Eventually, he fell from power and all of his reforms collapsed with him into ruin. He was fortunate enough to escape to Italy, where he settled quietly in Piacenza for the remainder of his days. His only consolation, he was fond of saying, was his good reputation.

Elisabetta did not stretch out her hand to help the once powerful minister. Nonetheless, she remained faithful to what he had taught her concerning a certain political technique the secret of which Alberoni—the erstwhile *"abbé* of the sausages" —alone knew. In later years, she became a cold, calculating woman, so much so that it appeared to the rest of Europe as though the spirit of Hapsburg imperialism had been revived in her and in the Italian and Parmesan coterie which surrounded her. In old age, she devoted herself entirely to the joys of maternal love; she died happily after having seen one of her sons ascend the ducal throne of Parma.

XIII

Don Antonio:
The Last of the Farnese

Don Antonio Farnese was in the middle of a banquet when the news came of his ducal brother Francesco's death. He was in Reggio Emilia, eating a quail pie with great gusto. Eating was his favorite pastime, as his two hundred and fifty pounds demonstrated, and his table was always kept supplied with delicate and savory foods. To see him at table was a spectacle; he ate seriously, sampling with his nose before tasting with his mouth, because, as he said, the first virtue of good food is its odor. He supervised the preparation of the various dishes, he thought about them for days, and finally, after testing them, he offered elaborate criticism. He was very demanding.

During carnival, Don Antonio loved to go to Reggio Emilia because in Parma his brooding and melancholic sister-in-law Dorotea Sofia forbade masques and public festivities at a time when other towns pullulated with merriment. Reggio Emilia was then the residence of Francesco d'Este, hereditary ruler of the duchy of Modena. Unlike his father Rinaldo, who was a tormented introvert, Francesco d'Este loved to live, and in this he was helped by his wife Carlotta Aglae, daughter of Philippe

275

d'Orléans, regent of France. Philippe himself had been a spirited man, fascinating, unconventional. An Anglophile, and possessed by "a heroic impiety," it was his custom to read Rabelais during Mass; and with the help of an alchemist he sought to find the philosopher's stone.

Thanks to Carlotta, life was gay in Reggio Emilia and all believers in the good life were warmly welcomed. Among them, Don Antonio Farnese was the most appreciated. Short, obese to the point of deformity, swaddled in silk suits, triple-chinned, his big head surmounted by a huge wig whose curls draped onto a magnificent enormous lace collar, he was a true academician of pleasure. From the time he could reason, he had taken on the task of dividing everything into two categories: the pleasurable and the boring. Then, disregarding the latter, he had arranged the various elements of the first in combinations that were either harmonious or pleasantly discordant; and he did it with such skill that he may be described as an inverted saint, a martyr to pleasure.

While Francesco Farnese usually lived in Colorno, Don Antonio preferred the castle of Sala, which he enlarged and decorated and where, serene and fulfilled among a gathering of happy Arcadians, he allowed himself all the luxuries of the *dolce vita*. He would not have been a Farnese if he had not been attracted to women, and attracted in the most carnal of ways and without an iota of romantic fantasy. To be sure, he allowed himself to be adored and dominated by his favorite, Countess Margherita Borri Giusti, who publicly seemed detached and aristocratically aloof but who was secretly involved in obscure intrigues all motivated by self-interest—an overwhelming self-interest that allowed her to close her eyes each time her lover, with pudgy and nimble fingers, undid the laces of some compliant damsel's corset. Don Antonio had never known any other kind of life. The grand tour through Europe which he had made at eighteen, with the purpose of establishing relations with the best of European society and of broadening and maturing himself, had ended up as a sort of protracted vacation, and an expensive one at that. Don Antonio had spent 1,580,000 lire on it, as is indicated in his secretary's account book.

Though Antonio's almost monstrous fatness at times seemed to slow him down both physically and mentally, he was clever enough. But his brother never exploited this cleverness, either in politics or in diplomacy or in matters of government. The lazy, easy-going Don Antonio, devoid of interest in anything but himself, could not have cared less. Amiable and superficial, he never knew the suffering and violence of passion; for him, there was no problem that could not be solved, no sin that could not be pardoned, no difficulty that could not be smoothed over. To use one of Goldoni's expressions, "he never let trouble disturb his dinner." His castle of Sala was a perfect microcosm of eighteenth-century society, which is to say that the time was spent in playing Arcadian games, acting out comedies, dancing minuets, and declaiming poetry. Love affairs were directionless, placid, ruining neither health nor appetite. Courtships were protracted, for good taste demanded long resistance; the years passed and the lovers found themselves with gray hair at the end of a *comédie galante* which had been only a waste of time.

Don Antonio considered the duchy his personal pleasure park, and he lived only for hunting, the theater, and endless games of faro. He surrounded himself with a band of well-dressed, tireless gentlemen, courtiers with very flexible backs (there were 236 varieties of bows), lords who drank fifty kinds of wines for dinner, ladies followed by their *cicisbei* (carrying vials of perfumes, fans, lap dogs and prayer books), and comic actors, dandified cardinals, poets with their pockets full of poems, composers in search of fame, somber chapelmasters, fat, rosy singers—all kinds of jovial sycophants in search of a free meal. The most affable flatterer of all of these was the poet Carlo Innocenzo Frugoni, known in Arcadia as Comante Eginetico, the epitome of the eighteen-century *abbé*. They belonged as much to their century as do cats to the smoky kitchens of Flemish paintings. In Rome they were referred to as *leccapiatti* [plate-lickers]. Once they had broken into the exclusive aristocratic circles, no salon could do without them. The *abbés* were extremely decorative, with their black capes and shiny shoes with gold buckles and red heels. They were usually florid, mincing, and charming, good minuet dancers, excellent conversationalists, politically tolerant, and so insensitive to melancholy and the world's troubles that nature seemed to have made them with "hearts colder than a cat's nose."

Carlo Innocenzo Frugoni—who, together with Bettinelli and Algarotti formed a trinity of poets, of which he was indisputably the best—had been made court poet. To repay the great hospitality given him in Parma and Sala, the former altar boy, hitherto accustomed only to his cell in the monastery of the Somaschi fathers of Piacenza, ground out sonnet after sonnet, ode after ode for all occasions: for weddings, funerals, births and birthdays, academic honors, takings of the veil, banquets, women's beautiful eyes, gifts of tobacco and woodcocks, recovery of health, and disasters avoided. Torrents of boring verse filled a dozen volumes, but it was not too much for an era in which poetry was essentially occasional and was written with great casualness by men, women, nuns, priests, doctors, barbers, and even scullery maids. Anyone who could hold a pen was entitled to aspire to Arcadia.

Parma was to Frugoni what Ferrara had been to Tasso: a daily spiritual magic, a town sometimes hated but always loved and rarely left. Don Antonio held him in great esteem and, as he did with everyone else who surrounded him, he let him live pleasurefully, except when he demanded that he turn out a melodrama, a genre for which Comante Eginetico felt himself little talented.

*

It is understandable, considering Don Antonio's intense hedonism, how the sudden death of Duke Francesco affected him more unpleasantly than sorrowfully by reminding him of his duties toward the dynasty. But his annoyance and perplexity were short-lived. Dressed in black, still dazed from his latest carousing, he went to Parma. He attended the funeral, shed some tears—more for the sake of ritual than for sorrow—heard a number of magniloquent elegies, offered his subjects a view of his noble, sad profile, and immediately after his coronation returned to his old life. "He thinks only of pleasure," we read in a chronicle. "Late lunch, conversation and card playing in the house of Countess Margherita Borri, whose salon was open to the ladies and gentlemen of the city only when the duke was in Parma; dinner at his palace at one hour before dawn; sleep until noon; later a carriage ride outside of town, sometimes a little falconry; another ride in the carriage with the noblemen of the town until about lunchtime." From all these duties he then would take a long vacation in the castle of Sala.

Life passed lazily and apparently prosperously. The government was paralyzed, more inactive and backward than ever. Don Antonio continued to eat delicious and indigestible food, and Countess Borri increased her power over this fifty-year-old man who was too flaccid and old to change his way of life.

A few months after the coronation, and with the problem of succession still unsolved, the court urged the new duke to marry and produce an heir. But Don Antonio was not looking forward to either. "Sacrifice your comfort for the public good," the pope sent word to him, "and do not forget how much your family owes to the Holy See. Be moved by the tears of your subjects, listen to the prayers of all of Italy." Don Antonio sighed desolately and resigned himself.

In her concern with suffering the least inconvenience from her lover's marriage, Countess Borri, with the help of Count Anvidi, the secretary of state—the two were the best-informed and the most powerful people in the government—chose the twenty-four-year-old Enrichetta d'Este to be Don Antonio's wife. Enrichetta was an anemic blonde, insipid and prissy, dulled by an almost nunlike education. Her father was that Duke Rinaldo of Modena who at forty had been compelled to divest himself of his cardinal's robes for the sake of the dynasty and who, ever since, in mourning for his lost splendor, wore black frocklike suits buttoned to the collar. Under her father's influence, Enrichetta (and her two sisters) had learned to conceal her true feelings under an austere manner, growing into a timid, docile woman—exactly what Countess Borri thought would suit her fat and jolly lord. Don Antonio examined her miniature, found her attractive but not exactly beautiful. Yet, she would do; she would bring some freshness to his stale middle age.

On July 21, 1727, the marriage contract was signed and Parma and Piacenza intoned their chorus of praise and thanks. Frugoni was commissioned to write poems for the nuptials. In addition, he was to compile an anthology of epithalamiums to which anyone in Italy who could count syllables and make rhymes was allowed to contribute. What resulted was a pastiche of 652 pages, the effort of 232 poets, with verses in Latin, Italian, French, Greek, and even Hebrew. It was enough to satisfy even Don Antonio's vanity and the era's desire that the quantity, though not necessarily the quality, of poetry should be in proportion to the importance of the occasion for which it was written. After a few months of postponements—Rinaldo d'Este was annoyed, but he hesitated to protest for fear of losing this opportunity of marrying off one of his three daughters—

the wedding finally took place. The future of the Farnese dynasty now rested entirely on the slender shoulders of Enrichetta d'Este.

Enrichetta's new subjects found her beautiful and at first sight they thought her worthy of the throne. In the court of Parma, in the palace of Colorno, and in the castle of Sala, among parties and hunts and surrounded by poets, she found happiness in exploring an unknown and fascinating world that made her forget that her husband was a gambler and a glutton, and that his life was being shortened by his appetites. Time stood still for her, the hands of the clock always fixed at the hour of dining and entertainment. The duke, when he was not busy playing faro or basset, was a thoughtful husband; Donna Margherita Borri was a most polite lady in waiting; Frugoni was a most affable court poet, always ready to compose a sonnet at the drop of a hat. And those years of novenas and rosaries in Modena were so distant that, on looking back, Enrichetta sometimes thought she had been dreaming. The lack of an heir was the only cloud on her horizon.

Europe had its eye on both the duchy of Parma and Piacenza and the grand duchy of Tuscany, where Giangastone de' Medici (as fat, dissipated, and sterile as Don Antonio Farnese) was chewing away what little remained of his life. It was enough for these two heirless rulers to sneeze three times in succession or to take laxatives with any frequency to send European chancelleries into ferment. Long-rooted dynastic struggles nourished the fever of a sick continent; the wars of succession were Europe's perennial malady, and Spain's alone had drenched half of Europe in blood. Doubtlessly, even a throne of half the importance of that of Madrid would have whetted already ravenous political appetites. In 1718, in London, a treaty was concluded among the kings of France, Holland, and Great Britain and the emperor of Austria, providing that, in the event that the Medicis and the Farneses should become extinct, the crowns of Parma and Piacenza and Florence would go to the son of Elisabetta of Spain, Don Carlos of Bourbon, who in turn would become the emperor's vassal.

This quadruple alliance, thought by everyone a reasonable attempt to make peace and a good way of resolving the conflicts with intelligence and diplomacy, actually became the spark of new discord. Charles VI of Austria, whose life was a catalogue of disillusionments and failures, darkened at the very thought of what he had promised with his signature: to introduce a Spanish enclave into his Italian dominions. Elisabetta, on the other hand, trembled with rage at the thought of her son's future vassalage and could not sleep because of what she considered a check on her son's brilliant future. Yet, she hoped the Farneses would not have the heir longed for by a Europe tired of wars; by Parma and Piacenza, which were little inclined to a change; by the pope, who was politically interested in the continuation of the Farnese dynasty; by Don Antonio, who was beginning to curse his obesity and sterility; and naturally, by Donna Enrichetta, envious of other princesses who had no problem bearing children.

In 1729, Elisabetta of Spain, now certain that the rulers of Parma and Florence would never have children, moved to accelerate events for fear that the emperor of Austria would break his promise. In Seville she signed a pact with France and England which, voiding the agreement made in London, provided that six thousand Spanish soldiers immediately occupy the fortresses of Livorno and Portoferraio, Parma, and Piacenza, without waiting for the death of the two princes.

In Vienna, at that time, Charles VI was most interested in obtaining the recognition of the European states for his abolition of the Salic law of succession, an abolition which would permit his daughter Maria Theresa to succeed him should there be no male heirs. Apart from this concern, Charles spent his days in gloomy boredom, mourning the loss of the Spanish crown and hardening his knees in prayers. The treaty of Seville, which neither took into account his august person nor mentioned the imperial vassalage of the two Italian states, offended him and roused him into action. Persuaded by his ministers, he decided to station forty thousand German soldiers in the territory of Mantua and Milan, ready to be sent to Parma, Piacenza, and Florence before the Spaniards arrived. The troops were to remain there until Don Carlos of Bourbon adhered to the stipulations of the original treaty and brought home his army.

At this point, Don Antonio Farnese died. On January 18, 1731, he had been confined to bed with a boil under his ear, caused, it was said, by frequently wearing "a wig that was too hot for him." On the nineteenth he was blessed with a relic of Saint Bernard. Toward evening of that day he received communion and extreme unction. On the following day, after getting temporary relief on the closet stool, he died. He was fifty-one and had governed only four years. Parma and Piacenza were disconsolate at his death, for it seemed to them that Don Antonio had been a model ruler, a lovable prince of such generosity that, had he lived longer, his entire patrimony would have been spent in charity. In this sense, they were not altogether wrong, for Don Antonio's extravagance was such that after his death the duchy found itself bankrupt.

On January 22, 1731, the Duke's body, fitted into a Franciscan habit, was exposed to the public. The nobility dusted off their mourning suits, and Frugoni sat down with a sigh to produce an elegy. In the cathedral, elaborate funeral services began. Four days later—the couriers had not yet left to bring the news to the various European courts—the duchy was occupied by German troops commanded by Count Carlo Stampa, artillery commander of the state of Milan, whom Charles VI had authorized to take possession of the Farnese state and hold until Don Carlos had complied with the Treaty of London—a treaty that Charles VI said he himself would religiously respect.

The rapidity with which the Germans had crossed the border showed clearly how efficient their spies had been. Under the dismayed eyes of the population, on the piazzas of Parma and Piacenza occupied by German foot soldiers and cavalry were affixed proclamations from the emperor. The sound of trumpets spoke to all in a voice of sorrow and despair, a voice well known among the people who could remember how often their tiny country had been coveted and threatened but which always had been ready to defend its right to exist among the great powers. Silently, the citizens prepared themselves to bear the weight of this new foreign occupation and cursed the imminent loss of money and property, the soldiers, thieves of chickens and eggs, the war profiteers, the drunken officers coarsely flirting with the girls of the town.

With the Germans at home and the Spaniards about to arrive, the situation seemed to settle for the moment in a precarious balance, when a bombshell exploded at the opening of Don Antonio's will. The late duke had left his state to "the pregnant stomach" of his wife Enrichetta and further, he had delegated a regent who would govern until his son—because it had to be a boy—with the help of God, became of age.

In Europe the reactions to this news were naturally divided according to the various interests and aspirations of those concerned. Parma and Piacenza, at the height of their joy, saw in this the confirmation of their belief in the nobility and longevity of the Farnese dynasty. Charles VI found it a good thing, just perfect to gain time and to keep his troops in the duchy without having to comply with what would have allowed the Spaniards to return to Italy. The pope, Clement XIII, did not believe in the pregnancy but publicly stated that he waited for it with joy.

The French king did not believe in it either but, unlike the pope, amused himself by expressing his incredulity through the ironical dispatches of his diplomats. Elisabetta of Spain, who could become quite vulgar when she was angry, shouted that Enrichetta's pregnancy was a fake and nothing would stop her from becoming the mother of a ruler. From Piacenza, where she lived, the German Dorotea Sofia of Neuburg demanded that she should be made regent until her grandson Don Carlos became of legal age.

In all that turmoil, amid the comings and goings of ambassadors, the prayers and novenas for a happy outcome to the pregnancy, the public demonstrations of joy and the inevitable sonnets of Frugoni—unusually inspired by the present event— Donna Enrichetta was perplexed and intimidated. The death of her husband had brusquely closed a brief but magical phase of her life. The problems, she felt, were just beginning. Incredible as it may seem, she herself was not certain whether she was pregnant. Don Antonio, like all the Farneses, was a devotee of alchemy and had always surrounded himself with *spargirici*— quacks and charlatans who pretended to have a secret remedy for everything, including Enrichetta's sterility. With her usual docility she had allowed herself to be given strong laxatives and strange concoctions; and ever since then she had been affected "by strange physical irregularities which from time to time made her think she was pregnant."

The alleged pregnancy rapidly assumed the proportions of an international *cause célèbre*. Parma became a meeting place for foreign emissaries, spies, ministers, political observers, doctors, famous scientists, and playboys of every nation, who came "to see the outcomes of a matter that kept all of Europe waiting." In the palace, the pregnancy was discussed with much fervor, and the courtiers found themselves divided into two factions: those who denied that Enrichetta was pregnant expected to win honors and privileges from Spain; and the others, believing in it, counted on the gratitude of the Farneses. Nonetheless, everyone was secretly torn by hopes, fears, and aimless plans. Between Donna Enrichetta and the Duchess Dorotea formalities no longer counted and their relationship was very tense. Their respective ladies in waiting, infected by the hostile atmosphere, presently stopped greeting each other. The young widow spent her day examining herself, trying to make sense of what, so simple for other women, was so complicated and mysterious for her. Her thinking led her over and again to the suspicion and, in her more lucid moments, to the belief that her mysterious ovarian malfunction was being exploited by the highest powers of Europe.

From Modena, Enrichetta's father, to whom she turned for help and advice, merely sent her some doctors and midwives; they only made her uncertainty greater by exaggerating her few symptoms in favor of the pregnancy and minimizing the many indications to the contrary. Defensive and anxious, Donna Enrichetta listened attentively to the encouraging discourses of the doctors and the assurances of the midwives. But the one who reassured her most was Count Carlo Stampa, His Imperial Majesty's commissioner in Parma. Every time that strong and determined man entered her room, preceded by the tramp of his boots, she felt protected against Dorotea's malice, the imprecations of the queen of Spain, political intrigues, and the danger of ending up deprived of her dignity and dowry. When she was with him, she believed in her pregnancy, but as soon as she was alone her gnawing doubts returned to her and she felt she did not have one valid argument in favor of the pregnancy.

Carlo Stampa of Soncino, Count of Montecastello, marshal of the German army, was a Lombardian patrician who as a very young man had entered the service of the emperor of Austria. He was the exemplar of the cold, calculating mentality avid for power and luxury which was typical of the German governorship in Milan and of the politicians in Vienna, both of which were firmly resolved to prevent the return of the Spaniards in Italy by any means, if necessary even the most unorthodox. And Donna Enrichetta's simulated childbirth was not considered the most dishonest one. They were inclined to this "solution" because of the character of the young widow, her mediocre intelligence, her impressionability, the certainty that it would not be too difficult—as in fact it was not—to sow in her a psychogenic pregnancy. So Enrichetta, who was at the time of life when emotionally a woman needs to have a child, ended up by convincing herself that she was expecting. When her doubts were reawakened, there came Carlo Stampa with fatherly words, to calm her anxiety and reinspire in her a confident, patient expectation.

It was destined that the story of Donna Enrichetta's pregnancy would be an important historical factor. Charles VI gave it a decisive twist. The emperor of Austria lived, as we have said, completely obsessed by the idea of the pragmatic sanction, which would enable his daughter to succeed him. He did not realize that this would become one of the most important documents in the history of Europe, and for all the trouble it caused it could have been rewritten a million times over with the blood that it cost succeeding generations. He had dedicated his life to obtaining for this decree the sanction of the princes and electors of the empire and of the European powers. He labored over it for twenty years, notwithstanding his many sacrifices and the opposition of his own ministers, who believed the sanction useless and irrelevant. After much consideration—keeping in mind that the queen of Spain threatened to veto his pragmatic sanction—Charles VI found it convenient to come to terms with Donna Enrichetta's condition by turning the nagging problem over to medical science. This resolution, in sharp contrast to the policy of the Vienna ministers, then induced Count Stampa and his colleagues to formulate, unknown to the emperor, a secret plan based on the logic of corruption, which for them, at that moment, seemed to spring from the very philosophy of the *raison d'état*. It was immediately necessary to bribe the doctors chosen to examine Donna Enrichetta, to buy the silence of the maids and servants, and to pay off the midwives in order to keep them from telling the truth. Presently, they were all bought off: the surgeons of the court of Parma, the doctors sent by the emperor, the chambermaids, the midwives, even the personal obstetrician of the queen of Spain and the one sent by Duke Rinaldo d'Este.

The day of the consultation, May 31, 1731, finally arrived. In the duchess's room, people settled themselves, coughing politely as if they were in a theater moments before the curtain rises. There were three Spanish ministers, the gentlemen of the regency, and Dorotea of Neuburg surrounded by matrons of the highest nobility and by splendidly arrayed ladies in waiting. Missing was the pope's representative, Monsignor Oddi, who was absent not because of embarrassment at the prospect of watching a gynecological examination but because "the event has been ordered by the emperor and not by the pope." While everyone in the room held his breath in a solemn pause, the wretched Enrichetta, "adjusting herself in the most decent position possible," her eyes closed, muttering a prayer, gave herself to the inspection of the unusual tribunal.

The testimony of five midwives was drawn up and made public to those present, and it is still to be found in the archives of Milan. It is a document of a certain interest in the history of obstetrics. The conclusion reads that, "according to all the known symptoms," the duchess was seven months pregnant. One of the midwives added that she was ready to pay with her head if Donna Enrichetta would not give birth. The investigation brought the matter back to where it had started. In Parma, festivities were happily resumed. Charles VI's conscience was again in peace. The pope thought that time would take care of everything; one had only to wait. Elisabetta, in a black, vindictive mood, as usual, bleated insults. Her mother, Dorotea Sofia, who before the consultation had treated Enrichetta coolly but respectfully, now wore her hardest, most bilious expression. Frugoni continued to write poetry. Count Stampa was ecstatic.

The birth was expected for the end of July. The only question was whether the child would be a boy or a girl. Donna Enrichetta had become pale, languorous, weak, but she seemed tranquil—"her natural sincere self"—although her stomach did not grow any larger. Presently, symptoms incompatible with pregnancy forced her back to her old uncertainties: "Everything is ready," she wrote to her father, "we are now in God's hands; as for my health, I suffer from fainting spells and a great weariness. Gioconda continues to hope for the best and so does my surgeon, but one can never be sure."

There were two more months of doubts, delays, slanderous rumors. In that hot summer—a time when life in Parma usually stood still, the nobility in its country homes, the townspeople dozing behind closed shutters, the rich bourgeois napping between shop hours—curiosity gripped the city. The people were betting, and in every household, from palace to hovel, they argued passionately. They argued in the foreign courts and chancelleries, in salons and monasteries, and in the Vatican. Everyone had his own opinion, some believing, some disbelieving, some finding it a great mystery. All of Italy was whispering, laughing, giggling, rolling eyes, and shaking heads. In the imminence of the birth, half-seriously half-jokingly called "the conclave," rivalries sharpened. The great game that had for its stakes the Farnese duchy was coming to its end. The two major players, the queen of Spain and Count Stampa, knowing that it was the last hand, grew sharper, studying every movement to weigh the chances and their consequences. Stampa's weapons were bribery and threats; the queen countered by doubling her spies.

The count probably would have won if one day Enrichetta had not stopped to chat with the pregnant wife of a palace gardener. Elisabetta, promptly informed by her spies of this casual meeting, interpreted it as part of a plot. She immediately demanded of Charles VI that Enrichetta give birth in the presence of the diplomatic corps, "with all the formalities used by the queens of England to avoid any suspicion of simulated childbirth."

Duke Rinaldo of Modena was shocked by the news: the idea that his daughter might have been tricked made his head spin. He thought of the scandal, the dishonor to the d'Este family, and of the queen of Spain's revenge. But in his great embarrassment he could think of nothing better to do than to abuse the midwife Bertacchini and to fire the surgeon Trotti who, on that very same day, from the sheer weight of disgrace, had a fit of apoplexy.

Meanwhile, the palace was overflowing with people. Foreign ministers, town delegates, doctors, ladies in waiting, all spent their nights there, waiting for the great moment. Cannon were ready to signal the happy news. In Enrichetta's room everything was ready: the bed, the swaddling, the crib, the basin for hot water, the *porte-enfant,* and the wet nurse. A master of ceremonies was empowered to assign seats to the guests; but even so, there were problems about precedence. Monsieur de la Batue, the French delegate, declared that he would not come unless he was first informed in which order he would be received with respect to the other ministers. The tension was indescribable, and the days went by slowly and suspensefully.

Count Stampa, incredibly self-contained, continued his intrigues, securing the complicity of all those who would be beside the duchess at the moment of delivery. Above all, he trusted the able and shrewd Gioconda Guerri, the chief midwife, to deceive everyone, including the ministers, by staging, for example, a brief labor for Enrichetta—perhaps while everyone was having dinner. The queen of Spain could threaten that an unwitnessed birth would not be recognized, but Count Stampa was unconcerned. The important thing for the moment was to produce a Farnese heir—and he would take care of the rest later. He needed to convince Enrichetta that, in the event some accident "interrupted" the pregnancy—heaven forbid—the best solution for the love of her subjects and for the peace of Europe, was a simulated birth.

Donna Enrichetta finally understood. In that instant she lost her last illusion. Impulsively without telling anyone, for the first time she made a decision on her own and wrote to the emperor and to the Duchess Dorotea, informing them of the bitter truth. But Count Stampa still did not lose control of the situation. He counterattacked. He sent couriers everywhere confirming the pregnancy, and then he gently scolded the duchess for having been thoughtless and hasty. With the help of Gioconda, and never at loss for arguments, he slowly and laboriously revived Enrichetta's belief in the pregnancy. To the Duke of Modena he sent word that everything was going well. "God in his mysterious ways," he wrote, "has chosen to keep us in suspense until the last moment and has combined in Her Highness the most complicated problems of pregnancy, problems which women usually have one at the time." The duke should not worry, however, because Gioconda had examined Donna Enrichetta carefully, and there was no doubt that the duchess must be considered "really and truly pregnant."

From that moment everything rushed to a conclusion. In Madrid the queen, at the apex of impatience and anger, ordered that legal action be taken against Enrichetta and accused her of fraud and of withholding her son's rights. At the same time, a council of German ministers met in Vienna with Prince Eugene of Savoy, commander-in-chief of the German army, who was vitally interested in preventing Spain from returning to Italy. The problem was becoming more unbearable every day; though her father had sent a trusted counselor to support her in her difficult time, Donna Enrichetta could hardly speak any more and she merely nodded when others spoke. A life that had been once carefree and vibrant was now insufferably long, dense with crushing troubles. The truth of her "pregnancy" had become clear to the duchess the day Count Stampa had ordered her to keep her doubts secret until the beginning of the eleventh month from the time of her husband's last sickness. To wait sixty days beyond the time any woman takes to bear a child, she thought in despair, "was to deliberately dishonor herself, and to be exposed to the greatest ridicule." With her last strength she humbly wrote again to Vienna, clearing up once and for all the facts of her case.

Count Stampa finally understood that, without the cooperation of Donna Enrichetta, the plan for the simulated birth was unthinkable. Pressed by time and by the necessity to bring the great imbroglio to a conclusion before it was discovered, and utterly weary of continuing the farce, he wrote to the emperor that there was to be no Farnese heir. He managed to have his letter precede that of Donna Enrichetta. On September 13, 1731, the pregnancy was officially called off, and Donna Enrichetta emerged from the tragicomedy with her reputation almost unscathed. In the following months common sense prevailed in the European chancelleries. The emperor of Austria and the queen of Spain decided to resolve their differences peacefully, in order "not to worsen the precarious state of European affairs."

On December 29, Don Carlos' investiture solemnly took place in Parma, where the vassals of the duchy swore their allegiance to the new Spanish ruler, who was represented by his grandmother Dorotea Sofia. The people were given bread, meat, wine, and silver coins, and therefore they expressed their gratitude by appearing happy. Donna Enrichetta remained alone in her rooms, sad and annoyed by the people's show of happiness. After a few days she went to Piacenza. In time, she married a German nobleman, a colonel of a regiment of cuirassiers, and lived a quiet life in the quiet town of Borgo San Donnino, among affectionate and respectful people.

In Madrid, Queen Elisabetta read over and again the good news from Parma and at last felt entitled to rest from her labors. One who did not participate in the general euphoria was Frugoni—that poor poet, tossed by the waves of events—who was now busy looking for recommendations to put him in favor with the new rulers. "Sad days are ahead for me. On my bald crown I find only few dried-out laurel leaves," he wrote to a friend. "I am perfectly aware of everything, and with moral strength I yield to time and resign myself to my destiny." Yet the desire to return to Parma, from where he had been excluded, if not banished, became so strong that he sent a "poetic dedication" to Duchess Dorotea, who received it coldly. His *L'Orano Espugnato*, an elaborate epic that praised the heroism of a Spanish expedition in Africa and was dedicated to Their Catholic Majesties of Spain, had better fortune. It was a clever poem, "full of subtle and polished artifice," so wisely adulatory that it could hardly miss. Comante Eginetico was in fact told that on reading it the hard blue eyes of Duchess Dorotea had softened in an expression of appreciation. And so he too began to wait for Don Carlos.

And Don Carlos arrived one morning in October of the following year, having passed through the d'Este territory, where Duke Rinaldo had the dusty roads watered-down for the procession. Don Carlos was hardly twenty, charming, and rather handsome in spite of his pox marks, with a large nose—one of those aristocratic noses that carry at least three centuries of history with them—and a physique that held the promise of a powerful man. He had come to learn about the country and the people, to investigate and to feel out the situation. His new subjects, having forgotten their past master and curious about the new one, were well-disposed toward him because he was handsome and the son of a Parmesan princess. After so many vicissitudes, his arrival gave them hope for a better future. They had only to see him ride through the city, under a canopy of gold and silver brocade, preceded by cuirassiers, Irish guards, noblemen, priests, and knights, to applaud him as if they had been waiting for him forever.

With that applause the long Farnese cycle ended. Two centuries had passed since Pier Luigi had settled down on the banks of the Po. The *fortunazza paolina* had run out. In the Duchy of Parma and Piacenza, history turned a page and began a fresh one.

BIBLIOGRAPHY

Affò, I. *Vita di Pier Luigi Farnese I duca di Parma.* Giusti, Milan, 1821. *Memorie storiche di Colorno.* Fratelli Gozzi, Parma, 1800. *Memorie degli scrittori e letterati parmigiani,* Vol. VI. Stamperia Reale, Parma, 1789.

Albèri, E. *Relazioni degli ambasciatori veneti.* Tipografia all'Insegna di Clio, Florence, 1839–63.

Alcari, C. *Il giardino pubblico di Parma.* La Bodoniana, Parma, 1925.

Balestrieri, L. *Feste e spettacoli alla corte dei Farnese.* Tipografie Riunite Donati, Parma, 1909.

Barilli, A. *Ranuccio Farnese abbindolato da un alchimistra.* Aurea Parma, 1913. *Un duca di Parma stregato.* Aurea Parma, 1949. *Lettere d'amore di Gianbattista Masi, conte di Felino.* Parma. *Suor Maura Lucenia.* Archivio Storico delle Provincie Parmensi, Vols. XXII–b, XXIII, 1922–23. *Lettere anonime contro il mal-*

governo di Ranuccio I Farnese. Porta, Piacenza, 1939. *Una pagina nera nella storia dei Farnese.* Lodi, 1909. *La congiura di Parma del 1611 e le confessioni dei congiurati.* Archivio Storico delle Provincie Parmensi, Vol. I, 1936. *I Piacentini nella congiura di Parma del 1611.* Fresching, Parma, 1949. *La Gran Giustizia sulla piazza di Parma.* Aurea Parma, 1912.

Bellonci, M. *Segreti dei Gonzaga.* Mondadori, Milan, 1947.

Benassi, U. *Storia di Parma dal 1545 al 1860.* Battei, Parma, 1907–1908. *Ambizioni ignorate di Ranuccio I Farnese.* Archivio Storico delle Provincie Parmensi, 1909. *Pareri politici intorno alle nozze di Ranuccio I Farnese.* Archivio Storico delle Provincie Parmensi, 1909. *Le relazioni ispano-farnesiane.* Archivio Storico Italiano, 1922.

Bezzi, A. *Annotazioni in margine alla congiura di Parma del 1611.* Aurea Parma, 1949.

Bicchieri, E. *Vita di Ottavio Farnese.* Monumenti di Storia Patria delle Provincie Modenesi e Parmensi, 1884.

Calandrini, I. *Vita Laudativa di Odoardo Farnese.* Manuscript folio 737, Biblioteca Palatina, Parma.

Capasso, C. *Paolo III.* Principato, Messina, 1924. *Odoardo Farnese.* Archivio Storico delle Provincie Parmensi, 1909.

Castagnoli, P. *Il Cardinale Alberoni.* Ferrari, Rome, 1929.

Cerri, L. *Il conte Teodoro Scotti nella congiura di Parma del 1611.* Solari, Piacenza, 1922.

Costa, E. *Spigolature artistiche e letterarie.* Parma, 1887.

De Navenne, F. *Rome, le palais Farnese et les Farnese.* Michel, Paris, 1914.

Drei, G. *I Farnese, grandezza e decadenza di una dinastia italiana.* Libreria dello Stato, Rome, 1954.

Edoari Da Erba, A.M. *Miscellanea di cose storiche parmigiane.* Manuscript, Biblioteca Palatina di Parma.

Fea, P. *Alessandro Farnese.* Fratelli Bocca, Rome, 1886.

Giacobassi Di Viotarino, L. *Enrichetta d'Este duchessa di Parma.* Garzanti, Novara, 1941.

Guerrieri, G. *Mecenatismo farnesiano.* Archivio Storico delle Provincie Parmensi, Third Series, Vols. VI, VII, VIII, 1942.

Intra, G. B. *Margherita Farnese, principessa di Mantova.* Rassegna Nazionale, Vol. LXI, 1891. *Una pagina della giovinezza di Vincenzo Gonzaga.* Archivio Storico Italiano, Vol. XVIII, 1886.

Litta, P. *Celebri Famiglie d'Italia.* Giusti, Milan, 1819–73.

Lombardi, G. *Il teatro Farnese di Parma.* Archivio Storico delle Provincie Parmensi, Vol. IX, 1909.

Maylender, M. *Storia delle Accademie d'Italia.* Cappelli, Bologna, 1926.

Melegari, F. *Storia inedita della congiura del 1611 contro i Farnese.* Manuscript, Biblioteca Palatina di Parma.

Minucci Del Rosso. *Le nozze di Margherita de' Medici con Odoardo Farnese.* Rassegna Nazionale, Vols. XXI, XXII, XXIII. Florence, 1885.

BIBLIOGRAPHY

Odorici, F. *Barbara di Sanvitale e la congiura del 1611 contro i Farnese*. Ripamonti, Milan, 1863.

Pastor, L. *Storia dei Papi*. Vol. V. Desclée, Rome, 1910–33.

Poggiali, C. *Memorie Storiche di Piacenza*. Giacobazzi, Piacenza, 1766.

Quazza, R. *Una vertenza fra principi italiani del '600*. Rivista Storica Italiana, 1930.

Ronchini, A. *Vita di Barbara Sanseverino, contessa di Sala*. Monumenti di Storia Patria delle Provincie Modenesi e Parmensi, 1863. *Cento lettere del capitano Francesco Marchi. Delle relazioni di Tiziano con i Farnese*. Monumenti di Storia Patria delle Provincie Modenesi e Parmensi, Vol. III, 1865. *Giovanni Boscoli e la Pilotta*. Monumenti di Storia Patria delle Provincie Modenesi e Parmensi, Vol. VII, 1876.

Tiraboschi, G. *Storia della letteratura italiana*. Società Tipografica, Modena, 1783.

INDEX

A NOTE ABOUT THIS BOOK

The title page and chapter titles are set in
the monophoto version of Bembo. The
original typeface was named for Pietro
Bembo, who was created Cardinal by
Pope Paul III in 1539. Cut by Francesco
Griffo for the Venetian printer Aldus
Manutius, this face was first used in
Bembo's *De Aetna,* published in 1495.
The text is set in Intertype Baskerville,
derived from John Baskerville's original
design. The typography and binding were
designed by Angela Pozzi.

J